JONAH

JONAH

ZONDERVAN
Exegetical
Commentary
ON THE
Old Testament

A DISCOURSE ANALYSIS OF THE HEBREW BIBLE

KEVIN J. YOUNGBLOOD

DANIEL I. BLOCK
General Editor

ZONDERVAN

Jonah
Copyright © 2013 by Kevin Youngblood

This content was previously published as the *Jonah* volume in the Hearing the Message of Scripture series.

Requests for information should be addressed to:

Zondervan, 3900 Sparks Dr. SE, *Grand Rapids, Michigan 49546*

This edition: ISBN: 978-0-310-52835-7

The Library of Congress cataloged the original edition as follows:

Youngblood, Kevin J., 1969–
    Jonah : God's scandalous mercy / Kevin J. Youngblood.
       pages cm. — (Hearing the message of Scripture commentary series)
    Includes bibliographical references and indexes.
    ISBN 978-0-310-28299-0 (hardcover)
    1. Bible. Jonah—Commentaries. I. Title.
  BS1605.53.Y68 2014
  224'.92077—dc23
                      2013017553

Cover design: Tammy Johnson
Cover photography: The Bridgeman Art Library; Masterfile; Moti Meiri/iStockphoto;
Rob Friedman/iStockphoto
Interior illustration/production: Beth Shagene
Interior design: Mark Sheeres

Printed in the United States of America

15 16 17 18 19 20 21 22 /DCI/ 25 24 23 22 21 20 19 18 17 16 15 14 13 12 11 10 9 8 7 6 5 4 3 2 1

To Karissa and Khyle,
whose capacity for mercy daily convicts me,
challenges me, and inspires me

Contents

Series Introduction

Prospectus

Modern audiences are often taken in by the oratorical skill and creativity of preachers and teachers. However, they tend to forget that the authority of proclamation is directly related to the correspondence of the key points of the sermon to the message the biblical authors were trying to communicate. Since we confess that "all Scripture [including the entirety of the OT] is God-breathed and useful for teaching, rebuking, correcting and training in righteousness, so that [all God's people] may be thoroughly equipped for every good work" (2 Tim 3:16 – 17 NIV), it seems essential that those who proclaim its message should pay close attention to the rhetorical agendas of biblical authors. Too often modern readers, including preachers, are either baffled by OT texts, or they simply get out of them that for which they are looking. Many commentaries available to pastors and teachers try to resolve the dilemma either through word-by-word and verse-by-verse analysis or synthetic theological reflections on the text without careful attention to the flow and argument of that text.

The commentators in this series recognize that too little attention has been paid to biblical authors as rhetoricians, to their larger rhetorical and theological agendas, and especially to the means by which they tried to achieve their goals. Like effective communicators in every age, biblical authors were driven by a passion to communicate a message. So we must inquire not only what that message was, but also what strategies they used to impress their message on their hearers' ears. This reference to "hearers" rather than to readers is intentional, since the biblical texts were written to be heard. Not only were the Hebrew and Christian Scriptures composed to be heard in the public gathering of God's people, but also before the invention of moveable type few would have had access to their own copies of the Scriptures. While the contributors to this series acknowledge with Paul that every Scripture — that is, every passage in the Hebrew Bible — is God-breathed, we also recognize that the inspired authors possessed a vast repertoire of rhetorical and literary strategies. These included not only the special use of words and figures of speech, but also the deliberate selection, arrangement, and shaping of ideas.

The primary goal of this commentary series is to help serious students of Scripture, as well as those charged with preaching and teaching the Word of God, to hear the messages of Scripture as biblical authors intended them to be heard. While we recognize the timelessness of the biblical message, the validity of our interpretation and the authority with which we teach the Scriptures are related directly to the extent to which we have grasped the message intended by the author in the first place. Accordingly, when dealing with specific texts, the authors of the commentaries in this series are concerned with three principal questions: (1) What are the principal theological points the biblical writers are making? (2) How do biblical writers make those points? (3) What significance does the message of the present text have for understanding the message of the biblical book within which it is embedded and the message of the Scriptures as a whole? The achievement of these goals requires careful attention to the way ideas are expressed in the OT, including the selection and arrangement of materials and the syntactical shaping of the text.

To most readers syntax operates primarily at the sentence level. But recent developments in biblical study, particularly advances in rhetorical and discourse analysis, have alerted us to the fact that syntax operates also at the levels of the paragraph, the literary unit being analyzed, and the composition as a whole. Rather than focusing on words or phrases, contributors to this series will concentrate on the flow of thought in the biblical writings, both at the macroscopic level of entire compositions and at the microscopic level of individual text units; in so doing we hope to help other readers of Scripture grasp both the message and the rhetorical force of OT texts. When we hear the message of Scripture, we gain access to the mind of God.

Format of the Commentary

The format of this series is designed to achieve the goals summarized above. Accordingly, each volume in the series will begin with an introduction to the book being explored. In addition to answering the usual questions of date, authorship, and provenance of the composition, commentators will highlight what they consider to be the main theological themes of the book, and then discuss broadly how the style and structure of the book develop those themes. This discussion will include a coherent outline of the contents of the book, demonstrating the contribution each part makes to the development of the principal themes.

The commentaries on individual text units that follow will repeat this process in greater detail. Although complex literary units will be broken down further, the commentators will address the following issues.

1. **The Main Idea of the Passage**: A one- or two-sentence summary of the key ideas the biblical author seeks to communicate.
2. **Literary Context**: A brief discussion of the relationship of the specific text to the book as a whole and to its place within the broader arguments.

3. **Translation and Exegetical Outline**: Commentators will provide their own translations of each text, formatted to highlight the discourse structure of the text and accompanied by a coherent outline that reflects the flow and argument of the text.

4. **Structure and Literary Form**: An introductory survey of the literary structure and rhetorical style adopted by the biblical author, highlighting how these features contribute to the communication of the main idea of the passage.

5. **Explanation of the Text**: A detailed commentary on the passage, paying particular attention to how the biblical authors select and arrange their materials and how they work with words, phrases, and syntax to communicate their messages. This will take up the bulk of most commentaries.

6. **Canonical and Practical Significance**: The commentary on each unit will conclude by building bridges between the world of the biblical author and other biblical authors and with reflections on the contribution made by this unit to the development of broader issues in biblical theology — particularly on how later OT and NT authors have adapted and reused the motifs in question. The discussion will also include brief reflections on the significance of the message of the passage for readers today.

The way in which this series treats biblical books will be uneven. Commentators on smaller books will have sufficient scope to answer fully each of the issues listed above on each unit of text. However, limitations of space preclude full treatment of every text for the larger books. Instead, commentators will guide readers through ## 1 – 4 and 6 for every literary unit, but "Full Explanation of the Text" (#5) will be selective, generally limited to twelve to fifteen literary units deemed most critical for hearing the message of the book.

In addition to these general introductory comments, we should alert readers of this series to several conventions that we follow. First, unless otherwise indicated, the English translations of biblical texts are the commentators' own.

Second, the divine name in the OT is presented as YHWH. The form of the name — represented by the Tetragrammaton, יהוה — is a particular problem for scholars. The practice of rendering the divine name in Greek as κύριος (= Heb. אֲדֹנָי, "Adonay") is carried over into English translations as "Lᴏʀᴅ" or "Lᴏʀᴅ," which reflects the Hebrew יהוה, and distinguishes it from "Lord," which reflects Hebrew אֲדֹן. But this creates interpretive problems, for the connotations and implications of referring to someone by name or by title are quite different. When rendered as a name, English translations have traditionally vocalized יהוה as "Jehovah," which combines the consonants of יהוה with the vowels of אֲדֹנָי. However, today non-Jewish scholars often render the name as "Yahweh," recognizing that "Jehovah" is an artificial construct.

Third, frequently the verse numbers in the Hebrew Bible differ from those in our

English translations. Since the commentaries in this series are based on the Hebrew text, the Hebrew numbers will be the default numbers. Where the English numbers differ, they will be provided in square brackets (e.g., Joel 4:12[3:12]).

Fourth, when discussing specific biblical words or phrases, these will be represented both in transliteration and in translation. The electronic version of this commentary series will also include the Hebrew font.

Author's Preface and Acknowledgments

Rarely does a work of literature have as broad an appeal as does the book of Jonah. The plot is simple enough to be grasped by children, and yet the story unfolds with such literary and theological sophistication that it continues to enthrall seasoned scholars and theologians. Jonah's account of the odyssey that led him from the depths of the sea to the desert outside of Nineveh is embraced by all three of the monotheistic faiths: Judaism, Christianity, and Islam.

It is not surprising, therefore, that the book of Jonah has generated a plethora of commentaries, monographs, and articles, all wrestling with aspects of the interpretation of this masterpiece. One wonders what could possibly be left to say about this intriguing little book. I have asked myself that very question at many points during my own attempt to understand and explain this book's message and rhetorical strategy. Yet, at every turn I found that my predecessors were cheering me on, exhorting me to take the baton and run the next leg of the interpretive relay. Good commentaries on Jonah don't bring the discussion of the book's meaning to an end; rather, they take the discussion to a new level. I have found this to be true of much of the history of the interpretation of this biblical book up to the present.

The niche that the present volume attempts to fill is one created by recent advances in the application of text linguistics and rhetorical analysis to biblical interpretation. To date few commentaries have attempted a detailed exposition of the entire book driven primarily by this combination of methods in a way that is accessible to a general audience. This is the vision of the Zondervan Exegetical Commentary on the Old Testament (ZECOT) series.

Jonah was selected as the subject of one of the first volumes for the series because it contains a relatively brief narrative in the style of classical Hebrew, a genre in which many of the greatest advances and the most assured results of text linguistic analysis have been achieved. In addition, the book contains a psalm suitable for piloting a text linguistic approach to the exegesis of Hebrew poetry.

My love for the book of Jonah began when I translated it as a second-year Hebrew student in college. Since that time I have had the privilege of introducing many of my own students to the Hebrew text of Jonah. It is an ideal book for beginners of biblical Hebrew to cut their teeth on. With each reading I have become increasingly fascinated with the book's profound message and compelling rhetoric.

The completion of this commentary would not have been possible without the help and support of many people. I am deeply indebted to Daniel Block, who invited me to join the ZECOT team. His encouragement, guidance, and patience enabled me to break through many impasses and kept me going. His scholarship and his faith in his students are truly an inspiration. My treasured friend and colleague Miles Van Pelt, who first read the full manuscript, offered the perfect combination of critique and encouragement. His suggestions greatly influenced my work and vastly improved the finished product. In fact, I could not have asked for a more supportive and stimulating group of colleagues than the ZECOT editorial board.

Katya Covrett and Verlyn Verbrugge of Zondervan lead a world class team who have turned a dream into reality. Their practical advice, technical support, and careful eyes averted many blunders I otherwise would have made. I thank them profusely for saving me from many embarrassments.

My colleagues in the College of Bible and Ministry at Harding University have faithfully upheld me in prayer. Their encouragement, wisdom, and camaraderie have sustained me through the challenge of maintaining a full teaching load while bringing this work to completion. May the Lord give us many years of service together in his kingdom.

I have been blessed the past two years with the indispensible aid of two of the brightest and most helpful student workers imaginable: my grader, Melissa Dykes, and my graduate assistant, Andrew Sowers. Their diligence and thoughtfulness saved me time and effort, allowing me the opportunity to conduct my research and writing.

Finally and most importantly, I must thank my family. My wife, Becky, has never failed to support me in my ministry of scholarship, teaching, and preaching despite the fact that it often places a significant burden on her. Without her love there would be no book and there would be far less of me. My daughter, Karissa, regularly lifts my spirits with her indefatigable faith in her father, and my son, Khyle, reminds me on a daily basis the importance of joy and of balancing work and play.

My prayer is that this commentary, along with the entire ZECOT series, will aid preachers and teachers of Jonah's message in unleashing the power of the Scriptures in the church to the glory of God the Father and of his Son, Jesus Christ.

Abbreviations

Abbreviations for books of the Bible, pseudepigrapha, rabbinic works, papyri, classical works, and the like are readily available in sources such as the *SBL Handbook of Style* and are not included here.

AB	Anchor Bible
ABD	*Anchor Bible Dictionary*
AfO	Archiv für Orientforschung
AJBI	*Annual of the Japanese Biblical Institute*
ANET	*Ancient Near Eastern Texts*, ed. J. Pritchard
ATANT	Abhandlungen zur Theologie des Alten und Neuen Testaments
BAR	*Biblical Archaeology Review*
BBR	*Bulletin for Biblical Research*
BDB	*A Hebrew and English Lexicon of the Old Testament*, ed. F. Brown, S. R. Driver, and C. A. Briggs.
BerO	Berit Olam
BHHB	Baylor Handbook on the Hebrew Bible
Bib	*Biblica*
BIS	Biblical Interpretation Series
BN	*Biblische Notizen*
BSac	*Bibliotheca sacra*
BZ	*Biblische Zeitschrift*
BZAW	Beihefte zur Zeitschrift für die alttestamentliche Wissenschaft
CANE	*Civilizations of the Ancient Near East*, ed. Jack Sasson
CBQ	*Catholic Biblical Quarterly*
ConBNT	Coniectanea biblica: New Testament Series
COS	*Context of Scripture*, ed. W. W. Hallo, 3 vols.
DAI	Dissertation Abstracts International
EBC	*Expositor's Bible Commentary*, rev. ed., ed. Tremper Longman III and David E. Garland
ETL	*Ephemerides theologicae lovanienses*
FOTL	Forms of the Old Testament Literature
GBSOT	Guides to Biblical Scholarship: Old Testament series
GKC	*Gesenius' Hebrew Grammar*, ed. E. Kautsch and A. E. Cowley

HALOT	*Hebrew and Aramaic Lexicon of the Old Testament*, ed. Ludwig Kohler, Walter Baumgartner, and J. J. Stamm
HBT	Horizons in Biblical Theology
HS	*Hebrew Studies*
HSMP	Harvard Semitic Museum Publications
HSS	Harvard Semitic Studies
HTR	*Harvard Theological Review*
Int	*Interpretation*
ISBL	*Indiana Studies in Biblical Literature*
JBL	*Journal of Biblical Literature*
JE	*Jewish Encyclopedia*
JETS	*Journal of the Evangelical Theological Society*
JHS	*Journal of Hebrew Scriptures*
JPS	Jewish Publication Society
JSOT	*Journal for the Study of the Old Testament*
JSNTSup	Journal for the Study of the New Testament Supplements
JSOTSup	Journal for the Study of the Old Testament Supplements
KAT	Kommentar zum Alten Testament
KTU	*Die keilalphabetischen Texte aus Ugarit*, ed. M. Dietrich, O. Loretz, and J. Sanmartin
NIB	*New Interpreters Bible*
NICNT	New International Commentary on the New Testament
NICOT	New International Commentary on the Old Testament
NIDOTTE	*New International Dictionary of Old Testament Theology and Exegesis*, ed. Willem VanGemeren.
OIP	Oriental Institute Publications
OTL	Old Testament Library
OTP	*Old Testament Pseudepigrapha*, ed. J. H. Charlesworth
RB	*Revue biblique*
SBLMS	Society of Biblical Literature Monograph Series
TBC	Tools for Biblical Study
TDOT	*Theological Dictionary of the Old Testament*, ed. G. Johannes Botterweck and Helmer Ringgren
TynBul	*Tyndale Bulletin*
VT	*Vetus Testamentum*
WBC	Word Biblical Commentary
WMANT	Wissenschaftliche Monographien zum Alten und Neuen Testament
WW	*Word and World*
ZAW	Zeitschrift für die alttestamentliche Wissenschaft
ZIBBCOT	*Zondervan Illustrated Bible Backgrounds Commentary on the Old Testament*

Select Bibliography

Ackerman, James S. "Satire and Symbolism in the Song of Jonah." Pages 213–46 in *Traditions in Transformation: Turning Points in Biblical Faith.* Edited by Bruce Halpern and Jon D. Levenson. Winona Lake, IN: Eisenbrauns, 1981.

Alexander, T. Desmond. "Jonah and Genre." *TynBul* 36 (1985): 35–59.

Allen, Leslie C. *The Books of Joel, Obadiah, Jonah, and Micah.* Grand Rapids: Eerdmans, 1976.

Andersen, Francis I. *The Sentence in Biblical Hebrew.* Janua Linguarum, Series Practica 231. The Hague: Mouton, 1974.

Bickerman, E. J. *Four Strange Books of the Bible: Jonah, Daniel, Koheleth, Esther.* New York, Schocken, 1968.

Chow, Simon. *The Sign of Jonah Reconsidered: A Study of Its Meaning in the Gospel Traditions.* ConBNT 27. Stockholm: Almqvist & Wiksell, 1995.

Cooper, Alan. "In Praise of Divine Caprice: The Significance of the Book of Jonah." Pages 144–63 in *Among the Prophets: Language, Image and Structure in the Prophetic Writings.* Edited by P. R. Davies and D. J. A. Clines. Sheffield: JSOT, 1993.

Cross, Frank Moore. *From Epic to Canon: History and Literature in Ancient Israel.* Baltimore: Johns Hopkins University Press, 2000.

Dozeman, Thomas B. "Inner-biblical Interpretation of Yahweh's Gracious and Compassionate Character." *JBL* 108 (1989): 207–23.

Dyck, Elmer. "Jonah among the Prophets: A Study in Canonical Context." *JETS* 33 (1990): 63–73.

Estelle, Bryan D. *Salvation through Judgment and Mercy: The Gospel according to Jonah.* Phillipsburg, NJ: Presbyterian & Reformed, 2005.

Eynikel, Erik. "One Day, Three Days, and Forty Days in the Book of Jonah." Pages 65–76 in *One Text, a Thousand Methods.* Edited by P. C. Counet and U. Berges. Boston: Brill, 2005.

Ferguson, Paul. "Who Was the 'King of Nineveh' in Jonah 3:6?" *TynBul* 47 (1996): 301–14.

Fokkelman, Jan. *Reading Biblical Narrative: An Introductory Guide.* Translated by Ineke Smit. TBC. Louisville: Westminster John Knox, 1999.

Fretheim, Terence E. *The Message of Jonah: A Theological Commentary.* Minneapolis: Augsburg, 1977.

Fuller, Russell Earl. "The Minor Prophets Manuscripts from Qumrân, Cave IV." DAI 49, no. 10 (1989): 3012A–3012B.

Gitay, Yehoshua. "Jonah: The Prophecy of Anti-rhetoric." Pages 197–206 in *Fortunate the Eyes That See.* Edited by Astrid B. Beck et al. Grand Rapids: Eerdmans, 1995.

Glueck, Nelson. *Hesed in the Bible.* Translated by Alfred Gottschalk. Edited by Elias L. Epstein. Cincinnati: Hebrew Union College Press, 1967.

Goldstein, Elizabeth. "On the Use of the Name of God in the Book of Jonah." Pages 77–83 in *Milk and Honey: Essays on Ancient Israel and the Bible*. Edited by Sarah Malena and David Miano. Winona Lake, IN: Eisenbrauns, 2007.

Guillaume, Philippe. "The Unlikely Malachi-Jonah Sequence (4QXIIa)." *JHS* 7 (2007): 2–10.

Habel, Norman C. "Form and Significance of the Call Narratives." *ZAW* 77 (1965): 297–323.

Heimerdinger, Jean-Marc. *Topic, Focus and Foreground in Ancient Hebrew Narratives*. JSOTSup 295. Sheffield: Sheffield Academic, 1999.

Hesse, Eric W., and Isaac M. Kikiwada. "Jonah and Genesis 11-1." *AJBI* 10 (1984): 3–19.

Holbert, John C. "'Deliverance Belongs to Yahweh': Satire in the Book of Jonah." *JSOT* 21 (1981): 59–81.

Hunter, Alastair G. "Jonah from the Whale: Exodus Motifs in Jonah 2." Pages 142–58 in *The Elusive Prophet: The Prophet as a Historical Person, Literary Character and Anonymous Artist*. Edited by Johannes C. de Moor. Leiden: Brill, 2001.

Jenson, Philip Peter. *Obadiah, Jonah, Micah: A Theological Commentary*. New York: T&T Clark, 2008. http://site.ebrary.com/id/10489977.

Joüon, Paul. *A Grammar of Biblical Hebrew*. Translated and revised by T. Muraoka. Rome: Pontifical Biblical Institute, 1993.

Kamp, Albert H. *Inner Worlds: A Cognitive Linguistic Approach to the Book of Jonah*. Translated by David Orton. BIS 68. Boston: Brill, 2004.

Kaufmann, Y. *The Religion of Israel: From Its Beginnings to the Babylonian Exile*. Translated and abridged by Moshe Greenberg. Chicago: University of Chicago Press, 1960.

Köhler, Ludwig, et al. *The Hebrew and Aramaic Lexicon of the Old Testament*. Leiden: Brill, 1994.

L'Hour, Jean. "Yahweh Elohim." *RB* 81 (1974): 525–56.

Landes, George M. "Kerygma of the Book of Jonah: The Contextual Interpretation of the Jonah Psalm." *Int* 21 (1967): 3–31.

———. "Textual 'Information Gaps' and 'Dissonances' in the Interpretation of the Book of Jonah." Pages 273–93 in *Ki Baruch Hu: Ancient Near Eastern, Biblical, and Judaic Studies in Honor of Baruch A. Levine*. Edited by R. Chazan, W. W. Hallo, and L. H. Schiffman. Winona Lake, IN: Eisenbrauns, 1999.

———. "Three Days and Three Nights Motif in Jonah 2:1." *JBL* 86 (1967): 446–50.

Levine, Étan, and Jonathan ben Uzziel. *The Aramaic Version of Jonah*. Jerusalem: Jerusalem Academic Press, 1975.

Lichtert, Claude. "Par terre et par mer! analyse rhétorique de Jonas 1." *ETL* 78 (2002): 5–24.

Limburg, James. *Jonah: A Commentary*. OTL. Louisville: Westminster John Knox, 1993.

Lohfink, Norbert. "Jona ging zur Stadt hinaus (Jon 4:5)." *BZ* 5 (1961): 185–203.

Longacre, Robert E., and Shin Ja J. Hwang. "A Textlinguistic Approach to the Biblical Hebrew Narrative of Jonah." Pages 336–58 in *Biblical Hebrew and Discourse Linguistics*. Edited by Robert D. Bergen. Dallas: Summer Institute of Linguistics, 1994.

Longman, Tremper III, and David E Garland, ed.. *Daniel-Malachi. EBC* 8. Grand Rapids: Zondervan, 2009.

Lunn, Nicholas P. *Word-order Variation in Biblical Hebrew Poetry: Differentiating Pragmatics and Poetics*. Milton Keynes, UK: Paternoster, 2006.

Lutz, Hans Martin. *Jahwe, Jerusalem und die Völker: Zur Vorgeschichte von Sach 12, 1-8 und 14,1-5*. WMANT. Neukirchen-Vluyn: Neukirchener Verlag, 1968.

Magonet, Jonathan. *Form and Meaning: Studies in Literary Techniques in the Book of Jonah*. Sheffield: Almond, 1983.

Merwe, C. H. J. van der, Jacobus A. Naudé, and Jan Hendrik Kroeze. *A Biblical Hebrew Reference Grammar*. Sheffield: Sheffield Academic, 1999.

Miller, Cynthia L. *The Representation of Speech in Biblical Hebrew Narrative: A Linguistic Analysis*. Atlanta: Scholars, 1996.

Miller, J. Maxwell, and John H. Hayes. *A History of Ancient Israel and Judah*. Philadelphia: Westminster, 1986.

Moberly, Walter. "Jonah, God's Objectionable Mercy, and the Way of Wisdom." Pages 154–68 in *Reading Texts: Seeking Wisdom*. Edited by David F. Ford and Graham Stanton. Grand Rapids: Eerdmans, 2003.

Neusner, Jacob. *Habakkuk, Jonah, Nahum and Obadiah in Talmud and Midrash: A Source Book*. Studies in Judaism. Lanham, MD: University Press of America, 2007.

Nogalski, James. *Redactional Processes in the Book of the Twelve*. BZAW 218. Berlin; de Gruyter, 1993.

———. *The Book of the Twelve: Hosea-Jonah*. Smyth & Helwys Bible Commentary. Macon, GA: Smyth & Helwy, 2011.

Nogalski, James D., and Ehud Ben Zvi. *Two Sides of a Coin: Juxtaposing Views on Interpreting the Book of the Twelve*. Analecta Gorgiana. Piscataway, NJ: Gorgias, 2009.

Perry, T Anthony. *The Honeymoon Is Over: Jonah's Argument with God*. Peabody, MA: Hendrickson, 2006.

Powell, M. A. "Echoes of Jonah in the New Testament." *WW* 27 (2007): 157–64.

Rad, Gerhard von. *Der Prophet Jona*. Nürnberg: Laetare Verlag, 1950.

Rocine, B. M. *Learning Biblical Hebrew: A New Approach Using Discourse Analysis*. Macon, GA: Smyth & Helwys, 2000.

Sakenfeld, Katharine D.. *The Meaning of Hesed in the Hebrew Bible: A New Inquiry*. HSMP. Missoula, MT: Scholars, 1978.

Sasson, Jack M. *Jonah: A New Translation and Commentary*. AB 24B. New York: Doubleday, 1990.

Shemesh, Yael. "'And Many Beasts' (Jonah 4:11): The Function and Status of Animals in the Book of Jonah." Accessed April 10, 2013. www.jhsonline.org/Articles/article_134.pdf.

Sherwood, Yvonne. A Biblical Text and Its Afterlives: The Survival of Jonah in Western Culture. Cambridge: Cambridge University Press, 2000.

Simon, Uriel. *Jonah: The Traditional Hebrew Text with the New JPS Translation*. Translated by Lenn J. Schramm. JPS Bible Commentary. Philadelphia: Jewish Publication Society, 1999.

Sternberg, Meir. *The Poetics of Biblical Narrative: Ideological Literature and the Drama of Reading*. ISBL. Bloomington, IN: Indiana University Press, 1987.

Strawn, Brent A. "Jonah's Sailors and Their Lot Casting: A Rhetorical-Critical Observation." *Bib* 91 (2010): 66–76.

Stuart, Douglas K. *Hosea-Jonah*. WBC 31. Waco, TX: Word, 1987.

Sweeney, Marvin A. *The Twelve Prophets*. BerO. Collegeville, MN: Liturgical, 2000.

Trible, Phyllis. *Rhetorical Criticism: Context, Method, and the Book of Jonah*. GBSOT. Minneapolis, MN: Fortress, 1994.

———. "The Book of Jonah." Pages 463–529 in vol. 7, *NIB*. Nashville, TN: Abingdon, 1994.

Tucker, W. Dennis, Jr. *Jonah: A Handbook on the Hebrew Text*. BHHB. Waco, TX: Baylor University Press, 2006.

Waltke, Bruce K., and Michael Patrick O'Connor. *An Introduction to Biblical Hebrew Syntax.* Winona Lake, IN: Eisenbrauns, 1990.

Walton, John H. "The Object Lesson of Jonah 4:5-7 and the Purpose of the Book of Jonah." *BBR* 2 (1992): 47–57.

Wendland, Ernst R. "Text Analysis and the Genre of Jonah, Part I." *JETS* 39 (1996): 191–206.

———. "Text Analysis and the Genre of Jonah, Part II." *JETS* 39 (1996): 373–95.

Willis, John T. "The 'Repentance' of God in the Books of Samuel, Jeremiah and Jonah." *HBT* 16 (1994): 156–75.

Wiseman, D. J. "Jonah's Nineveh." *TynBul* 30 (1979): 29–51.

Wolde, Ellen van. "The Verbless Clause and Its Textual Function." Pages 321–36 in *The Verbless Clause in Biblical Hebrew: Linguistic Approaches.* Edited by Cynthia L. Miller. Winona Lake, IN: Eisenbrauns, 1999.

Wolff, Hans Walter. *Obadiah and Jonah: A Commentary.* Translated by Margaret Kohl. Minneapolis: Augsburg, 1986.

Zvi, Ehud ben. *Signs of Jonah: Reading and Rereading in Ancient Yehud .* JSNTSup 367. London: Sheffield Academic , 2003.

Translation of Jonah

Jonah 1

¹YHWH's word came to Jonah, Amittai's son, as follows: ²"Up! Go to Nineveh, that great metropolis, and condemn it because their evil has ascended before me!"

³So Jonah got up to flee to Tarshish, away from YHWH's presence. He descended to Joppa. He found a ship bound for Tarshish. He paid its hire, and he descended into it to accompany them to Tarshish, away from YHWH's presence.

⁴Meanwhile, YHWH flung a great gale toward the sea. A great storm ensued on the sea. As for the ship, it threatened to burst apart. ⁵The mariners feared, and each one cried out to his god, and they flung the cargo that was on the ship to the sea to lighten for themselves.

But as for Jonah, he had descended into the bowels of the ship's hold. And there he lay down and fell fast asleep. ⁶The helmsman approached him and said to him, "How can you be sleeping? Up! Cry out to your god! Perhaps the deity will consider our plight so that we are not destroyed."

⁷Then each one said to his shipmate, "Come! And let us cast lots that we might discover on whose account this disaster has befallen us." So they cast lots, and the lot fell on Jonah. ⁸They inquired of him, "Please, tell us on whose account this disaster has befallen us. What is your occupation? And from where do you come? What country do you claim? And to which of its people do you belong?"

⁹And he responded, "I am a Hebrew, and YHWH, the god of heaven, I fear, who made the sea and the dry land."

¹⁰Then the men feared a great fear, and they asked him, "What have you done?" For the men knew that he was fleeing YHWH's presence because he had told them so.

¹¹So they asked him, "What must we do with you so that the sea might settle down for us?" For the sea was raging on relentlessly.

¹²He replied, "Pick me up, and fling me to the sea so that the sea might settle down for you. For I realize that on my account this disaster has befallen you."

¹³The men dug in to return to dry land. But they could not do it because the sea raged against them with growing intensity. ¹⁴So they cried out to YHWH, "We beg of

you, YHWH! Please don't destroy us on account of this man! Nor hold us accountable for innocent blood. For you are YHWH; just as you pleased, you have done." [15]So they lifted Jonah and flung him to the sea, and the sea ceased its raging. [16]Then the men feared YHWH with great fear. They offered sacrifices to YHWH, and they vowed vows.

Jonah 2

[1]Then YHWH appointed a great fish to swallow Jonah. Now Jonah was in the fish's belly for three days and three nights, [2]and Jonah prayed to YHWH, his god, from the fish's womb [3]and said:

I cried out, because of my distress, to YHWH, and he answered me;
> from Sheol's belly I screamed for help, you heeded my voice.

[4]You had cast me down to the deep, into the heart of the sea,
> where the river swirled about me.
> All your breakers and waves passed over me.

[5]As for me, I said,
> "I have been banished from your sight;
> nevertheless, I will try again to gaze toward your holy temple!

[6]The waters had enclosed me, threatening my life;
> the deep had enveloped me;
> reeds had wrapped around my head.

[7]To the base of the mountains I had descended,
> to the land whose bars would trap me forever.

Then you restored from the pit my life, YHWH, my God.
> [8]Just when I had felt myself succumbing to death,

YHWH I had remembered.

My petition had reached you;
> (it had reached) your holy temple.

[9]Devotees of useless idols forsake their experience of mercy,
> [10]but, as for me, with a grateful voice I will sacrifice to you;
> what I have vowed I will pay.

Deliverance belongs to YHWH!

[11]Then YHWH spoke to the fish, and it vomited Jonah on to the dry ground.

Jonah 3

[1]Yahweh's word came to Jonah again: [2]"Up! Go to Nineveh, that great metropolis, and proclaim to them the proclamation that I am about to speak to you."

[3]So Jonah got up and went to Nineveh as Yahweh commanded. Now Nineveh

was a great metropolis belonging to God. (It was) a three-day journey. [4]Jonah had just begun making his way into the city, a single day's journey, when he announced, "Forty days until Nineveh is overturned." [5]Then the men of Nineveh trusted God and announced a fast and wore sackcloth from the greatest of them to the least of them.

[6]The message reached the king of Nineveh, and he arose from his throne and disrobed and clothed himself with sackcloth and sat upon the dust. [7]Then he issued a proclamation and said in Nineveh by royal authority with the help of his officials,

"Both man and beast, both herds and flocks must taste nothing.

They must not graze.

They must not drink water.

[8]They must cover themselves with sackcloth, both man and beast.

They must cry out to God earnestly.

They must repent, each one, of his wicked behavior and the violence that he performs with his own hands.

[9]Who knows?

God may change his mind

and relent

and recover from his intense anger so that we will not perish."

[10]Then God saw their deeds, that they repented of their wicked behavior. So he relented concerning the disaster that he threatened to perform against them, and he did not do it.

Jonah 4

[1]This displeased Jonah with great displeasure. And it infuriated him. [2]So he prayed to YHWH, "Alas! YHWH. Was this not my concern while I was in my homeland? Therefore I hastened to flee to Tarshish because I knew that you are a gracious and compassionate god, slow to anger and full of mercy and one who relents from punishment. [3]So now, YHWH, take my life from me. For my death would be better than my life."

[4]Then YHWH asked, "Is your anger that intense?"

[5]Jonah departed from the city, and sat east of the city. He built himself a hut there, and sat under it in the shade until he could see what would happen in the city.

[6]Then YHWH God appointed a plant, and it grew over Jonah to serve as a shade over his head to deliver him from his misery. Jonah rejoiced over the plant with great joy. [7]Then God appointed a worm. When dawn came the next day, it attacked the plant, and the plant withered. [8]As the sun climbed higher, God appointed a cutting, easterly wind, and the sun attacked Jonah's head. He grew faint, and asked himself to die. He said, "My death is better than my life."

[9]God asked Jonah, "Is your anger over the plant that intense?"

He answered, "My anger is so intense I could die!"

[10]YHWH said, "As for you, you pitied the plant, over which you exerted no effort, nor did you grow it, which overnight appeared and overnight perished. [11]But as for me, must I not pity Nineveh, the great metropolis, in which live more than 120,000 persons who do not know their right from their left, as well as many animals?"

Introduction to Jonah

The profound cultural impact of the book of Jonah is out of all proportion to its small size. This brief narrative of four short chapters has captured the imaginations of authors, painters, poets, and musicians like few other stories have.[1] Even in our own time the book of Jonah continues to fascinate as is evident from its most recent cultural reference in a new song by Bruce Springsteen entitled "Swallowed Up (in the Belly of the Whale)."[2]

What accounts for this story's enduring impact? Why does it have such a powerful and universal appeal? Jewish, Christian, and Islamic traditions all bear witness to the relevance of Jonah's message for people of faith, and its repeated appearances in secular literature and the arts attest to its enduring influence even among those who claim no religious affiliation.[3] Perhaps one reason for this story's ability to transcend the normal barriers of cultural and religious differences is its emphasis on the universal scope of God's sovereignty and mercy. Furthermore, the book's subtlety and open-endedness lend the story to a multiplicity of interpretations as is apparent from the vast number of commentaries purporting to expound the book's message.

The present work is yet another attempt to understand this intriguing little book of the Bible. By building on the insights found in the wealth of literature on Jonah and by taking advantage of recent developments in our understanding of how Hebrew narrative works, this commentary strives to advance the discussion regarding Jonah's message. A number of preliminary considerations, however, deserve attention before turning to the detailed exegesis. An understanding of three overlapping contexts — canonical, historical, and literary — is critical to the book's interpretation. The following orientation to each of these contexts will acquaint readers with the historical, cultural, linguistic, rhetorical, and theological forces that shaped the book of Jonah.

---

1. References to the book of Jonah as a "story" are not meant to indicate that the book relates a purely fictional account. To some the word "story" connotes fantasy or perhaps even deliberate falsification. The word "story," however, can be considered synonymous with "narrative" and can be used with reference to "the recounting of a series of facts or events and the establishing of some connection between them." Cf. Angus Ross, "Narrative," in *The Routledge Dictionary of Literary Terms* (ed. Peter Childs and Roger Fowler; London: Routledge, 2006), 224, 148.

2. Bruce Springsteen, "Swallowed Up (in the Belly of the Whale," in the album *Wrecking Ball*, produced by Ron Aniello in association with Columbia Records, 2012.

3. For an excellent survey of Jonah's cultural impact, see Yvonne Sherwood, *A Biblical Text and Its Afterlives: The Survival of Jonah in Western Culture* (Cambridge: Cambridge University Press, 2000).

The Canonical Context

Jonah among the Twelve Minor Prophets

Interpreters have often noted that the book of Jonah seems oddly out of place among the prophetic books of the Hebrew Bible.[4] It is, after all, a narrative instead of a collection of oracles as one usually finds in the writing prophets. Furthermore, the one oracle that it does include bears little resemblance to those we find in books like Isaiah, Jeremiah, or Ezekiel. The book's main character, the prophet Jonah, is never explicitly referred to as a prophet within the framework of the story, and Jonah's behavior is certainly not what one would expect of a prophet of YHWH. One wonders if this account isn't better suited for the books of Kings, where we find similar accounts of the exploits of prophets like Elijah and Elisha. Or perhaps it would better fit in the Writings, where we find similar brief accounts of encounters between God's people and foreigners, often with surprisingly sympathetic portrayals of those outside the covenant community (e.g., Ruth, Esther, and Daniel).

Whatever our speculations might be regarding where the book of Jonah best fits within the threefold division of the Hebrew Bible, it has come to us as part of a collection known in Jewish tradition as "The Book of the Twelve," or in Christian tradition as "The Twelve Minor Prophets." As a member of this collection, Jews, Christians, and Muslims alike have always considered the character Jonah to be a prophet and have included this book as part of Israel's prophetic corpus. Interpretation of the book, therefore, ought to begin within the context of this prophetic corpus and the prophetic tradition of Israel and Judah that it represents.

Scholars differ, however, regarding how "The Book of the Twelve" serves as a context for interpreting the contents of Jonah. Marvin Sweeney and James Nogalski, for example, have each attempted a commentary that treats the twelve Minor Prophets as a literary or redactional unity on the basis that, in Jewish tradition, these twelve writings constitute a single scroll.[5] These scholars, therefore, focus on "isolating unifying elements that transcend the individual writings (including catchwords, themes, and motifs) and take on new significance when the Book of the Twelve becomes a single collection rather than twelve distinct writings."[6] Often, these "unifying elements" are understood to be late redactional changes to the individual books designed to impose a unity on the collection.[7]

Others, however, are critical of interpreting the twelve Minor Prophets as a redactional unity because of the speculative nature of the theories regarding their

4. See, e.g., E. Bickerman, _Four Strange Books in the Bible: Jonah, Daniel, Koheleth, Esther_ (New York: Schoken, 1967).

5. Marvin A. Sweeney, _The Twelve Prophets_ (BerO; Collegeville, MN: Liturgical, 2000); James D. Nogalski, _The Book of the Twelve: Hosea–Jonah_ (Smyth & Helwys Bible Commentary; Macon, GA: Smyth & Helwys, 2011).

6. Nogalski, _The Book of the Twelve_, 1.

7. James Nogalski, _Redactional Processes in the Book of the Twelve_ (Berlin: de Gruyter, 1993).

arrangement and final editing. Ehud ben Zvi, for example, argues that it is far more likely that ancient readers understood the twelve Minor Prophets as discreet prophetic books, each one on an equal footing with the books of Isaiah, Jeremiah, and Ezekiel. He points to the commentaries discovered at Qumran as an example. No commentary on the Book of the Twelve has been discovered among the Qumran scrolls; rather, what we find are commentaries on the individual prophets, such as the Habakkuk Pesher (1QpHab).[8]

The book of Jonah in particular presents challenges to theories of redactional or literary unity with respect to the twelve Minor Prophets since its content seems independent. Furthermore, the book's interpretation does not rest on any presumed relationship with other prophetic books. In fact, Jonah's placement among the Minor Prophets is the most fluid of the twelve books, assuming no less than four different positions in four known arrangements. In the traditional Jewish and Protestant order (the MT) Jonah is listed fifth, after Obadiah and before Micah. In the order of the oldest Greek codices (Vaticanus, Sinaiticus, and Alexandrinus), however, Jonah occurs sixth after Obadiah and before Nahum.[9] The pseudepigraphical *Martyrdom and Ascension of Isaiah* also places Jonah sixth but has it after Nahum and before Obadiah, thus reversing the sequence in the oldest Greek codices. Finally and most surprisingly, a Qumran fragment containing portions of Malachi and Jonah (4QXII[a]) appears to place Jonah last in the sequence of the Minor Prophets.[10] These four arrangements are listed in parallel columns below.

The variations in canonical sequence are difficult to explain, but they seem to

Table 1.1: Jonah's Placement in the Book of the Twelve			
	MT	**Septuagint**	**M & A of Isaiah**	**4QXII[a]**
1	Hosea	Hosea	Amos	?
2	Joel	Amos	Hosea	?
3	Amos	Micah	Micah	?
4	Obadiah	Joel	Joel	?
5	Jonah	Obadiah	Nahum	?
6	Micah	Jonah	Jonah	?
7	Nahum	Nahum	Obadiah	?
8	Habakkuk	Habakkuk	Habakkuk	?
9	Zephaniah	Zephaniah	Haggai	?
10	Haggai	Haggai	Zephaniah	?
11	Zechariah	Zechariah	Zechariah	Malachi
12	Malachi	Malachi	Malachi	Jonah

8. Ehud ben Zvi and James D. Nogalski, *Two Sides of a Coin: Juxtaposing Views on Interpreting the Book of the Twelve/the Twelve Prophetic Books* (Piscataway, NJ: Gorgias, 2009), 60 – 70.

9. The order of the Minor Prophets found in the Greek co-

dices is first attested in 2 Esdras 1:39 (in Latin known as *4 Ezra* 1:39) which is usually dated ca. AD 70.

10. This placement of Jonah in 4QXII[a] was first proposed by R. E. Fuller in his 1988 dissertation and is based on his own

indicate that interpretations of Jonah were not dependent on its position within the Minor Prophets.

Jonah among the Prophets

Given these data, it is best to read Jonah on its own terms and then relate its distinctive themes to the common motifs of the prophetic literature in general. That Jonah is conversant with the prophetic tradition is evident from the book's numerous literary allusions to other prophetic books such as Joel, Jeremiah, and Nahum as well as to the stories of Elijah found in 1 and 2 Kings. The propriety of designating the book of Jonah as a work of prophecy, however, is often questioned on the grounds that the book bears little resemblance to the classical prophetic literature.[11] Despite the judgment of modern scholars, the book of Jonah was always considered part of Israel's/Judah's prophetic tradition, as indicated by early attestation of its inclusion within the prophetic corpus in 4QXII[a] (second century BC) and in the apocryphal book Ben Sirach.[12] Furthermore, Jonah is explicitly identified as a prophet in 2 Kings 14:25, which suggests that the book that bears his name and features him as the protagonist was written as a work of prophecy.[13] This is confirmed by early references to this book that describe the main character as a prophet. For example, Tobit 14:4 includes Jonah among the prophets that predicted Nineveh's destruction,[14] and Jesus in Matthew 12:39 refers to Jonah by the title "prophet."

Jonah's place among the prophets, therefore, is secure. Nonetheless, the book's radical departure from the norms of prophetic literature calls for some explanation. One reason for this book's unique character may be its canonical function as a summary of and commentary on the prophetic tradition in general.[15] The book of Jonah focuses on two questions that preoccupied all of the prophets: (1) How do divine mercy and divine justice interact without canceling each other out? (2) How do God's universal sovereignty and his particular covenant with Israel interact without

---

reconstruction of the fragment (see his "The Minor Prophets Manuscript from Qumran, Cave IV"; PhD diss., Harvard, 1988; published Ann Arbor: UMI, 1995). This reconstruction and proposal has since been questioned by Phillippe Guillaume ["The Unlikely Malachi-Jonah Sequence (4QXII[a])," *JHS* 7 (2007): 1 – 10.]. Guillaume, however, acknowledges the possibility that Jonah did come after Malachi on this scroll. He simply questions the confidence with which this reconstruction has been embraced and subsequently used to prove certain redactional theories of the Book of the Twelve.

11. Karl Budde, for example, proposed that the only reason Jonah was included among the Minor Prophets was to raise the number of books in the collection to twelve so that it would correspond to the number of Israel's patriarchs and tribes. K. Budde, "Jonah, Book of," *JE* 7 (1904), 229.

12. Ben Sirach, also known as Ecclesiasticus, states in 49:10, "May the bones of the Twelve Prophets send forth new life from where they lie, for they comforted the people of Jacob and delivered them with confident hope" (NRSV). The reference to twelve Minor Prophets seems to indicate Jonah's inclusion well before the writing of Ben Sirach, which was likely composed in the early part of the second century BC.

13. Elmer Dyck, "Jonah among the Prophets: A Study in Canonical Context," *JETS* 33 (1990): 64.

14. This reading is based on Codex Vaticanus and Codex Alexandrinus. Other manuscripts read "Nahum."

15. Ehud Ben Zvi, "Atypicality and the Meta-prophetic Character of the Book of Jonah," in *Signs of Jonah: Reading and Rereading in Ancient Yehud* (Sheffield: Sheffield Academic, 2003), 89 – 107.

canceling each other out? By emphasizing these two questions, the book of Jonah provides a theological focal point for reading the vast and varied literature of the prophetic corpus.

Jonah and the Christian Bible

The Synoptic Gospels compare Jesus to Jonah primarily on the basis of Jesus' teaching regarding Jonah as a sign of his resurrection (Matt 12:39 – 41; 16:4; Luke 11:29 – 32). The comparison seems as odd as the book of Jonah itself. Comparisons between Jonah and Jesus abound, however, likely because the book that tells Jonah's story so succinctly and powerfully summarizes the central issues of Hebrew prophecy. It contains all of the elements crucial to the mission Jesus came to launch: a journey from death back to life, an acknowledgment of the potential offensiveness of divine mercy, and a focus on YHWH's concern for the nations.

Jesus' references to the book of Jonah underscore its suitability as a lens through which to read not only the prophetic literature, but the entire Hebrew Bible. For such a short book, Jonah is remarkably dense with biblical references. Furthermore, its references and allusions represent every part of the Hebrew canon: Law, Prophets, and Writings. The book's fondness for the language and imagery of Genesis is unmistakable. Its rich tapestry of citations from the book of Psalms in Jonah 2 weaves together several of the psalms' most crucial themes. The narrative repeatedly appeals to nature as the theater of divine revelation and activity, recalling a foundational principle of Wisdom Literature. Finally, the book dramatically illustrates the principles of conditional prophecy and repentance outlined in Jer 18:7 – 12.

It is little wonder, then, that such a compact expression of biblical theology as the book of Jonah should feature so prominently in Jesus' teaching or that its themes resurface repeatedly throughout the New Testament. For example, Luke's account of Paul's sea voyage in Acts 27 bears many close similarities to Jonah 2. Furthermore, Paul captures the essence of the book of Jonah's message in Romans 11:28 – 36.

> As far as the gospel is concerned, they are enemies for your sake; but as far as election is concerned, they are loved on account of the patriarchs, for God's gifts and his call are irrevocable. *Just as you who were at one time disobedient to God have now received mercy as a result of their disobedience, so they too have now become disobedient in order that they too may now receive mercy as a result of God's mercy to you.* For God has bound everyone over to disobedience so that he may have mercy on them all.
>
> Oh, the depth of the riches of the wisdom and knowledge of God!
> How unsearchable his judgments,
> and his paths beyond tracing out!
> "Who has known the mind of the Lord?
> Or who has been his counselor?"

> "Who has ever given to God,
>   that God should repay them?"
> For from him and through him and for him are all things.
>   To him be the glory forever! Amen. (NIV, emphasis added)

With respect to canonical context, therefore, two principles will govern the interpretation offered here. First, the starting point for interpretation is the final or canonical form of the book of Jonah as it has been received and preserved by the community of faith. Theoretical editions or oral forms preceding the book as we know it are speculative at best and largely distract from hearing the message of the book as a whole. Second, once the message of Jonah has been determined by means of a careful analysis of the book's canonical form, this message will be related to the larger contexts of Israel's prophetic corpus, of the Old Testament in general, and finally of the Bible as a whole. Particular attention will be given to Jesus' and the Evangelists' references to the book of Jonah, which they understood to anticipate Jesus' ministry in significant ways.

The Historical Context

The book of Jonah assumes an early eighth-century BC setting in keeping with the mention of the prophet in 2 Kings 14:25. The narrative's focus on Nineveh indicates an imposing Assyrian presence throughout the Fertile Crescent consistent with the Neo-Assyrian hegemony that defined eighth-century Mesopotamian politics. Knowledge of this period, therefore, assists proper interpretation of the book. A curious fact about Jonah, however, is that the narrative has been mostly stripped of historical details. Other than Jonah and YHWH, no other character in the book is named. The only ruler mentioned is the mysterious "king of Nineveh," an odd epithet for the potentate of Assyria — one of the ancient Near East's most formidable superpowers. The text does not offer any clues as to which of the well-known Neo-Assyrian rulers this "king of Nineveh" might have been.

Furthermore, the narrative seems to operate under the assumption that Nineveh is the capital of Assyria. This, however, would not have been the case during Jonah's time (ca. 786 – 746). Nineveh did not become the capital of the Neo-Assyrian Empire until Sennacherib relocated the center of his government there at the end of the eighth century BC, some forty-five years after the period of Jonah's ministry under Jeroboam II of Israel.

Another curiosity of the narrative is its geographical orientation. Whereas 2 Kings 14:25 locates Jonah in the northern kingdom of Israel and identifies him as a native of Gath Hepher, the book of Jonah has a decidedly Judean orientation with a focus on Jerusalem. This is evident from Jonah's choice of Joppa as the port where he seeks passage to Tarshish. Joppa would not have been the logical point of departure if

Jonah received the divine call in his hometown of Gath Hepher. Instead, Acco would have been a much closer port. From Jerusalem, however, Joppa would have been the obvious point of departure for a voyage across the Mediterranean. Furthermore, Jonah's prayer in chapter 2 is strongly oriented toward the temple (2:4, 7).

What accounts for the book's lack of interest in historical details? Unlike most prophetic books, which go to some lengths to locate their protagonists in a specific historical setting and to relate their ministries to particular crises in the life of Israel or Judah, the book of Jonah achieves a state of near timelessness. Three reasons may be offered for the book's historical vagueness. First, the story appears to be written at some historical distance from the events recorded in the book. As a result, some details may have been lost in the story's transmission or simply deemed unimportant by comparison with the story's message.

Second, the narrative may have been stripped of historical details in order to highlight the universality of the book's message and to facilitate its appropriation by succeeding generations of God's people. The phenomenon of suppressing historical details in texts for the purpose of their incorporation into a liturgy or for their transmission to successive generations is well-known in the Hebrew Bible, especially in the psalms.[16]

Third, while the book of Jonah relates historical events, the book of Jonah was not written as strict historiography. Rather, since the author's interests were more theological and didactic than historical and chronological, the author chose a genre characterized by less historical detail — one that offered few distractions from the author's main point and one that allowed some freedom in shaping the material toward his theological purpose.

Meir Sternberg offers a helpful perspective regarding the relationship of biblical narrative to history that avoids a false dichotomy into which many interpreters fall.

> Biblical narrative emerges as a complex, because multifunctional, discourse. Functionally speaking, it is regulated by a set of three principles: ideological, historiographic, and aesthetic. How they *cooperate* is a tricky question…. But that they do operate is beyond question. For at some points — or from some viewpoints — we find each laid bare, as it were, asserting its claims and exerting its peculiar influence on narrative selection and arrangement.[17]

Sternberg's observations remind us that biblical narrative is a complex interweaving of theology, history, and literary art. Contemporary approaches tend to

---

16. Sigmund Mowinckel, "Psalm Criticism between 1900 and 1935," *VT* 5 (1955): 16–17. In explaining why so many of the psalms, even the historical ones, express themselves in such general, often stereotyped, phrases and metaphors, Mowinckel memorably commented, "Such a Psalm was meant to be used by 'Everyman' (*sic*) throughout all generations and would

therefore have to be put in such general terms as would suit 'Everyman.'"

17. Meir Sternberg, *The Poetics of Biblical Narrative: Ideological Literature and the Drama of Reading* (Bloomington: Indiana University Press, 1985), 41 (italics original).

oversimplify the interaction of these three facets especially with regard to the book of Jonah. The result is a false dichotomy between the aesthetics of the book of Jonah, which many interpreters wrongly assume to imply a fictional account, and the historicity of the book of Jonah, which others wrongly assume to preclude rhetorical features and creative shaping of the material in keeping with theological emphases.

As interpreters, it is our job to respect the inspired author's choice to suppress historical details for theological or rhetorical purposes without assuming that the author is composing fiction or falsifying history. The ancient Hebrews were characterized by a strong historical consciousness. Halpern helpfully reminds us regarding the Hebrew Bible that its "historical narrative is not to be handled as are folklore or the elements of dramatization in historical narrative ... a historian's conviction is not formal evidence of concoction."[18] Nonetheless, the form that their history writing took is quite different from modern historiography with its discounting of supernatural causation and its assumption of objectivity.[19] These principles should guide the reconstruction of Jonah's historical setting(s) based on clues within the book.

The Historical Background of the Narrative

The author of Jonah introduces the human protagonist by giving his full name, "Jonah Amittai's son." In doing so, the author links the narrative he is relating to the historical character mentioned in 2 Kings 14:25. This crucial link provides the historical background for the events narrated in the story. According to 2 Kings 14:25, Jonah prophesied during the reign of Jeroboam II (786–746 BC), making him roughly contemporary with Amos and Hosea.

Jeroboam II's long reign was characterized by peace and prosperity that rivaled the golden age of Solomon. Two political factors worked to Jeroboam's advantage. First, Adad-nirari III, upon assuming the Assyrian throne, launched a series of aggressive campaigns against the Arameans that eventually resulted in their capital, Damascus, being crushed and their military broken. Even after Assyria entered a period of decline, Aram was unable to resume campaigns against the northern kingdom of Israel because of a bitter rivalry with Zakir, the king of Hamath.[20] These two serendipities brought an end to many years of Aramean harassment in northern Israel and opened the way for Jeroboam II to reclaim Israelite territory that had been seized by Aramean rulers.

---

18. Baruch Halpern, _The First Historians: The Hebrew Bible and History_ (San Francisco: Harper & Row, 1988), xvii.

19. Oswalt notes, "It is often said that the accounts found in the Bible are only 'history-like.' In response, we will look at the characteristics of biblical narrative and compare them with the ancient Near Eastern approaches to the past. Once again, we will note that whatever the biblical narratives are, they are in a different category altogether. If they do not conform to all the canons of modern history writing, they are still much closer to what characterizes that genre than they are to anything in the ancient world." John N. Oswalt, _The Bible among the Myths: Unique Revelation or Just Ancient Literature?_ (Grand Rapids: Zondervan, 2009), 15.

20. "The Inscription of Zakkur, King of Hamath," translated by Alan Millard (_COS_ 2.35: 155).

Aram's paralysis by itself, however, could not have led to the resurgence of northern Israel under Jeroboam II. Northern Israel lay next in Assyria's path to domination of West Asia, and had not Assyria also entered a period of weakness at this time, Aramean harassment would simply have given way to Assyrian oppression and tyranny. Fortunately for Jeroboam II, however, Assyria was also beset with internal division and external threats, both of which served to distract her from her imperial ambitions, which included domination of West Asia as a path to Egypt. Internally, revolts had been brewing in Assyria since the end of Shalmaneser III's reign, including such powerful cities as Asshur, Nineveh, and Arbela. In fact, the revolts were so severe that Shalmaneser III's son had to fight for the throne for four years and was at last only able to secure it with Babylonian help.[21] Apparently, none of his successors were able to quell completely these rebellions at least until Tiglath-Pileser III came to the throne in 745 BC. In fact, beginning with the reign of Adad-nirari III, Assyria experienced epidemics, famines, revolts, and succession problems for a period of nearly forty years.[22]

Externally, Assyria was threatened by the growing power of Urartu, the kingdom to her north. By the beginning of the eighth century BC, Urartu rivaled Assyria in both size and strength. Since the succession of the Urartian king Sarduri I, Urartu began to threaten Assyria's expanding empire.[23] With a series of weak kings (Shalmaneser IV, Asshur-dan III, and Asshur-nirari V) following Adad-nirari III, however, the Urartian threat became critical and occupied all of Assyria's time and resources.

These two political realities allowed Jeroboam II the freedom necessary to expand Israel's borders to the same extent enjoyed under Solomon's reign. Second Kings 14:23 – 25 ascribes this great success to the mercy of YHWH, who announced through his prophet Jonah the successes that Jeroboam would enjoy despite the king's wickedness.

Another important aspect of this historical sketch is that it identifies Assyria's condition during Jonah's ministry, conditions that may well have led citizens of the great empire, like those in Nineveh, to question why Assyria's fortunes had taken such a turn for the worse. A few commentators have pointed to the historical suitability of this time frame for Jonah's mission.[24] In fact, some have suggested that a solar eclipse that occurred in the tenth year of Asshur-dan III (June 15, 763 BC) may have been YHWH's way of preparing Nineveh for Jonah's proclamation and of paving the way for the dramatic repentance displayed in Jonah 3.[25] Such circumstances as these could have played a role in predisposing the people of Nineveh to believe

21. Amélie Kuhrt, *The Ancient Near East* (London: Routledge, 1995), 2:490.

22. Ibid., 2:492.

23. Marc Van De Mieroop, *A History of the Ancient Near East* (Malden, MA: Blackwell, 2007), 215.

24. Douglas Stuart, *Hosea – Jonah* (WBC 31; Waco, TX: Word, 1987), 290 – 91, and John H. Walton, "Jonah" (*ZIBBCOT* 5; ed. John H. Walton; Grand Rapids: Zondervan, 2009), 115.

25. Stuart, *Hosea – Jonah*, 491.

and respond to Jonah's message. Though the biblical text mentions none of these historical factors, the backdrop of Assyrian weakness in the early eighth century supports the plausibility of the events narrated in the book of Jonah.

The Historical Background of Jonah's Author and Audience

Though the historical setting of the events recorded in Jonah is fairly easy to determine, the circumstances that prompted the book's composition is another matter entirely. Suggestions for the date of composition range from 750 BC,[26] shortly after the events it describes, to 250 BC,[27] shortly before the earliest known references to Jonah in Ben Sirach 49:10 and 4QXII[a]. Others have left the question open, allowing for a date anywhere within this spectrum.[28]

While any date within this range is possible, certain aspects of the book suggest that the Persian period of Judah is the most likely setting. First, the book of Jonah appears to assume the reader's familiarity with 1 and 2 Kings.[29] For example, the book's lack of a historical superscription is likely due to the presumption that readers know Jonah and his historical setting from 2 Kings 14:25. Furthermore, the author appears to invite comparison of Jonah with Elijah, particularly in Jonah 4, where Jonah's experience with the miraculous plant and worm bear marked similarities with Elijah's wilderness journey (1 Kings 19:4–5). Since the books of Kings were likely written between 560 BC and 538 BC,[30] the account of Jonah probably reached its final written form sometime after this.

A second consideration is that the book's vocabulary and syntax are more consistent with postexilic Hebrew than it is with preexilic Hebrew. Though dating ancient literature on a linguistic basis can be tricky, recent advances in the typology of the Hebrew language and clarification of the criteria that accurately distinguish later Hebrew from earlier has placed linguistic dating on firmer ground.[31] For its small size, the book of Jonah has a large number of late features, including vocabulary known elsewhere only in postexilic contexts[32] and spelling practices adopted in later biblical and postbiblical texts.[33]

---

26. The early date is, perhaps, most famously espoused by Kaufmann. Cf. Yehezkel Kaufmann, *The Religion of Israel: From Its Beginnings to the Babylonian Exile* (trans. Moshe Greenberg; New York: Schocken, 1972), 282.

27. Nogalski, *Redactional Processes*, 272.

28. Stuart, *Hosea – Jonah*, 432.

29. John Day, "Problems in the Interpretation of the Book of Jonah," in *In Quest of the Past: Studies on Israelite Religion, Literature, and Prophetism* (Leiden: Brill, 1990), 34 – 35.

30. Traditionally, the books of Kings are dated on the basis of the last recorded event, Jehoiachin's release from prison in 560 BC, and on the fact that the narrative makes no mention of the return from exile, an event that the author would likely

have included had it transpired by the time of writing. See Philip E. Satterthwaite and J. Gordon McConville, *Exploring the Old Testament: A Guide to the Historical Books* (Downers Grove, IL: InterVarsity Press, 2007), 188.

31. Avi Hurvitz, "Can Biblical Texts Be Dated Linguistically? Chronological Perspectives in the Historical Study of Biblical Hebrew," in *Supplements to Vetus Testamentum: Congress Volume, Oslo 1998* (vol. 80; ed. A. Lemaire and M. Sæbø; Leiden: Brill, 2000): 143 – 60.

32. For a recent, detailed list see Day, "Problems in the Interpretation of the Book of Jonah," 34 – 36.

33. Of particular interest is the rare spelling *nāqî'* for "innocent" in Jonah 1:14. The word is normally spelled *nāqî*, though

The possible chronological distance between the events recorded in the book and the book's composition should not, however, deter readers from taking the narrative seriously. A brief and dramatic account like that of the prophet Jonah could easily have been preserved in Israel's memory, having first circulated in northern Israel and then eventually making its way to postexilic Judah. It was finally combined with Judean prophetic traditions, at which point it was committed to writing with consummate artistic skill.[34]

Furthermore, the context of postexilic Judah is a particularly suitable occasion for the finalizing of Jonah's account in written form. Judah's attempt to understand and learn from her experience of captivity resulted in much reflection on the principle of divine retribution. In fact, 1 and 2 Kings explain both Israel's and Judah's captivity in largely retributive terms. The principle of divine retribution, however, can easily be distorted through oversimplification, which results in a conceptual tension between divine mercy and divine justice. Postexilic Judah was vulnerable to such mechanistic conceptions of divine retribution especially with regard to her desire for vengeance on the nations that had humiliated her.

The people's accusation against YHWH in Mal 2:17 provides one good example. Apparently frustrated with delays in YHWH's execution of justice, Judeans in Malachi's day were saying, "All who do evil are good in the eyes of the Lord, and he is pleased with them" (NIV). They also asked impatiently, "Where is the God of justice?" Other texts from this same period reflect similar sentiments.[35] The concept of divine retribution, therefore, was susceptible to distortion and misinterpretation and needed to be balanced with texts emphasizing divine mercy. One need only recall the people's reaction to Jesus' synagogue sermon in Nazareth recorded in Luke 4:16 – 29 to see an example of this sort of distorted reading of the prophets and 1 and 2 Kings. The deeply held misconceptions on display in Luke 4 likely had roots extending back to the time of Jonah's composition.

It is for this reason that the text where the prophet Jonah first appears is remarkable in the narrative of 1 and 2 Kings. The brief paragraph summarizing Jeroboam II's reign in 2 Kings 14:23 – 27 serves to balance the emphasis on the retributive principle found throughout 1 and 2 Kings by relating an instance of divine mercy. Despite Jeroboam II's wickedness, YHWH blessed his reign and announced his successes through the prophet Jonah son of Amittai apart from any repentance. The

---

it is frequently spelled with final *ʾālep* in the Qumran scrolls. Cf. Francis I. Andersen and A. Dean Forbes, *Spelling in the Hebrew Bible* (Rome: Biblical Institute, 1986), 84; Ziony Zevit, "What a Difference a Year Makes: Can Biblical Texts Be Dated Linguistically?" *HS* 47 (2006): 83 – 91; and Elisha Qimron, *The Hebrew of the Dead Sea Scrolls* (HSS 29; Atlanta: Scholars, 1986), 20 – 21.

34. For one explanation of how northern and southern prophetic traditions may have combined, see Robert R. Wilson, *Prophecy and Society in Ancient Israel* (Minneapolis: Fortress, 1980), 305 – 6.

35. Cf. Psalm 137:7 – 9; the prophecy of Nahum.

book of Jonah underscores and expands on this principle of mercy evident in 2 Kings 14:23 – 27 by extending it to the Gentiles, even to the most despised and feared Gentiles in Israel's memory — the Assyrians. The book of Jonah, therefore, preserves an account that offers a corrective to simplistic, mechanistic conceptions of divine justice especially with regard to the nations.

Literary Context

Genre and Structure of the Book of Jonah

Jonah has proven difficult to classify in terms of genre. Scholars have suggested such varying classifications as parable, midrash, tragedy, novella, and satire.[36] The wide variety of genre suggestions underscores the book's complexity and sophistication. Genre identification, however, is especially important for an interpretation based on discourse analysis. Only after identifying the type of discourse can one know which grammatical and syntactical signals to look for in determining the book's structure and the interrelationship of its clauses.

The book of Jonah conforms to the basic principles of Hebrew narrative with the exception of chapter 2, which consists almost entirely of poetry. The prose narrative nature of the book is indicated by the preponderance of Hebrew narrative verb forms (*wayyiqtol*) that serve as the plotline's backbone and advance the story through a sequence of reported events.[37] The narrative verb form always occupies first position in the clause. Thus, typical word order in narrative clauses is verb-(subject)-object. Clauses displaying this word order and marked with the narrative verb form are typically referred to as mainline clauses. Interruptions to this plotline are referred to as offline clauses and may be indicated by direct speech (dialogue or monologue by the characters), clauses beginning with some verb form other than the narrative verb, or by a change in the typical word order.[38] When an interruption to the plotline occurs, the narrative slows down or pauses altogether in order to report an important conversation or speech, to provide background information, to report simultaneous or antecedent events, or to shift to a new scene or episode. These are the signals that guide the analysis of structure and meaning in the commentary.

Narrative is a broad designation that easily subdivides into a wide variety of genres. It is possible, therefore, to identify the genre of Jonah with even greater precision — a precision that can potentially improve the accuracy of interpretation. Closer examination of this book reveals that it bears a striking resemblance to prophetic

---

36. T. D. Alexander, "Jonah and Genre," *TynBul* 36 (1985): 35 – 59.

37. W. Dennis Tucker, *Jonah: A Handbook on the Hebrew Text* (BHHB; Waco, TX: Baylor University Press, 2006), 5.

38. Bryan M. Rocine, *Learning Biblical Hebrew: A New Approach Using Discourse Analysis* (Macon, GA: Smyth & Helwys, 2000), 424.

accounts like those centering on the activity of Elijah and Elisha. A prophetic account is a third person narrative that recounts the notable exploits of one of YHWH's prophets typically for the purpose of demonstrating the prophet's exemplary religious devotion, extolling his ethical behavior, or exploring a divine attribute of YHWH.[39] In the case of the book of Jonah the emphasis of the prophetic account falls on YHWH's attribute of mercy expressed toward a hostile people. The book, however, employs the genre with a hint of satire since the exemplary behavior in the book is displayed not by the prophet Jonah, but by the idolatrous Gentile mariners and the wicked people of Nineveh, who, in contrast to Jonah, respond properly to YHWH's word and mercy.[40] Thus, Jonah may be characterized as a gentle parody of the traditional prophetic account designed to challenge Judah's distorted notions of traditional prophetic themes such as divine justice and Israel's election.

The book's overarching genre may contain a number of subgenres that support the book's general purpose and style. For example, prophetic accounts frequently include commission narratives, in which YHWH appoints an agent to carry out a specific task. They may also contain elaborate prayers that conform to one of the many known psalm patterns (e.g., lament, thanksgiving psalm, historical psalm, hymn). They also frequently contain prophetic oracles that can be classified on the basis of several known forms of prophetic speech (doom oracle, parable, disputation speech, salvation oracle). All of these subgenres occur in Jonah's prophetic account and serve as a reminder that this analysis of the book's basic genre should be supplemented with a genre analysis of each of its units.

The Message of the Book of Jonah

Two problems intersect in the book of Jonah that prevent the prophet from fully enjoying and freely sharing divine mercy. The first is Jonah's inability to reconcile YHWH's concern for nations hostile to Israel with YHWH's election of Israel. The second is Jonah's inability to reconcile YHWH's justice with YHWH's mercy. The narrative's conclusion reveals that the deeper problem is a distorted understanding of both divine election and divine justice, which precludes joyful participation in YHWH's mercy.

The Structure and Rhetorical Strategy of the Book of Jonah

The book of Jonah is compelling because it combines a powerful and timely message with persuasive and captivating rhetoric. Six main devices reinforce the book's

39. Marvin A. Sweeney, *Isaiah 1–39 with an Introduction to Prophetic Literature* (FOTL 16; Grand Rapids: Eerdmans, 1996), 21.

40. Ben Zvi, "Atypicality and the Meta-prophetic Character," 91–92.

structure and message: parallelism, alternating scenes, verbal repetition, symbolic use of geography and climate, intertextuality, and textual information gaps.

Parallelism. The narrative unfolds in two parallel sections as indicated by the repetition of the phrase "Yahweh's word came to Jonah ..." at 1:1 and 3:1 (*wayĕhî dĕbar yhwh 'el yônâ*). Each of these halves consists of three parallel episodes: a stage-setting episode, a pre-peak episode, and a peak episode. The stage-setting episodes introduce the characters and the main conflict that drives the plot forward in each of the book's two parts. The pre-peak episodes build tension and suspense leading toward a climactic confrontation between the characters. Finally, the peak episodes bring the conflict to a head and reach a climax accompanied by a noticeable slowing of the narrative and marked by a dramatic increase in direct speech.[41]

Each main section begins with a nearly identical call narrative in which YHWH commissions the prophet to deliver a message to Nineveh (stage-setting episode). Both units proceed with an account of a journey involving Jonah's interacting with Gentiles (pre-peak episode), and both units conclude with Jonah's praying to YHWH (peak episode) as indicated by the repetition of the phrase "and Jonah prayed to YHWH" at 2:2 (2:1) and 4:2 (*wayyitpallēl yônâ 'el-yhwh*).

The two halves of the book, therefore, form an almost perfect symmetry with three parallel episodes each: a stage-setting episode, a pre-peak episode, and a peak episode. The one exception to the symmetry is that the second main section of the book includes a post-peak (4:5 – 11) episode, which has no parallel in the book's first main section. This post-peak episode interrupts, then resumes the final dialogue between YHWH and Jonah, delaying and dramatizing the book's denouement. Within this post-peak episode YHWH offers Jonah an object lesson in divine mercy and concludes with a rhetorical question that clarifies the book's message. The book's structure, therefore, displays a large-scale parallelism that resembles a staircase.[42] Within the overarching symmetry of the parallelism marked by repetition, there is strategically placed variation that both highlights key thematic elements and enhances the artistry of the story.[43]

---

41. Robert E. Longacre and Shin Ja Hwang, "A Text-Linguistic Approach to the Biblical Hebrew Narrative of Jonah," in *Biblical Hebrew and Discourse Analysis* (ed. Robert D. Bergen; Winona Lake, IN: Eisenbrauns, 1994), 336 – 58. This terminology comes from Longacre's and Hwang's analysis, the results of which form the basis of the structural outline adopted in this commentary.

42. Longacre and Hwang acknowledge the parallelism of Jonah's two halves, but they miss the staircase structure by collapsing 4:1 – 4 and 4:5 – 11 into a single episode. The two episodes are distinguished, however, by a return to narrative discourse in 4:5 and by a scene shift (from Nineveh to a location outside the city; see ibid., 342). A more accurate division

of the book's units on a text-linguistic basis is offered by Ernst R. Wendland, "Text Analysis and the Genre of Jonah, Part I." *JETS* 39 (1996): 191 – 206; idem, "Text Analysis and the Genre of Jonah, Part II," *JETS* 39 (1996): 373 – 95.

43. Jan Fokkelman perceptively notes, "Hebrew prose writers as well as poets like to use the device of repetition, and they use it systematically and deliberately. At the same time, they know very well that repetition for the sake of it soon degenerates into monotony. This is why they developed a sophisticated technique of *varied repetition*, with the primary purpose of expanding the richness of meanings and keeping all sorts of surprises in store for us." J. P. Fokkelman, *Reading Biblical Narrative: An Introductory Guide* (Louisville: Westminster John Knox, 1999), 112.

Figure 1.1: Staircase Structure of the Book of Jonah

First main section (1:1 — 2:11)

A Stage setting [1:1-4a]	B Pre-peak Episode [1:4b-2:1b (1:17b)]	C Peak Episode [2:1c(1:17c)-2:11 (2:10)]	

Second main section (3:1 — 4:11)

A′ Stage setting [3:1-3b]	**B′ Pre-peak Episode [3:3c-10]**	**C′ Peak Episode [4:1-4]**	D Post-Peak Episode[44] [4:5-11]

Alternating scenes. The staircase parallelism[45] is supported by alternating scenes in which Jonah interacts first with YHWH and then with foreigners. Each main section of the book contains the following pattern of interactions: Jonah with YHWH, Jonah with Gentiles, Jonah with YHWH. A rhythm is thus established in the narrative that creates expectation and reinforces the book's symmetry. Furthermore, the alternating interactions suggest that the two relations — Jonah with YHWH and Jonah with Gentiles — are interconnected. This interconnection and alternation drives the plot forward to Jonah's climactic argument with God regarding the proper limits for divine mercy.

Figure 1.2: Alternating Scenes in the Book of Jonah

FIRST HALF (1:1 – 2:11 [10])			**SECOND HALF (3:1 – 4:11)**		
Scene 1 (1:1-3) YHWH with Jonah	**Scene 2 (1:4-16) Jonah with Gentiles**	**Scene 3 (2:1-11) YHWH with Jonah**	**Scene 4 (3:1-3) YHWH with Jonah**	**Scene 5 (3:4-10) Jonah with Gentiles**	**Scene 6 (4:1-11) YHWH with Jonah**

Verbal repetition. The author also demonstrates a penchant for clever verbal repetitions that mark significant junctures in the book and tie together parallel episodes. For example, the pairing of verbs with nouns derived from the same root is a common occurrence (1:10, 16; 3:7; 4:1, 6). The clauses containing the construction are conspicuous and often have a significant structural or thematic function. For example, the high concentration of verbal cognates in 1:16 underscores the Gentile

---

44. Dorsey and I independently arrived at similar conclusions regarding Jonah's seven-part structure. His conclusions are based on literary analysis while mine are based on discourse analysis. See David A. Dorsey, *The Literary Structure of the Old Testament: A Commentary on Genesis-Malachi* (Grand Rapids: Baker, 1999), 292.

45. Staircase parallelism has long been recognized as a distinctive type of line-level parallelism occurring in Hebrew poetry. It has not, however, been widely recognized as occurring in larger structures such as narratives or whole books. I am adopting the term here for the proposed structure of the book of Jonah because of its descriptive and heuristic value. Cf. Wilfred G. E. Watson, *Classical Hebrew Poetry: A Guide to Its Techniques* (Sheffield: Sheffield Academic, 1984; London: T&T Clark, 2005), 150.

mariners' surprising demonstration of devotion to YHWH [1:4b – 2:1a (17a)]. The pertinent words are highlighted in the following examples.

wayyîrĕʾû hāʾănāšim yirʾâ gĕdôlâ ʾet-yhwh wayyizbĕḥû-zebaḥ layhwh wayyiddĕrû nĕdārîm
The men feared with great fear YHWH, and they sacrificed sacrifices to YHWH and they vowed vows.

These clauses are memorable due to the sound play and verbal repetition they contain. Therefore, they come readily to mind when reading the parallel example of Gentile piety demonstrated by the people of Nineveh (3:5 – 10). The construction thus reinforces the parallel episodes in the book and highlights a significant occurrence of foreshadowing.

Another example occurs at the central turning point of the book, where YHWH issues his commission to Jonah a second time (3:2c).

wiqĕrāʾ ʾēlêhā et-haqqĕrîʾâ
And proclaim to it the proclamation

In this case the repetition reinforces the book's structure joining with other significant rhetorical features to mark the opening of the book's second major division.

A final example is the way the repetition of the word "evil" (*rāʿâ*) constitutes a theme that refers not only to Assyria's evil (1:2), but also to the great storm (1:7), to YHWH's threat of punishment (3:10; 4:2), and to Jonah's displeasure (4:1, 6). The author brilliantly exploits the word's broad range of meanings in order to draw a close connection between Nineveh's evil, Jonah's evil/displeasure, and YHWH's threat of punishment against both Jonah and Nineveh. English translations necessarily obscure these connections due to the variety of English equivalents required to render the various nuances of *rāʿâ*. The play on this word in Hebrew, however, is clear and serves to tie the book together. The fact that the same word describes both Jonah and Nineveh may indicate that there is less of a moral distinction between the prophet and the Assyrians than Jonah imagined. Furthermore, the fact that the same word also describes YHWH's response to both Jonah's sin and Assyria's sin may indicate that Jonah and Assyria deserved the same fate.

Symbolic use of geography and climate. Another compelling aspect of the book's rhetoric is its symbolic use of space and climate. The geography and climate of the prophet's location in various scenes frequently serve as an indication of the prophet's disposition.[46] For example, in each of the scenes where Jonah receives his commission from YHWH, the prophet is located on "dry land" (*hayyabbāšâ*, 1:9, 13; 2:11) — the normal environment for human habitation. When the prophet is fleeing YHWH's commission in part 1, however, he is caught on the turbulent sea — an inhospitable environment. The stormy sea was widely recognized in the ancient Near

---

46. T. A. Perry, *The Honeymoon Is Over: Jonah's Argument with God* (Peabody, MA: Hendrickson, 2006), 80.

East as a symbol of chaos, death, and tension with the gods.[47] These associations of the sea with chaos, death, and divine judgment become explicit in Jonah's prayer in chapter 2. Similarly in part 2, when the prophet is seething over Nineveh's deliverance and distressed over the demise of the plant that shaded him from the sun, he is located in a hot, dry desert (4:7 – 9) — again, an inhospitable environment.

YHWH appears to place Jonah in inhospitable environments in order to externalize his faith condition and confront Jonah with the truth of his spiritual condition.[48] When Jonah is in communion with YHWH and is compliant with his word, Jonah resides on dry land. When, however, Jonah flees YHWH's presence and resists his word, he resides in the extreme and inhospitable environments of sea and desert — places of death and chaos that are hostile to creation and to the divine order.

Intertextuality. A significant aspect of the book's rhetorical strategy is its effective use of intertextuality. Intertextuality simply refers to the pervasive influence of prior texts through direct quotation, literary allusion, or subtle echoes detectable in words, phrases, or images that call prior texts to mind.[49] The book of Jonah is particularly rich in intertextual allusions, and many of these will be discussed in the commentary. Two examples bear mention by way of introduction, however, because of their significant impact on the book's structure and message.

The first example is Jonah's heavy dependence on Genesis 1 – 11. From its description of Nineveh as a "great metropolis" (Jonah 1:2; cf. Gen 10:10 – 12) to Jonah's use of the compound divine name, YHWH-God (*yhwh-'ĕlōhîm*, cf. Gen 2 – 3), the book of Jonah displays marked and deliberate dependence on the first eleven chapters of Genesis. Some scholars have even suggested that the sequence of events in Genesis 1 – 11 serves as the outline for the book of Jonah, though in reverse order.[50] Though some of these parallels are far-fetched, these scholars are certainly correct to see the pervasive influence of Genesis 1 – 11 in the book of Jonah. In fact, some of the text's idiosyncratic features may be explained on the basis of the author's attempt to invoke the pre-Israelite, pan-human setting of Genesis 1 – 11. For example, the odd and frequent pairing of human and beast throughout the account may serve as a reminder that humans and land animals were both made on the sixth day of creation and both are objects of divine care.

The author may have drawn extensively from Genesis in order to support his emphasis on the universality of divine mercy. The author recreates in Jonah a setting like that of Genesis 1 – 11 as a reminder that Israel's election serves a universal, divine purpose rather than a parochial, self-centered one.

The second example is the way the author implicitly contrasts Jonah with other

---

47. William P. Brown, *Seeing the Psalms: A Theology of Metaphor* (Louisville: Westminster John Knox, 2002), 106 – 21.

48. Ben Zvi, "Atypicality and the Meta-prophetic Character," 104 – 5.

49. Daniel Lea, "Intertextuality" in *Routledge Dictionary of Literary Terms* (London: Routledge, 2006), 121.

50. Eric W. Hesse and Isaac M. Kikiwada, "Jonah and Genesis 1 – 11," *AJBI* 10 (1984): 3 – 19.

iconic prophets. For example, Moses leveraged his own life against Israel's in a desperate attempt to talk YHWH out of destroying the people over their sin with the golden calf. In contrast, Jonah would rather die than see Nineveh spared. Similarly, Elijah sat under a broom tree and requested death because Israel would not repent. In contrast, Jonah sits under a plant and requests death because Nineveh did repent. These examples illustrate the author's clever exposé of some of the twisted interpretations of Israel's prophetic tradition circulating around the time of the book's composition. Jonah's misunderstanding of the content and purpose of his own oracle serves as a paradigm of the dangers of a superficial and distorted understanding of prophetic oracles of judgment.

Textual information gaps. The sixth pervasive rhetorical strategy is the author's use of textual information gaps. The author frequently withholds information at points in the narrative where the reader expects it only to reveal the information later.[51] The best example of this technique is the delayed disclosure of the motive behind Jonah's initial flight from the divine commission. The reader expects and desires to know Jonah's reason for fleeing immediately following the narration of the event (1:3). The author deliberately suppresses this information, however, until Jonah 4:1 – 3. This displacement serves two important rhetorical purposes. First, it moves the reason for Jonah's initial flight to the book's second peak episode, ensuring that this information receives particular emphasis as critical to the book's message. Second, it encourages readers to speculate regarding Jonah's reasons for fleeing, potentially exposing to readers their own objections to divine mercy and their complicity in Jonah's sinful disposition toward Nineveh and YHWH.

Numerous other examples of this technique occur throughout the narrative and will be pointed out in the commentary. In each case, however, the reader is left guessing regarding omitted details in the story. As a result, readers may often be surprised to discover that their assumptions about various characters or events are incorrect when the missing information appears later in the narrative. The device effectively creates suspense and exposes readers' biases as the narrative advances toward its climax.

Discourse Markers

The final consideration with regard to literary context is the text's structure and the identification of the discourse markers that determine where the major divisions occur. As was mentioned earlier, the book divides into two main sections [1:1 – 2:11 (2:10); 3:1 – 4:11] that can be identified by their identical opening lines "YHWH's word came to Jonah …" (*wayĕhî dĕbar yhwh-'el yônâ*).

---

51. George M. Landes, "Textual 'Information Gaps' and 'Dissonances' in the Interpretation of the Book of Jonah," *Ki Baruch Hu: Ancient Near Eastern, Biblical, and Judaic Studies* *in Honor of Baruch A. Levine* (Winona Lake, IN: Eisenbrauns, 1999), 273 – 93.

The first main section divides into three episodes [1:1 – 4a; 1:4b – 2:1b (1:17b); 2:1c (1:17c) – 2:11], each of which begins with the verb *wayĕhî,* "and it happened." This verb often serves as a discourse marker that introduces new information at the beginning of an episode.[52] The peak episode in part 1 [2:1c (1:17c) – 2:11] brings the first main section of the book to its climax by radically shifting the discourse from prose to poetry. The narrative comes to a complete standstill as Jonah extols the virtue of divine mercy in a beautiful thanksgiving psalm ironically sung from the fish's belly. The unit as a whole traces Jonah's journey from dry land to stormy sea to the belly of Sheol as the prophet chooses death over obedience to YHWH's call. At the conclusion of the unit, however, Jonah is forced to acknowledge his dependence on and gratitude for YHWH's expansive mercy.

The second main section divides into four episodes. The first of these (3:1 – 3b) begins with *wayĕhî,* which once again indicates a new chapter in the narrative and closely corresponds to 1:1 – 4a. YHWH renews Jonah's commission, and this time Jonah obeys.

The second episode in part 2 begins by interrupting the plotline with a noun-initial clause: "Now Nineveh was a great metropolis belonging to God" (*wĕnînĕwēh hāyĕtâ ʿîr-gĕdôlâ lēʾlōhîm*). By moving the noun "Nineveh" to the first position in the clause, the author indicates a change of topic from Jonah's actions to Nineveh's most notable characteristics — her great size and YHWH's claim on her.[53] A new episode focusing on the city of Nineveh and YHWH's interaction with her is thus introduced.

The conclusion to the second episode in part 2 provides the first syntactic clue to the beginning of episode 3. Episode 2 ends at 3:10 with the emphatic assertion that YHWH "relented concerning the disaster that he threatened to perform against them *and he did not do it.*" The final clause of 3:10 is remarkable in two respects. First, it is redundant. The narrative has already made clear that YHWH relented from the disaster he had planned. Seldom does Hebrew narrative stray from its normal economy of words to report the same event or fact twice. Second, the clause is negated, offering the negative corollary to the preceding clause "he relented." Normally, negated clauses occupy the background of Hebrew narrative, relegated to parenthetic remarks that serve as scene setting material for the main story line. In this case, however, a negated clause occupies a place of prominence, interrupting the narrative to clarify YHWH's unbelievable act of clemency. This clause brings decisive closure to both the threatened destruction and to the second episode of part 2.[54]

The boundary between episodes 2 and 3 is thus clearly marked. Episode 3 begins at 4:1 with an emphasis on Jonah's angry reaction to the clemency YHWH extended to Nineveh. Jonah has been absent from the narrative since 3:5. So his reappearance

---

52. Christo van der Merwe, Jackie Naudé, and Jan H. Kroeze, *A Biblical Hebrew Reference Grammar* (Sheffield: Sheffield Academic, 2000), 333.

53. Rocine, *Learning Biblical Hebrew*, 424.
54. Tucker, *Jonah*, 84.

in 4:1 constitutes a significant shift of attention from Nineveh's obedient repentance to Jonah's disobedient resentment. Furthermore, 4:2 marks the onset of the peak episode in part 2 with the same verb that marked the peak episode in part 1 — "and Jonah prayed" (*wayyitpallēl yônâ*). These two prayers, however, stand in sharp contrast to each other. Whereas Jonah's prayer in the first main section of the book was a prayer of thanksgiving for YHWH's mercy, his prayer in the second main section of the book is a prayer of complaint against YHWH's mercy. The book's main theological issue begins to come into focus.

The final episode of part 2 resumes the narrative after Jonah's second prayer and YHWH's response. The beginning of a new episode is confirmed by a scene shift (from Nineveh to the desert east of Nineveh) and by the parallels evident between episodes 3 and 4. In both episodes Jonah requests death, and in both episodes YHWH questions the intensity of Jonah's anger. The fourth episode of part 2 breaks the symmetry of the rest of the book. It has no parallel episode in part 1. In the logic of the staircase parallelism this indicates that the burden of the book's message falls primarily on this final episode. The object lesson involving the plant, the worm, the wind, and the sun must therefore play a significant role in communicating the book's message.

The outline based on this discourse analysis is offered in the table on the next page. The first (far left) column indicates, by means of word count, the amount of narrative space devoted to each section. The second column indicates, by means of shading, the thematic density of each section — the degree to which each section emphasizes and reinforces the book's message. This provides a basis of comparison with the discourse analysis regarding where the emphasis in the narrative falls relative to the lengths of the sections. As the table demonstrates, part 1, episode 2 (1:4b – 2:1b [1:17b]) is by far the longest section of the book, yet it does not carry the thematic weight of the much shorter final episode. This apparent discrepancy between episode length and thematic significance may be due to the deliberate protraction of the first pre-peak episode for the purposes of characterization and conflict development. This section, more than any other, develops the characters of Jonah, the Gentiles, and YHWH. Furthermore, it intensifies and clarifies the depth of the conflict between Jonah and YHWH.

	Table 1.2 : God's Scandalous Mercy	
	The Structure of Jonah	
66	**I. From Silent Resistance to Jubilant Acceptance: The Compelling Nature of God's Mercy (1:1–2:11 [2:10], Macro Unit 1)**	
	A. A Silent Escape from God's Mercy (1:1–4a, Stage setting)	
	1. The commission: a challenge to parochial prophecy (1:1a–2d)	
	2. The objection: an unexplained, reckless flight (1:3)	
	3. The rebuke: YHWH's conspiracy with wind and waves (1:4a)	
219	B. The Relentless Pursuit of God's Severe Mercy (1:4b–2:1b [1:17b], Pre-peak episode)	
	1. The wrath of YHWH's severe mercy (1:4b–5d)	
	2. The futility of ignoring YHWH's severe mercy (1:5e–6g)	
	3. The revelation of YHWH's sovereign, severe mercy (1:7–9)	
	4. The fear due YHWH's sovereign, severe mercy (1:10–12)	
	5. The futility of escaping YHWH's severe mercy (1:13–14)	
	6. The relenting wrath of YHWH's relentless mercy (1:15a–2:1b [1:17b])	
128	C. A Prayer of Praise for God's Mercy (2:1c–11 [1:17c –2:10], Peak episode)	
	1. Jonah's reversal regarding his preference for judgment over obedience (2:1c–7b)	
	2. Jonah's partial and prideful response to grace (2:7c–11b)	
48	**II. From Compliant Acceptance to Angry Resentment: The Offense of God's Mercy (3:1–4:11, Macro Unit 2)**	
	A. A Second Chance at Compliance with God's Mercy (3:1–3b, Stage setting)	
	1. The commission: a second chance to learn the scope of God's mercy (3:1–2)	
	2. The compliance: a concession to God's mercy (3:3a–b)	
125	B. Responsiveness to and the Responsiveness of God's Mercy (3:3c–10, Pre-peak episode)	
	1. The motives and methods of God's mercy (3:3c–6)	
	2. The goals of God's mercy (3:7–10)	
48	C. Resentment of God's Mercy (4:1–4, Peak episode)	
	1. Jonah's anger over YHWH's mercy (4:1)	
	2. Jonah's complaint against YHWH's mercy (4:2–3)	
	3. YHWH's challenge to Jonah's anger (4:4)	
116	D. An Object Lesson on the Divine Mercy and Divine Justice (4:5–11, Post-peak episode)	
	1. Jonah's vigil for YHWH's response (4:5)	
	2. YHWH's object lesson on divine mercy (4:6–8)	
	3. God's final challenge to Jonah's anger (4:9–11)	

I. From Silent Resistance to Jubilant Acceptance:
The Compelling Nature of God's Mercy

CHAPTER 1

Jonah 1:1 – 4a

A. A Silent Escape from God's Mercy

Main Idea of the Passage

Jonah 1:1 – 3 introduces a surprising commission from God from which Jonah flees. His flight, however, takes a downward direction, and Jonah begins descending toward the realm of chaos and death.

Literary Context

The book of Jonah's opening phrase, "YHWH's word came to Jonah, Amittai's son" (*wayěhî děbar yhwh 'el yônâ*), serves as a common introduction to episodes in biblical narrative that focus on a divine commission and its fulfillment.[1] Only in the book of Jonah, however, does this phrase stand at the beginning of a book.[2] In its other occurrences, the phrase serves to introduce a new episode in a narrative already in progress.[3]

The effect of this uncommon opening on the reader is somewhat disorienting. One enters this book with little sense of the precise location or time of the narrative. The suppression of historical and geographical details is atypical for the openings of prophetic books and may be a rhetorical device designed to facilitate the narrative's appropriation by audiences of any historical and geographical setting (cf. Introduction, pp. 30 – 36).

---

1. See, e.g., 1 Sam 15:10; 2 Sam 7:4; 1 Kgs 6:11; 16:1; 17:2, 8 (esp. close resemblance to Jonah 1:1); 21:17, 28; 2 Chr 11:2; Isa 38:4; Jer 28:12; 29:30; 32:26; 33:1, 19; 34:12; 35:12; 36:27; 37:6; 42:7; 43:8; Hag 2:20; Zech 7:8.

2. Other prophetic books begin with a similar introduction (*dābār yhwh 'ăšer hāyâ 'el* ... [lit., "the word of YHWH that was to ..."]). The syntax, however, is different from Jonah's opening line and serves in these cases to mark the beginning of a collection of oracles rather than a narrative episode. Thus, this more typical formula for the introduction of prophetic books serves as a heading or title for the entire collection.

3. Uriel Simon, *Jonah* (JPS Bible Commentary; Philadelphia: Jewish Publication Society, 1999), 3.

This abrupt introduction also serves to highlight the divine word as the precipitating event that sets the narrative in motion. The reader is immediately confronted with a challenging word from YHWH and perhaps senses some of Jonah's surprise at God's unexpected and unwelcome commission. This opening may also alert the reader to a prior relationship between Jonah and YHWH (cf. 2 Kgs 14:23 – 25).[4] Jonah is already a prophet called into YHWH's service, but his vocation now broadens beyond the borders of Israel, borders incidentally that Jonah had announced would return to their Solomonic dimensions under the reign of Jeroboam II (2 Kgs 14:23 – 25).

The form and wording of 1:1 – 3 recur at 3:1 – 3 when YHWH reissues the commission that Jonah initially disobeyed. These two texts serve as pillars for the book's structure and establish the parallelism that exists between the two halves of the book. Jonah 1:1 – 3 sets the stage and introduces the major characters and the major conflict that will drive the plot toward its first peak episode (2:1c – 11 [1:17c – 2:10]).[5] The outline below demonstrates the relationship of Jonah 1:1 – 3 to the larger structure of the first main section of the book.

I. From Silent Resistance to Jubilant Acceptance: The Compelling Nature of God's Mercy (1:1 – 2:11 [2:10], Macro Unit 1)

➡ **A. A Silent Escape from God's Mercy (1:1 – 4a, Stage setting)**
1. The commission: a challenge to parochial prophecy (1:1 – 2)
2. The objection: an unexplained, reckless flight (1:3)
3. The rebuke: YHWH's conspiracy with wind and waves (1:4a)
B. The Relentless Pursuit of God's Severe Mercy (1:4b – 2:1b (1:17b), Pre-peak episode)
C. A Prayer of Praise for God's Mercy (2:1c – 11 [1:17c – 2:10]), Peak episode)
II. From Compliant Acceptance to Angry Resentment: The Offense of God's Mercy (3:1 – 4:11, Macro Unit 2)

Translation and Outline

(See next page.)

---

4. Since the phrase *wyhy dbr yhwh ʾl* elsewhere marks the continuation of a narrative, the syntax here reinforces the intertextual connection with 2 Kgs 14:23 – 25. Furthermore, the information gaps relative to the narrative's location and time period may be due to the author's assumption of the readers' familiarity with 2 Kgs 14:23 – 25. See Yehoshua Gitay, "Jonah: The Prophecy of Antirhetoric," in *Fortunate the Eyes That See: Essays in Honor of David Noel Freedman in Honor of His Seven-* *tieth Birthday* (Grand Rapids: Eerdmans, 1995), 198, and Landes, "Textual 'Information Gaps,'" 276 – 77. Landes argues that the omission of geographical and temporal information in the introduction to Jonah is due to the author's lack of interest in such matters. It is, however, equally plausible that these omissions reinforce the connection to 2 Kgs 14:23 – 25.

5. Longacre and Hwang, "A Text-Linguistic Approach," 342.

Jonah 1:1–4a

1:1	YHWH's word came to Jonah, Amittai's son, as follows:
1:2a	↑ Up!
1:2b	Go to Nineveh, that great metropolis,
1:2c	and condemn it
1:2d	↑ because their evil has ascended before me!
1:3a	So Jonah got up
1:3b	↑ to flee to Tarshish, away from YHWH's presence.
1:3c	He descended to Joppa.
1:3d	He found a ship bound for Tarshish.
1:3e	He paid its hire,
1:3f	and he descended into it
1:3g	↑ ↑ to accompany them to Tarshish, away from YHWH's presence.
1:4a	Meanwhile, YHWH flung a great gale toward the sea.

A. A Silent Escape from God's Mercy (1:1-4a)

  1. The commission: a challenge to parochial prophecy (1:1-2)
    a. The suddenness of the commission (1:1)
    b. The urgency of the commission (1:2a)
    c. The surprising destination of the commission (1:2b)
    d. The reason for the commission (1:2c-d)

  2. The objection: an unexplained, reckless flight (1:3)
    a. The silent defiance of the flight (1:3a-b)
    b. The downward direction of the flight (1:3c)
    c. The destination of the flight (1:3d-e)

    d. The intent of the flight (1:3f-g)

  3. The rebuke: YHWH's conspiracy with wind and waves (1:4a)

Structure and Literary Form

The opening words, "YHWH's word came to Jonah, Amittai's son, as follows …," help readers identify the genre of this passage. Since the phrase is so common in prophetic narratives, many scholars designate it as a formula for Hebrew narrative called the "prophetic word formula."[6] Typically this formula indicates the divine origin of a call or commission. Its presence at the beginning of 1:1 – 3 followed by YHWH's command to Jonah to go to Nineveh indicates that this text is a commission narrative. Commission narratives are a common feature of prophetic accounts and often serve as their starting point (cf., e.g., 1 Sam 16; 1 Kgs 17:2 – 6)

Commission narratives in the Old Testament follow a typical pattern that finds its classical expression in YHWH's commission of Moses in Exodus 3 – 4. First, YHWH commissions an individual to a particular task (divine commission). Following this commission, the individual usually objects that he is inadequate for the task in question (objection to commission). God responds to these objections with both a rebuke and reassurance of divine presence and power (rebuke and reassurance). At this point, God typically engages in a ritual or sign act that confirms the commission and prepares the individual for the task (ritual/sign). Finally, God describes or clarifies the commission (clarification of commission).[7]

Not every commission narrative contains each of these elements, and a number of variations are possible, but the elements are relatively stable, especially the divine

---

6. Burk O. Long, *1 Kings with an Introduction to Historical Literature* (FOTL; Grand Rapids: Eerdmans, 1984), 265.

7. Norman C. Habel, "The Form and Significance of the Call Narratives," *ZAW* 77 (1965): 297 – 323.

commission, the objections to the commission, and the description/clarification of the commission. In the case of Jonah, the commission narrative is protracted due to Jonah's unexplained flight and extends beyond 1:1 – 4a into the next two episodes (1:4b – 2:1b; 2:1c – 11). The table below offers a side by side comparison of the typical commission narrative (Exod 3 – 4) with Jonah 1:1 – 3:2.

Table 2.1: A Comparison of the Commission Narratives in Exodus 3 – 4 and Jonah 1:1 – 3:2		
Elements of a Commission Narrative	**Exod 3 – 4**	**Jonah 1:1 – 3:2**
Divine commission	Exodus 3:10	Jonah 1:2
Objection to commission	Exodus 3:11 – 4:13	Jonah 1:3
Divine rebuke and reassurance	Exodus 4:14 – 16	Jonah 1:4 – 16
Ritual/symbolic act	Exodus 4:1 – 5, 17	Jonah 2:1 (1:17)
Clarification of Commission	Exodus 4:14 – 16	Jonah 3:2

While Jonah 1:1 – 4a fits this general scheme, it also departs from the typical commission narrative in a significant way. Jonah's objection to the commission is nonverbal. He simply flees the commission without comment or explanation. This response to the divine commission interrupts the pattern so thoroughly that the commission narrative gives way to YHWH's pursuit of Jonah in the second and third episodes (1:4 – 2:11), finally resuming in Jonah 3:1 – 2, where the original commission is repeated. While episodes 2 and 3 at first sight appear to derail the commission narrative, they may represent ironic expressions of the divine rebuke/reassurance and the ritual/symbolic act, thus advancing the commission narrative, though in an unexpected way, to its conclusion — the clarification of the commission (3:1 – 2).

Following YHWH's commission, Jonah's rebellious actions are succinctly reported in a keyword chiasm (inverted structure) that draws attention to the destination of Jonah's desperate flight (1:3).[8] The effect of this textual arrangement is demonstrated below.

Figure 2.1: The Keyword Chiasm in Jonah 1:3

A Jonah got up to flee to Tarshish, away from YHWH's presence
  B He descended to Joppa
    X He found a ship bound for Tarshish and paid its hire
  B´ He descended into it
A´   to accompany them for Tarshish, away from YHWH's presence

The first key word is the mainline narrative verb "he descended" (*wayyēred*). The repetition of this verb indicates that Jonah's westward journey is, spiritually speaking,

---

8. Norbert Lohfink, "Jona ging zur Stadt hinaus (Jona 4,5)," *BZ* 5 (1961): 200 – 201.

a downward journey. The verb recurs in the next unit (1:5e), serving to tie the two episodes together with this common theme. The next key words are "Tarshish" and "away from YHWH's presence." They normally occur together and provide a significant clue as to the author's assessment of Jonah's journey. Jonah foolishly tried to escape his calling by fleeing in the opposite direction, to the remotest place he knew — a place where YHWH had not yet been revealed (cf. Isa 66:19) and, presumably, where no challenging word from YHWH would come.

Explanation of the Text

1. The Commission: A Challenge to Parochial Prophecy (1:1a – 2d)

The book of Jonah places the divine word at the front (1:1) and center (3:1) of its narrative. Immediately the reader, like Jonah, is confronted with a challenging message from YHWH commanding an unprecedented prophetic mission. That YHWH's word is the precipitating event for all that follows in the narrative is evident by its predicate — "it came" (wayĕhî). This verb is actually a form of the verb "to be," and it is frequently used in Hebrew narrative to mark the onset of a new episode within a story.[9] In the case of 1:1 the verb introduces a word-event formula announcing a divine commission.[10] Only in 1:1, however, does this formula stand at the very beginning of a biblical book. This unusual introduction, therefore, highlights the sudden and unexpected nature of the commission.[11] YHWH's word comes without

warning, and it launches a journey Jonah has never anticipated.

The phrase "YHWH's word" (dĕbar yhwh) occurs frequently in the Old Testament (242 times),[12] especially in the prophetic literature. In fact, "almost everywhere it occurs dĕbar yhwh is a technical term for the prophetic word of revelation."[13] The phrase may be applied to a single utterance, an extended prophetic speech, an entire book, a revelatory act, or even to the entirety of God's revelation (cf., e.g., Ps 33:4).[14]

With few exceptions, the phrase "YHWH's word" introduces an oracle that the prophet is to convey on YHWH's behalf to a particular audience, usually YHWH's covenant people, Israel. In the present case, however, it introduces a royal commission issued directly from YHWH to his servant Jonah. Similar instances of this unusual construction with the phrase "YHWH's word" occur in the Samuel and Elijah narratives (cf. 1 Sam 15:10; 1 Kgs

---

9. Albert Kamp, *Inner Worlds: A Cognitive Linguistic Approach to the Book of Jonah* (BIS 68; trans. David Orton; Leiden: Brill, 2004), 89. Kamp argues that this verb form divides Jonah into four episodes per each of its occurrences. This fails to take into account, however, the different functions this verb has in each of these contexts.

10. Van der Merwe, Naudé, and Kroeze, *A Biblical Hebrew Reference Grammar*, 333. Van der Merwe, Naudé, and Kroeze rightly distinguish between *wyhy* as a discourse marker indicating episode boundaries and its function as an ordinary predicate. The occurrence in Jonah 1:1 would fall under this latter category according to their criteria. Cf. also Jean-Marc

Heimerdinger, *Topic, Focus, and Foreground in Ancient Hebrew Narratives* (JSOTSup, 295; Sheffield: Sheffield Academic, 1999), 234. Heimerdinger recognizes that *wyhy* forms part of an idiom in Jonah 1:1 and therefore does not function independently as a discourse marker.

11. Phyllis Trible, *Rhetorical Criticism: Context, Method, and the Book of Jonah* (Minneapolis: Fortress, 1994), 124 – 25.

12. Frank Ritchel Ames, "*dbr*," NIDOTTE, 1:912 – 15.

13. O. Grether, *Name und Wort Gottes im alten Testament* (BZAW, 64; Giessen: A. Toppelmann, 1934), 62, 66, 76, quoted in G. Mayer, "*dābhar; dābhār*," TDOT, 3: 111.

14. Ames, "*dbr*," 1:913.

17:2, 8; 18:1; 21:17).[15] These examples bear close resemblance to the commission found in Jonah 1:1 – 3 and suggest a close relationship between these prophetic accounts and the narrative of Jonah.

Jonah's name (*yônâ*) is the Hebrew word for "dove." Personal names derived from animal nomenclature are well attested in Hebrew as well as in other Afro-Asiatic languages.[16] Their significance, however, is unknown. The prophet Jonah is the only Old Testament character to wear this name.

His father's name, *'ămittay*, appears to derive from the noun *'ĕmet* ("truth" or "faithfulness"), followed by an abbreviated form of the divine name YHWH, yielding a meaning like "YHWH is faithful/true."[17] The mention of Jonah's surname clarifies that he is the same prophet who predicted Jeroboam's successful expansion of Israel's borders (2 Kgs 14:23 – 25) and may serve to anchor the story that follows to that historical situation.

YHWH's commission to Jonah is an embedded discourse in which imperatives, rather than narrative verbs, serve as the backbone of communication. The shift to direct discourse is marked by the words "as follows," corresponding to the infinitive *lē'mōr*, which typically introduces quoted speech.

As is often the case in divine commissions, YHWH's speech betrays a sense of urgency. The imperative "Up!" (*qûm*), when closely linked with other commands, frequently serves as an interjection or exclamation underscoring the force of the following imperatives. It appears to have that function here, indicating the need for haste in carrying out the following two commands: "go" (*lēk*) and "condemn" (*qĕrā'*).[18] The JPS and NRSV capture the idea with the expression "Go at once to Nineveh." The reason for this urgency will become clear in the causal clause following the actual commission (1:2d).

The identification of Nineveh as YHWH's target audience is remarkable on two counts. First, the commissioning of a prophet to visit and to preach to a foreign nation was unprecedented in Hebrew prophecy. Most prophets delivered oracles of judgment addressed to foreign nations, but they did so rhetorically as part of their message to Israel to serve as harbingers of Israel's deliverance from foreign oppression (e.g., Obadiah and Nahum), to warn Israel/Judah of the disastrous consequences of dependence on alliances with foreign nations (Isaiah 13 – 24), or to humble Israel by reducing her to the status of one of the nations in need of YHWH's judgment (e.g., Amos 1 – 2).[19] Against this background, YHWH's commission to Jonah to travel to Nineveh and deliver an oracle of doom directly to the nation in question is truly unique. This commission breaks new ground in Hebrew prophecy.

Second, Nineveh, though historically a city of some renown, was not, during Jonah's time, the capital of Assyria.[20] Nonetheless, it is treated

---

15. Jack M. Sasson, *Jonah* (AB 24B; New York: Doubleday, 1990), 68.

16. Ibid.

17. Jeaneane D. Fowler, *Theophoric Personal Names in Ancient Hebrew: A Comparative Study* (JSOTSup, 49; Sheffield: Sheffield Academic, 1988), 165. For an alternative interpretation of the suffix at the end of the name *'ămittay*, see Stuart, *Hosea – Jonah*, 447.

18. Bruce K. Waltke and M. O'Connor, *An Introduction to Biblical Hebrew Syntax* (Winona Lake, IN: Eisenbrauns, 1990), 574.

19. John H. Hays, "The Usage of the Oracles against Foreign Nations in Ancient Israel," *JBL* 87 (1968): 81 – 92. Cf. also Hans-Martin Lutz, *Jahwe, Jerusalem und die Völker: Zur Vorgeschichte von Sach 12, 1 – 8 und 14, 1 — 5* (Neukirchen-Vluyn: Neukirchener, 1968), 147 – 204.

20. The capital of Assyria throughout the ninth and most of the eighth centuries was Kalhu (modern Nimrud). Later, in 717 BC, Sargon II established a new capital at Dur Sharrukin (modern Khorsabad). Only after Sennacherib ascended to the throne did Nineveh (modern Mosul) become the capital of the Neo-Assyrian Empire (ca. 700 BC). Cf. Van De Mieroop, *A History of the Ancient Near East*, 233 – 36.

throughout the book as the representative city of the growing Assyrian empire despite the fact that Kalhu actually served as the administrative center in the early eighth century. Why then this urgent call to go to the more peripheral city of Nineveh? What about Nineveh warranted YHWH's and, consequently, Jonah's, attention?

The tradition regarding Nineveh's origin recorded in Gen 10:11 offers a significant clue. The text reads as follows: "From that land, Ashshur emerged and built Nineveh, that is the broadest city, and Calah, as well as Resen between Nineveh and Calah, which is the capital city."[21] Interestingly, Nineveh heads the list of cities attributed to Assyria's ancestor, Ashshur, which implies that Nineveh was the first of the great city states on which Assyria was founded. Thus, Nineveh was closely associated with the origins of Assyria as a nation and frequently served to represent Assyria as a whole as well as the Assyrian ideals of imperial expansion, national pride, and the indiscriminate use of power. YHWH's charge to Jonah to travel to Nineveh is rich with the symbolism of Assyria's origin and her reputation for unrestrained cruelty.

Nineveh's association with Assyrian cruelty made it an undesirable destination and an even more undesirable audience for Hebrew prophecy. The whole point of prophecy in Israel was to warn of impending judgment in order to encourage repentance and avert disaster (Amos 3:1 – 7; 5:3 – 6).

In the case of Assyria, however, few could believe that anything good would come from sparing such a ruthless enemy of Israel and Judah.

YHWH's description of Nineveh as a "great metropolis" (*hā'îr haggĕdôlâ*), repeated in 3:2, 3; and 4:11, anticipates this city's rise to prominence during the reign of Sennacherib. This phrase occurs in three other places in the Hebrew Bible outside of Jonah (Gen 10:12; Josh 10:2; Jer 22:8), each time with reference to a city that serves both as the capital of a district or nation and an important cultic center.[22] The expression appears to have the same significance in the case of Jonah 1:2b. The designation is deliberately anachronistic, reflecting the perspective of the author and his audience (see introduction, pp. 34 – 36), but it also emphasizes YHWH's anticipation of the resurgence of Assyrian power and the plans he had for this city by which he would discipline his own people (Isa 10:5). This may, in fact, have been YHWH's underlying motivation for commissioning Jonah — to avert the premature end of a city that had a significant role to play on the world stage under YHWH's governance.

The description of Nineveh as "great" may also recall the spies' description of the Canaanite city-states that so intimidated them. In Num 13:28 ten of the spies report to the people, "and the cities are well-fortified and very intimidating" (*wĕhe'ārîm bĕṣurôt gĕdōlōt mĕ'ōd*). No doubt Jonah's con-

---

21. In my translation of Gen 10:11, I understand *'aššûr* to be the subject of the verb "built," and I interpret it as a reference to the ancestor and namesake of Assyria (cf. Victor P. Hamilton, *The Book of Genesis, Chapters 1 – 17* [NICOT; Grand Rapids: Eerdmans, 1990], 340). Furthermore, I agree with Sasson in taking the phrase *wĕ'et-rĕḥōbōt 'îr* to be in apposition to "Nineveh," meaning "the broadest city" (Jack M. Sasson, "*Rĕḥōbōt 'îr*," *RB* 90 1983. : 94 – 96).

22. Genesis 10:12 identifies Calah as the capital city (*hā'îr haggĕdōlâ*) of Assyria. This would have been during the reign of Asshurnasirpal II. It was also the cult center for the worship of Ninurta, the Assyrian war god. The same phrase describes

Gibeon in Joshua 10:2 because of its role as the chief city of the Hivite tetrapolis (Gibeon, Beeroth, Chephirah, and Kiriath Yearim) that spanned the main thoroughfare connecting the Jordan rift with the Mediterranean coast. It also appears to have functioned early in the monarchy as an important sanctuary for YHWH worship (1 Kgs 3:4ff.; 2 Chr 1:3). In fact, Blenkinsopp argues convincingly that Gibeon served as Saul's capital after his victory over the Philistines (cf. Joseph Blenkinsopp, "Did Saul Make Gibeon His Capital?" *VT* 24 (1974): 1 – 7). Finally, Jer 22:8 applies the same phrase to Jerusalem, identifying it as both capital of the Davidic dynasty and the location of YHWH's temple.

temporaries in both Israel and Judah felt at least as much trepidation regarding the chief Assyrian cities like Nineveh as they had the Canaanite cities they faced in the conquest.

Furthermore, the phrase "great metropolis" echoes Sennacherib's own description of Nineveh after he rebuilt it as his capital.[23] In his annals he praises Nineveh with a string of honorific epitaphs:

> At that time, Nineveh, the noble metropolis, the city bemercyd of Ishtar wherein are all the meeting-places of gods and goddesses ... the eternal foundation, the plan of which has been drawn from of old in the firmament ... where the kings who went before had exercised lordship over Assyria and had received yearly, without interruption, never ending tribute from the princes of the four quarters.[24]

Sennacherib's praise of Nineveh is self-congratulatory in tone as he accepts credit for the city's magnificence as the result of his renovations and his rededication of the metropolis to its patron deity, Ishtar. The author of the book of Jonah asserts, however, that before Sennacherib ever came to power or ever thought about making Nineveh his capital, YHWH had already designated the city as a "great metropolis." In other words, Nineveh's status as the chief city of Assyria and the center of a new world power is due neither to Sennacherib nor to Ishtar but to YHWH, who designated the city an instrument of his sovereign purposes.

The final imperative in the series is "condemn" (*qārā' 'al*). The combination of the verb "to cry out" (*qārā'*) with the preposition "against" (*'al*)

connotes disapproval and warning.[25] This is the climactic command in YHWH's commission. The trip to Nineveh is merely prerequisite to the main task of publicly, unequivocally expressing YHWH's holy wrath against the ancient city.

The rationale for this task follows immediately ("because," *kî*). Nineveh's wickedness had reached a critical point and divine intervention was required. YHWH expressed this state of affairs through an interesting and rare idiom. He said, "their evil has ascended before me," (*'ālĕtâ rā'ātām lĕpānāy*). The idiom suggests a reckless racking up of offenses until YHWH can no longer abide the wickedness. It emphasizes the blatant nature of Assyria's crimes, which they had shamelessly put on display. The grotesque nature of Assyria's cruelty in the eighth century is confirmed by the numerous inscriptions that the Assyrian kings left to commemorate their brutality.[26] Perhaps it is to such proud, public displays of evil that YHWH is responding. Whatever the case, YHWH's justice can wait no longer. The purpose clause expresses the reason for immediate action and recalls the hint of urgency in the exclamatory "Up!" with which the commission began.

The word "evil" (*rā'â*) has a broad range of meanings in Hebrew and can refer not only to moral evil, but also to natural disasters, harm or injury, troubling times, negative emotions, and divine acts of judgment.[27] The word's precise meaning must, therefore, be contextually determined each time it occurs. In 1:2 the term clearly refers to human wickedness and the gloss "evil" is appropriate.

---

23. Sennacherib describes Nineveh as *ma-ha-zu¹ ṣi-i-ru*, which Frahm translates "der erhabenen Kultmetropole" or "the great city-shrine." This description aligns well with the use of the phrase *hā'îr haggĕdôlâ,*) throughout the Hebrew Bible. Cf. Eckart Frahm, *Einleitung in die Sanherib-Inschriften* (AfO Beiheft 26; Vienna: Eigentümer und Verlerger, 1997), 55 – 60.

24. D. D. Luckenbill, *The Annals of Sennacherib* (OIP 2; Chicago: Chicago University Press, 1924), 94.

25. D. J. A. Clines, *Concise Dictionary of Classical Hebrew* (Sheffield: Sheffield Phoenix, 2009), 401; Sasson, *Jonah*, 72 – 75.

26. Erika Bleibtreu, "Grisly Assyrian Record of Torture and Death," *BAR* 17.1 (Jan/Feb 1991): 52 – 61.

27. Clines, *Concise Dictionary*, 425.

As pointed out in the introduction, however, this term constitutes a major theme that permeates the book. The author exploits the word's broad range of meaning for rhetorical purposes. Though it would be desirable to use the same English equivalent for each occurrence of *rāʿâ* in order to track the development of this theme, it is nearly impossible to do so without distorting the word's meaning in context. The translations in the commentary, therefore, will use various equivalents as required by context, but repetitions of *rāʿâ* will be noted in the commentary itself.

2. The Objection: An Unexplained, Reckless Flight (1:3)

The mainline verb Jonah "got up" (*wayyāqom*) resumes the narrative initiated by the verb "it came" (*wayĕhî*) in 1:1a. Jonah's response to this unprecedented commission is the new focus as indicated by the explicit subject "Jonah" following the verb.[28] Divine commissions in Hebrew narrative are typically followed by reports of the addressee's obedience in terms that exactly parallel the wording of the commission itself.[29] The initial verb of 1:3a, "he got up" (*wayyāqom*) baits the reader to expect the usual report of obedience in that it echoes the initial imperative of YHWH's call, "Up!" (*qûm*). These expectations are immediately dashed, however, with the purpose clause that follows. Jonah does *not* get up to carry out his commission; rather, he gets up "to flee" (*librōaḥ*).

With this action, the commission narrative is abruptly interrupted. The expected verbal objection is replaced with flight. Oddly, the author offers no explanation for Jonah's disobedience. The focus is firmly fixed on his actions. The silence regarding Jonah's motives is likely intentional. The author of the book of Jonah frequently suppresses information where the reader most expects or desires it in order to reveal it later when least expected. This technique, called information gapping, builds suspense and sometimes exposes readers' assumptions and prejudices.[30] Jonah will reveal his motives later (4:2). First the author directs the reader's attention to Jonah's actions and their consequences.

Though his motives remain hidden for the time being, Jonah's destination is not hidden. His eyes are set on Tarshish. The precise location of Tarshish remains uncertain. Suggestions include Tartessus in southwest Spain (a Phoenician colony along the Guadalquiver River),[31] Carthage, and a town on the island of Sardinia.[32]

More important than its exact location, however, is Tarshish's general orientation and associations. Tarshish is typically associated with the West (Gen 10:2 – 5; Pss 48:7; 72:10; Isa 23:6, 10). It thus lies in the opposite direction of Nineveh and indicates Jonah's firm resistance to the divine commission. Furthermore, Tarshish was a distant and exotic locale — a place occupying the very edge of Israel's geographic awareness. According to 2 Chr 9:21, a round trip to Tarshish required three years. It was considered well worth the time and trouble, however, because of Tarshish's precious metals and

---

28. Hebrew often marks new paragraphs by joining a *wayyiqtol* verb with an explicit subject. Subsequent *wayyiqtol* verbs within the paragraph lack an explicit subject, assuming the same actor throughout. Thus, the explicit subject "Jonah" marks a new paragraph in the episode that resumes the narrative following YHWH's speech. Cf. Francis I. Andersen, *The Sentence in Biblical Hebrew* (Janua Linguarum, Series Practica 231; The Hague: Mouton, 1974), 64.

29. Trible, *Rhetorical Criticism*, 127 – 28.

30. Landes, "Textual 'Information Gaps,'" 273 – 93.

31. W. F. Albright, "The Role of the Canaanites in the History of Civilization," in *The Bible in the Ancient Near East* (ed. G. E. Wright; Garden City, NY: Doubleday, 1961; repr., Winona Lake, IN: Eisenbrauns, 1979), 328 – 62.

32. David W. Baker, "Tarshish," n.p., *ABD on CD-ROM* Version 2.0c. 1995, 1996.

exotica. Its distance from Israel (and Nineveh), therefore, proved attractive for this fugitive.

Most significant for Jonah, however, was the fact that Tarshish was known as a location where YHWH had not yet revealed his glory or his word. It could, therefore, serve as a refuge from such disturbing and unwelcome commissions as the one Jonah had just received (Isa 66:19). Tarshish's reputation as a place not yet graced by YHWH's glory and revelation is underscored by the additional prepositional phrase "away from YHWH's presence" (*millipnê yhwh*). This is the true goal of Jonah's flight — banishment from the prophet's unique experience of the divine presence.

Readers should be careful not to misconstrue Jonah's flight as a simplistic, foolish attempt to find a place beyond the scope of YHWH's knowledge or sovereignty. As Jonah later confesses (1:9), the

sea and the dry land are YHWH's domain. Jonah knows this, and at no point does he seriously entertain the possibility of eluding YHWH's omnipresence. Rather, Jonah seeks to escape the revelation of God experienced in the particular place where YHWH chose for his name to dwell (Deut 12:5, 11).[33] Exile was, precisely for this reason, banishment from both YHWH's presence and his word (Lam 2:9).

Prophets in particular enjoyed the distinction of standing in YHWH's presence and witnessing the deliberations of the divine council from which they received their messages (1 Kgs 22:19 – 23; Isa 6:1 – 8; Jer 23:18 – 22). Elijah's description of his prophetic vocation in 1 Kgs 17:1 serves as a good counterpoint to Jonah's flight.[34] Elijah's threat of drought directed at Ahab begins with the following oath formula: "As YHWH, the God of Israel, lives,

Figure 2.2: Possible Locations of Tarshish

---

33. Yehezkel Kaufmann helpfully distinguishes between the universalism of YHWH's sovereignty and the particularity of his self-revelation to Israel as his elect people. He sees this dynamic at work particularly in the book of Jonah. Cf. Yehezkel

Kaufmann, *The Religion of Israel*, 127 – 29.

34. Hans Walter Wolff, *Obadiah and Jonah* (Minneapolis: Augsburg, 1977), 103.

before whom I stand…" (*'ăšer 'āmadti lĕpānāyw*, italics added). Elijah expressed what prophets were supposed to do. They stood in attendance before YHWH in the divine council awaiting his orders. Jonah, however, abandoned his station, wishing to renounce the prophetic distinction of standing in the presence of the deity in the divine council.

Jonah began his journey by heading to Joppa. Joppa was located almost due west of Jerusalem and served as the main way station for travelers and merchants making their way to the region of Syria-Palestine.[35] In the eighth century, Joppa was not under Israelite control, but was the possession of Sidqia, king of Ashkelon.[36] Thus, Jonah was already outside of Israelite territory when he arrived at Joppa. Jonah apparently had no aversion to Gentiles per se, and he readily entered their territory and sought their assistance in his flight from YHWH.

Figure 2.3: Location of Joppa

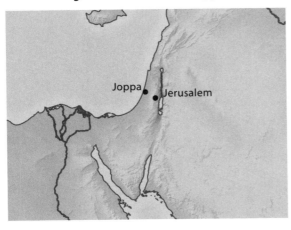

The author describes Jonah's journey to Joppa as a descent ("he descended," *yārad*), a characterization that will define the entirety of Jonah's at-

tempted escape marked by the repetition of this verb (1:3c, f, 5e). The author's choice of this verb is significant because it contrasts markedly with the initial imperative in YHWH's commission, "Up!" Whereas YHWH summoned Jonah "up," Jonah responds by going down. The contrast underscores the conflict between YHWH and Jonah.

The verb "to descend" also points to the potential result of Jonah's flight. Jonah's descent moved in the direction of death and conjures images of the grave and Sheol (cf. 2:3). Thus, though Jonah's geographical orientation is west, the author makes clear that his spiritual orientation is downward, moving in the direction of chaos and death. Much more is at stake in Jonah's flight from YHWH's presence than simply dodging an undesirable task. As YHWH made clear to Ezekiel, a prophet who neglects his calling and fails to warn those who are on the verge of divine judgment is held responsible for their blood and thus incurs death himself (Ezek 33:6 – 8). Jonah's downward trajectory indicates that he is in danger of such a fate. This may, however, be Jonah's intention. He may be attempting to force YHWH's hand in bringing judgment on him, which will ensure that he will never have to go to Nineveh and discharge his prophetic responsibility. This would explain the prophet's repeated requests that he be put to death (1:12; 4:3, 8, 9).

Upon his arrival, Jonah located a ship about to set sail (*bā'â*) for Tarshish. The participle *bā'â* is an unusual way of expressing a person's departure since the verb usually expresses motion toward the speaker. This is especially true in maritime contexts that clearly distinguish coming (the verb *bô'*) from going (the verb *hālak*; cf. 2 Chr 9:21).[37] The use of this unusual expression may be explained in terms

---

35. Jacob Kaplan and Haya Ritter Kaplan, "Joppa," n.p., *ABD on CD-ROM* Version 2.0c. 1995, 1996.

36. "Sennacherib and the Siege of Jerusalem," trans. A. Leo

Oppenheim (*ANET*, 287).

37. Sasson, *Jonah*, 82. Sasson tries to argue that (*bā'â*) should be understood here in its usual sense of motion toward

of its rhetorical effect. YHWH had commanded Jonah to go, using the typical verb for motion away from the speaker's vantage point (*hālak*). The author, however, describes Jonah's actions in terms of this verb's opposite (*bôʾ*). The rhetorical effect is to heighten the tension between YHWH's explicit command and Jonah's rebellious action.[38] Everything about Jonah's action is diametrically opposed to YHWH's commission. YHWH says, "Up!" and Jonah goes down. YHWH says "go to Nineveh" and Jonah leaves in the opposite direction, underscored by the clever use of a lexical infelicity.

Jonah had to pay for his passage, and he hired the ship and its crew for the long journey before boarding. Ancient Jewish tradition suggests that Jonah had to rent the entire ship for his journey.[39] This supposition finds some basis in the text. The text describes Jonah's payment as "her hire" (*śēkārāh*), with the feminine pronoun referring to the ship. The implication is that Jonah, in his haste, hired the entire ship and its crew for this journey rather than simply paying fare for a seat — a transaction more likely conveyed by a masculine pronoun "his payment" (*śēkārô*).[40] Disobedience is costly in more ways than one.

The author again emphasizes the downward orientation of Jonah's flight by stating that Jonah "descended" (*yārad*) into the ship. Thus, Jonah's continuing disobedience and its consequent danger remain in the reader's view. The recurrence of this verb as a description of Jonah's boarding the ship may well foreshadow the depths to which he is about to fall in the next episode. The same verb occurs in Ps 107:23 – 27 in order to indicate trouble at sea, from which only YHWH can rescue.

> Those who *descend* [*yôrĕdê*] to the sea in ships,
> who conduct business in immense bodies of
> > water,
> they have personally witnessed YHWH's deeds,
> His miracles in the deep.
> He spoke and the wind stood at attention.
> The tempest, it hoisted high its waves.
> They began scaling the heavens and *plummeting*
> > [*yērĕdû*] to the depths
> Their lives began ebbing away in the disaster.
> They began staggering and stumbling like a
> > drunk
> And all of their skill was stymied.

The psalm makes the same association between descent and a near-death experience at sea as does 1:3, 5e. The near disaster of the next episode is therefore anticipated in Jonah's downward trajectory. In fact, the author reiterates the prepositional phrase "away from YHWH's presence" to ensure that the reader remembers the true goal of Jonah's flight — distance from YHWH's call to prophetic service.

---

the speaker. This is hard to maintain, however, in the light of the verb's second occurrence in 1:3g, where it clearly means to head for Tarshish away from Joppa and, presumably, away from the vantage point of the speaker.

38. Claude Lichtert, "Par terre et Par mer! Analyse Rhétorique de Jonas 1," *ETL* 78 (2002): 8.

39. *Bavli Nedarim* 4:3 III states, "Said R. Yohanan, 'All of the prophets were wealthy. How do we know it? From the cases of Moses, Samuel, Amos, and Jonah. Jonah: "And he found a ship going to Tarshish, so he paid the fare thereof and went down into it" (Jonah 1:3).' And in this connection noted R. Yohanan, 'He paid for the rent of the whole ship.' R. Romanus said, 'The fee to rent the whole ship was four thousand gold denarii.'" Cited in Jacob Neusner, *Habakkuk, Jonah, and Obadiah in Talmud and Midrash: A Source Book* (New York: University Press of America, 2007), 86.

40. Wolff, *Obadiah and Jonah*, 102. The LXX and the Targum both translate the Hebrew text as though vocalized *śēkārōh*, "his fare." Though it is possible for the 3ms pronominal suffix in Hebrew to take this form, it is rare, and the MT is best taken as vocalized, which indicates unambiguously a 3fs pronominal suffix. See Paul Joüon, S.J., and T. Muraoka, *A Grammar of Biblical Hebrew* (Subsidia Biblical 14/1; Rome: Pontifical Biblical Institute, 2005), 1:289.

3. The Rebuke: YHWH's Conspiracy with Wind and Waves (1:4a)

Jonah 1:4a pauses the narrative to highlight YHWH's response to Jonah's flight.[41] The grammatical subject, YHWH, has been moved to the front of the clause and is followed by a verb that conveys action simultaneous with Jonah's flight: "Meanwhile, YHWH flung …" (*wayhwh hēṭîl*).[42] The construction shifts attention abruptly from Jonah's actions to YHWH's actions, indicating an escalation of the tension between the two characters.

This clause advances the call narrative, though in an unconventional way. The objection stage of a call narrative is normally followed by a divine rebuke in which YHWH rejects the excuses offered by his chosen agent. In the case of Jonah's calling, the prophet's unconventional (i.e., nonverbal) objection provoked an equally unconventional (and nonverbal) rebuke. YHWH conspires with the wind and the sea to foil Jonah's attempted escape. The verb "flung" (*hēṭîl*) calls to mind the throwing of a spear (1 Sam 18:11; 20:33) and suggests that YHWH assumes the role of divine warrior. The projectile of choice in this case, however, is a gale rather than a spear. The wind, therefore, serves as YHWH's weapon and expresses his wrath at Jonah's rejection of the commission.

Wind often serves as a divine weapon either in defense of YHWH's covenant people or as an instrument for their chastisement.[43] The wind and the storm it provoked were like a warning shot across the bow. The divine warrior chastised his prophet as he nudged Jonah toward a new frontier of divine mercy.

YHWH's response to Jonah's flight sets in motion a chain of events that launches and sustains the next episode. This is evident in the repetition of the verb "to fling" (*hēṭîl*) throughout the next unit (1:5c; 1:12c; 1:15b). YHWH's flinging the wind toward the sea eventually results in the mariners' flinging Jonah into the sea. The point of this chain reaction is that YHWH has orchestrated a series of events that places both Jonah and the mariners entirely at his mercy. This final clause of the first episode, therefore, introduces a catchword that ties the two units together, ensuring the recognition of YHWH's persistent call as the common denominator of the first two units.

It was no ordinary wind that YHWH flung toward the sea. The author describes it as a "great gale" (*rûaḥ gĕdôlâ*). The author employs the same adjective he used in his description of Nineveh in 1:2b. In fact, this same adjective occurs twelve more times in the book (1:2, 4b, 10a, 12, 16a; 2:1a; 3:2, 3, 5, 7; 4:1, 6, 11) always with reference to obstacles that Jonah had to confront and overcome (Nineveh, the wind, the storm, Jonah's selfish anger, Jonah's selfish joy). The frequency of the adjective throughout the book may underscore the daunting nature of the divine call and the challenge it presented to Jonah's conventional thinking about divine election, divine mercy, and divine justice.

---

41. Van der Merwe, Naudé, and Kroeze, *A Biblical Hebrew Reference Grammar*, 347–48.

42. Ziony Zevit, *The Anterior Construction in Classical Hebrew* (SBLMS 50; Atlanta: Scholars, 1998), 14.

43. Exod 15:10; Ps 48:8 [7]; Isa 27:8; 59:18–19; Jer 4:11; 49:36; 51:1; Ezek 13:11–13; 27:26; Hos 13:15.

Canonical and Practical Significance

YHWH's Mercy out of Bounds

Second Kings 14:23 – 27 serves as a backdrop against which one should read the book of Jonah. The two texts are tied together by their similar descriptions of Israel and Nineveh as "evil" (*ra*ʿ, 2 Kgs 14:24; cf. Jonah 1:2). The narrative in 2 Kings portrays Jonah as a prophet of salvation who foretold the restoration of Israel's borders by the hand of Jeroboam II, despite his wickedness. Jonah's announcement of YHWH's gracious act of blessing Israel when in fact she deserved severe punishment provides a significant foil for the book of Jonah. YHWH's mercy for Israel despite her wickedness should prepare Jonah for a similar act of mercy extended toward Nineveh. The nature of Nineveh's wickedness in the form of aggression toward Israel and the reality of a unique covenant between Israel and YHWH, however, predispose Jonah to object to any overtures of mercy YHWH might make to such an exceedingly wicked people.[44]

Jonah's association with the restored borders of the Promised Land becomes ironic in Jonah 1:1 – 3 when YHWH commissions Jonah to cross those very borders in order to travel to Nineveh and condemn its evil. YHWH's mercy extends well beyond Israel's borders and well beyond Jonah's comfort zone. Jonah might have characterized YHWH's mercy as scandalously unjust. From Jonah's point of view, YHWH's commission jeopardized both his unique relationship to Israel and Israel's existence as an independent state.

YHWH's Challenge to Worldly Power Structures

YHWH's commission betrays a decidedly regal tone. Every command conveys majesty and asserts YHWH's sovereignty despite Assyrian claims. This impression is due to the fact that commission narratives originated in royal courts. Kings regularly sent emissaries with messages to vassals and other foreign nations with whom they had dealings, and accounts of these commissions follow the typical form outlined above.[45] In this sense, Jonah's journey to Nineveh serves as a counterpoint to Isaiah 36, where Sennacherib sends his emissary, the Rabshakeh, to Jerusalem with a stern

---

44. John C. Holbert, "'Deliverance Belongs to Yahweh!': Satire in the Book of Jonah," *JSOT* 21 (1981): 63.

45. The royal nature and background of commissions such as this one were first noted by Klaus Baltzer. He based this connection on the tomb inscriptions of Rekhmire, vizier under Thutmose III and Amenhotep II. Rekhmire's tomb inscriptions include descriptions of his installation as vizier in the context of Pharaoh's court. The striking similarities of these descriptions to commission narratives in Hebrew prophetic lit- erature led Baltzer to conclude that installation texts such as the one found in Rekhmire's tomb inscriptions were precur- sors to prophetic commission narratives and that both share the assumption of a royal courtroom setting. Cf. Klaus Baltzer, *Die Biographie der Propheten* (Neukirchen-Vluyn: Neukirch- ener Verlag, 1975), 137 – 57, and N. de G. Davies, *The Tomb of Rekh-mi-Re at Thebes* I (New York: Metropolitan Museum of Art, 1943; repr., New York: Arno Press, 1973), 79 – 83.

warning that Jerusalem had better "repent" of her anti-Assyrian rebellion and resume payment of tribute or else suffer Sennacherib's wrath.

An ironic twist occurs in the book of Jonah as YHWH's commission turns the tables on human kings and their pathetic power plays. The book of Jonah reminds us that before Sennacherib had the audacity to send a royal emissary to YHWH's city with threats and taunts, YHWH had sent his own royal emissary to Nineveh, Sennacherib's city, with a threat of judgment. To quote the psalmist, "To YHWH belongs the earth and its contents; the habitations of the world and those who live there" (Ps 24:1). The significance of the regal tone in this context, therefore, is the challenge it poses to imperial ideologies like that of Assyria. All human authority and freedom are circumscribed by YHWH's greater authority and freedom.

The Challenge of Living Coram Deo (Before God's Presence)

Jonah's flight underscores the truth that it is sometimes uncomfortable to live in the divine presence. God's uncompromising challenge to show mercy even to our enemies and thus become perfect as he is perfect (Matt 5:48) can be frightening and overwhelming. It can even drive us into hiding.

Jonah quickly discovered, however, that the presence he fled was the very presence he desperately needed. The only alternative to living in God's presence and embracing the challenge of YHWH's call is to descend into chaos and death. Jonah's rejection of the new frontiers opened up to him by YHWH's challenging word condemns him to the depths. He may think that he is headed for distant and exotic places (e.g., Tarshish) when he flees from YHWH, but in reality he is headed only to the grave.

But is it even possible to flee YHWH's presence? David offers the following beautiful meditation:

> Where can I go from your Spirit?
> > Where can I flee from your presence?
> If I go up to the heavens, you are there;
> > if I make my bed in the depths, you are there.
> If I rise on the wings of the dawn,
> > if I settle on the far side of the sea,
> even there your hand will guide me,
> > your right hand will hold me fast. (Ps 139:7 – 10, NIV)

In the light of such a confession, how could Jonah have entertained the possibility of escaping YHWH's presence? The answer may be found in Old Testament texts that prescribe banishment from YHWH's presence as a punishment for certain serious sins. Cain, for example, was condemned to a life of aimless wandering for the crime of killing his brother, Abel. When describing Cain's fate the text states, "So Cain departed from YHWH's presence [*millipnê yhwh*] and settled in the land of Nod, east of Eden" (Gen 4:16). Furthermore, Lev 22:3 prescribed banishment from YHWH's presence for anyone who approached holy offerings while in a state of ritual impurity:

> Anyone from all of your descendents throughout all your generations who approaches the holy donations that the Israelites sanctified for YHWH while still in a state of ritual impurity will be cut off from my presence [*millipnāy*]. I am YHWH! (Lev 22:3)

Clearly, YHWH may deny a member of the covenant community access to his presence. This certainly does not mean that those who incurred such punishment were banished to a place beyond YHWH's reach. Rather, it means that they were removed from YHWH's fellowship and denied the privileges of Israel's special relationship with YHWH. This no doubt would include denial of access to the temple and all of its sacred assemblies, but the real tragedy of such a fate is the loss of intimacy with YHWH, the cessation of his revelation (Lam 2:6 – 9). Disobedience can and will erode one's relationship with the covenant Lord, which results in a loss of intimacy and, eventually, the loss of the relationship altogether (Ps 78:59; Jer 7:29).

In all of these texts, however, banishment from YHWH's presence occurs at YHWH's initiative. It is a punishment he imposes rather than an escape a sinner may choose as an alternative to obedience. Perhaps Jonah, by fleeing his commission, is trying to force YHWH's hand to impose on him such a banishment and thus disqualify him from YHWH's service. Jonah believes that such a severe punishment is better than the consequences of fulfilling YHWH's commission regarding Nineveh. Such a perspective on Jonah's part is understandable, given the terror that Assyria inspired in the hearts of the inhabitants of West Asia. YHWH's commission is, from Jonah's perspective, simply unreasonable. At the same time, however, Jonah's flight reveals how far removed Jonah is from the faith of his great ancestor Abraham, who, when asked to obey the unreasonable command of sacrificing his own son's life to YHWH, obeyed, trusting that somehow YHWH would make good on his promises despite the seeming contradiction.

The Wages of Sin versus the Free Gift of Grace

The fact that Jonah had to pay for the vessel and its crew to carry him "away from YHWH's presence" contrasts sharply with the provision YHWH offers to those who submit to his commission. For example, when YHWH commanded Elijah to flee across the Jordan, he provided his prophet with water from the Wadi Cherith and food from the ravens. When the wadi dried up, he sent him to a widow of Zarephath, who met his needs by means of YHWH's provision (1 Kgs 17:4 – 16).[46]

---

46. Wolff, *Obadiah and Jonah*, 102.

Similarly, Jesus commanded his disciples to journey without staff, luggage, wallet, or food when he sent them out on their first kingdom commissions (Luke 9:3; 10:4, 7). Disciples sent to do the Lord's work enjoy divine provision and rely on the hospitality of those they serve because "the worker deserves his wages" (Luke 10:7 NIV). Jonah, however, must pay for his own transportation and provisions in his rebellious flight. Disobedience is costly, and the rejection of YHWH's presence necessarily means the forfeiture of his benefits.

Fleeing the Ministry

Jonah is not the only prophet who fled his calling. Elijah also fled his ministry when Jezebel threatened his life after his great victory over the prophets of Baal on Mount Carmel (1 Kgs 19:2). Elijah's flight, however, was toward the mountain of God, Sinai, where he sought to receive fresh revelation. Elijah sought refuge *in* God's presence, not escape *from* God's presence (19:8 – 9).[47] Jonah's flight was in a very different direction and for the opposite purpose. He sought escape from both God's revelation and God's presence.

Both prophets are rebuked for their flight and sent back into the fray of ministry. The two stories serve as a reminder that ministry is difficult for two distinct reasons. First, ministry is difficult because of the opposition God's servants face both inside and outside of the faith community. In the face of such opposition, even God's faithful servants are tempted to retreat into a cloistered spirituality.

Second, ministry is difficult because of the demanding nature of the divine mercy that God's servants are required to proclaim to unsavory and undeserving people. This sometimes brings God's servants into conflict with God himself, sending them running not toward but away from his presence and away from the ministry. Thankfully, YHWH's response in both cases is loving correction, reassurance, and redirection back into the fray of service to God.

---

47. Holbert, "'Deliverance Belongs to Yahweh!'" 64.

Jonah 1:4b – 2:1b [1:17b]

B. The Relentless Pursuit of God's Mercy

Main Idea of the Passage

Jonah's descent to chaos and death continues, but YHWH and creation conspire to prevent Jonah's escape. In the process, the Gentile mariners grow in their reverent fear of YHWH as they witness both the severity and the solace of his mercy.

Literary Context

Jonah 1:1 – 4a focused on Jonah's flight from YHWH's presence and YHWH's response. A new unit shifts the attention in 1:4b to the result of YHWH's response as indicated by the episode marker *wayĕhî* (see comments on 1:1) Another indication of the new unit is a new setting — the sea. The movement from the dry land to the sea and from the sea to the watery depths of Sheol serves to mark Jonah's downward progression toward chaos and death. The wind, the storm, and the tempestuous sea all serve as instruments of divine wrath and as symbols of the chaotic underworld where Jonah is headed.

The end of the unit is marked by a renewed focus on YHWH's activity, which, after his casting of the great gale in 1:4a, receded to the background of the narrative as the new episode shifted attention to the mariners' and Jonah's plight at sea. In 2:1a (1:17a), however, YHWH again acts to bring his wayward prophet back into line, this time by means of a divinely appointed fish. Thus the second unit concludes with YHWH's action just as the preceding unit did (1:4a). This boundary is confirmed by the fact that a new episode begins with 2:1c (1:17c), as indicated by the presence of the third new episode marker *wayĕhî*.[1]

The majority of the narrative focuses on Jonah's interaction with the Gentile

---

1. Van der Merwe, Naudé, and Kroeze, *A Biblical Hebrew Reference Grammar*, 332. Cf. also Kamp, *Inner Worlds*, 89.

mariners and their response to the storm. The mariners' pious response to YHWH's activity and their eventual worship of YHWH is a foreshadowing of what will take place in chapter 3, when Jonah enters Nineveh. Thus, 1:4b – 2:1b serves as the parallel to 3:1 – 10 in the overarching structure of the book.

The pre-peak episode that unfolds in Jonah 1:4b – 2:1b, though a distinct unit, maintains an important connection with the preceding stage-setting episode (1:1 – 4a) that is often overlooked. It continues the commission narrative begun in Jonah 1:1 – 4a. YHWH's challenging word first introduced in 1:2 continues to shape the narrative, and the commission narrative form remains discernible in the new unit, though its elements assume surprising and ironic shape. The details of how this form defines the pre-peak episode are included in the Form and Literary Structure section below. It is important to recognize at this point, however, that the commission narrative form continues into the next unit of the book even though it is interrupted by Jonah's flight.

The break that occurs at 1:4b serves to underscore Jonah's unprecedented response to YHWH's unprecedented commission, but it also picks up where the commission narrative left off, and the section as a whole keeps the commission from which Jonah is fleeing before the readers' eyes. This commission won't go away no matter what Jonah does or how far afield the narrative may wander. The outline below demonstrates where the unit falls within the larger context of Jonah 1:1 – 2:11 (2:10).

> I. From Silent Resistance to Jubilant Acceptance: The Compelling Nature of God's Mercy (1:1 – 2:11 [2:10], Macro Unit 1)
>
>   A. A Silent Escape from God's Mercy (1:1 – 4a, Stage setting)
>
> →   **B. The Relentless Pursuit of God's Severe Mercy (1:4b – 2:1b [1:17b], Pre-peak episode)**
>
>   **1. The wrath of YHWH's severe mercy (1:4b – 5d)**
>
>   **2. The futility of ignoring YHWH's severe mercy (1:5e – 6g)**
>
>   **3. The revelation of YHWH's sovereign, severe mercy (1:7 – 9)**
>
>   **4. The fear due YHWH's sovereign, severe mercy (1:10 – 12)**
>
>   **5. The futility of escaping YHWH's severe mercy (1:13 – 14)**
>
>   **6. The relenting wrath of YHWH's relentless mercy (1:15a – 2:1b [1:17b])**
>
>   C. A Prayer of Praise for God's Mercy (2:1c – 11b [1:17c – 2:10b], Peak episode)
>
> II. From Compliant Acceptance to Angry Resentment: The Offense of God's Mercy (3:1 – 4:11, Macro Unit 2)

Translation and Outline

Jonah 1:4b–2:1b

B. The Relentless Pursuit of God's Mercy (1:4b-2:1b [1:17b])

1:4b   A great storm ensued on the sea.

1:4c   As for the ship, it threatened to burst apart.

1:5a   The mariners feared,

1:5b   and each one cried out to his god,

1:5c   and they flung the cargo that was on the ship to the sea

1:5d   to lighten for themselves

1:5e   But as for Jonah, he had descended into the bowels of the ship's hold.

1:5f   And there he lay down

1:5g   and fell fast asleep.

1:6a   The helmsman approached him

1:6b   and said to him,

1:6c   How can you be sleeping?

1:6d   Up!

1:6e   Cry out to your god!

1:6f   Perhaps the deity will consider our plight

1:6g   so that we are not destroyed.

1:7a   Then each one said to his shipmate,

1:7b   Come!

1:7c   And let us cast lots

1:7d   that we might discover

1:7e   on whose account this disaster has befallen us.

1:7f   So they cast lots,

1:7g   and the lot fell on Jonah.

1:8a   They inquired of him,

1:8b   Please, tell us

1:8c   on whose account this disaster has befallen us.

1:8d   What is your occupation?

1:8e   And from where do you come?

1:8f   What country do you claim?

1:8g   And to which of its people do you belong?

1:9a   And he responded,

1:9b   I am a Hebrew,

1:9c   and YHWH, the god of heaven, I fear,

1:9d   who made the sea and the dry land.

1:10a   Then the men feared a great fear,

1:10b   and they asked him,

1:10c   What have you done?

1:10d   For the men knew that

1:10e   he was fleeing YHWH's presence

1:10f   because he had told them so.

1:11a   So they asked him,

1:11b   What must we do with you

1:11c   so that the sea might settle down for us?

1:11d   For the sea was raging on relentlessly.

1. The wrath of YHWH's severe mercy (1:4b-5d)
   a. Creation as the harbinger of divine wrath (1:4b-4c)
      i. The storm as YHWH's weapon (1:4b)
      ii. The sea as YHWH's battlefield (1:4c)
   b. Ignorant fear of divine wrath (1:5a-c)
      i. Ignorance of the source of wrath (1:5b)
      ii. Ignorance of the solution to wrath (1:5c)

2. The futility of ignoring YHWH's severe mercy (1:5e-1:6g)
   a. The determined descent to Sheol (1:5e)
   b. The desire to withdraw from prophetic responsibility (1:5f-g)
   c. The insistence on prophetic action (1:6)

3. The revelation of YHWH's sovereign, severe mercy (1:7a-9d)
   a. Jonah's reticence to reveal the storm's cause (1:7a-e)

   b. YHWH's readiness to reveal the storm's cause (1:7f-g)

   c. The mariner's desire to know the storm's cause (1:8)

   d. Jonah's confession and claim to devotion (1:9)

4. The fear due YHWH's sovereign, severe mercy (1:10a- 12f)

   a. The mariners' rebuke of Jonah's rebellion (1:10)

   b. The mariners' request for relief from God's wrath (1:11)

Continued on next page.

Continued from previous page.

1:12a	He replied,	c. Jonah's request for relief in the grave (1:12)
1:12b	Pick me up,	
1:12c	and fling me to the sea	
1:12d	so that the sea might settle down for you.	
1:12e	For I realize that	
1:12f	on my account this disaster has befallen you.	
1:13a	The men dug in	5. The futility of escaping YHWH's severe mercy (1:13-14)
1:13b	to return to dry land.	a. The inadequacy of human solutions to divine wrath (1:13)
1:13c	But they could not do it	
1:13d	because the sea raged against them with growing intensity.	
1:14a	So they cried out to YHWH,	b. The mariners cry out for divine mercy (1:14)
1:14b	We beg of you, YHWH!	
1:14c	Please don't destroy us on account of this man!	
1:14d	Nor hold us accountable for innocent blood.	
1:14e	For you are YHWH;	
1:14f	just as you pleased,	
1:14g	you have done.	
1:15a	So they lifted Jonah	6. The relenting wrath of YHWH's relentless mercy (1:15a-17b)
1:15b	and flung him to the sea,	a. YHWH's responsiveness to the cry for mercy(1:15)
1:15c	and the sea ceased its raging.	b. The mariners' responsiveness to YHWH's mercy (1:16)
1:16a	Then the men feared YHWH with great fear.	
1:16b	They offered sacrifices to YHWH,	
1:16c	and they vowed vows.	
2:1a	Then YHWH appointed a great fish	c. Creation as the harbinger of YHWH's relentless mercy (2:1a-b)
2:1b	to swallow Jonah.	

Structure and Literary Form

Jonah 1:4 – 17 consists of six subunits discernible primarily on the basis of shifts from narrative (primary discourse) to direct speech (embedded discourse). Dialogue plays a particularly important role in this section; the two exchanges between Jonah and the mariners (1:7 – 9 and 1:10 – 12) form the core of the unit. Surrounding these central dialogues are two requests preceded by introductory narratives. The first is the helmsman's request that Jonah rise from his slumber and intercede with his god on behalf of the crew (1:5e – 6g), and the second is the mariners' request that YHWH not hold them accountable for Jonah's life since they had no choice but to cast him to the sea (1:13a – 14g).

Framing the entire unit are two brief narrative sections. The first describes the onset of the storm followed by the mariners' panic-stricken response (1:4b – 5d, three consecutive *wayyiqtol* clauses). The second describes the mariners' tossing Jonah overboard, the cessation of the storm, the mariners' worship of YHWH, and YHWH's rescue of Jonah by means of the great fish (1:15 – 2:1b; seven consecutive *wayyiqtol* clauses).

The first (1:4b – 5d) and second subunits (1:5e – 6g) are separated by an interruption to the narrative flow marked by a noun initial clause: "but as for Jonah, he had descended …" (wĕ + noun + qatal, 1:5e). The first subunit focused on the mariners' initial response to the storm. Jonah 1:5e, however, shifts attention to Jonah and sets up a contrast between the frenzied activity of the frightened mariners and Jonah's resigned passivity.[2] The second subunit ends with the helmsman's direct address to Jonah, commanding him to wake up and intercede on behalf of the endangered crew (1:6c-g).

The third subunit resumes the narrative (wayyiqtol) following the helmsman's speech to Jonah. A dialogue then occurs among the mariners regarding casting lots in order to discover the reason for the storm. A brief narrative follows relating the process of casting lots and the revelation of Jonah as the storm's underlying cause. This discovery leads to the first exchange between the mariners and Jonah, which climaxes in Jonah's confession of faith in YHWH as the sovereign of land and sea.

The fourth subunit (1:10a – 12f) resumes the narrative after Jonah's confession of faith. The focus shifts to the mariners' intensified fear at the revelation that Jonah's God is a cosmic deity. This leads to the second exchange between the mariners and Jonah, in which they discuss what they should do to appease YHWH and find relief from the growing storm. The dialogue climaxes with Jonah's insistence that the mariners throw him overboard.

The fifth subunit (1:13a – 14f) again resumes the narrative following the exchange between Jonah and the mariners. Unwilling to resort to such drastic measures as throwing Jonah overboard, the mariners attempt to row back to land, but the storm is too strong. At last they are forced to heed Jonah's advice; but before they do, they ask YHWH to absolve them of any bloodguilt related to Jonah's fate in the sea. The fifth subunit thus parallels the second in terms of its structure — brief narrative followed by request.

The entire section closes by a final return to the narrative following the mariners' prayer. This section constitutes the denouement of the tense and exciting storm scene (1:15a – 2:1b) and parallels the first section in three respects. First, the opening subunit relates how the storm began while the final subunit relates how it ended. Second, in the initial subunit the mariners sacrifice to their various gods while in the final subunit they sacrifice to YHWH. Finally, the initial subunit focuses on YHWH's direct intervention (1:4a) in initiating the storm, and the closing subunit focuses on YHWH's direct intervention in ending the storm (2:1b).

Fretheim has argued convincingly that these six sections form a chiasm, highlighting the centrality of the two dialogues between the mariners and Jonah.[3] This

---

2. Heimerdinger, *Topic, Focus, and Foreground*, 209 – 10.   3. Terence E. Fretheim, *The Message of Jonah: A Theological Commentary* (Minneapolis: Augsburg Press, 1977), 73 – 74.

arrangement agrees with the linguistic structure outlined above and provides the simplest and most compelling explanation of the text's organization.[4] The structure is pictured below.[5]

Figure 3.1: Chiastic Structure of Jonah 1:4 – 2:1b

A *Narrative frame* — The wrath of YHWH's severe mercy (1:4a-5d)

　B *Narrative & Request* — The futility of ignoring YHWH's severe mercy (1:5e-6g).

　　C *Dialogue 1* — Jonah's revelation of YHWH's sovereign, severe mercy (1:7a-9d)

　　C′ *Dialogue 2* — The mariners' fear for YHWH's sovereign, severe mercy (1:10a-12f)

　B′ *Narrative & Request* — The futility of escaping YHWH's severe mercy (1:13a-14g)

A′ *Narrative frame* — The relenting wrath of YHWH's relentless mercy (1:15a-2:1b)

The chiastic structure suggested by Fretheim finds support in a number of word-plays and repetitions that serve to tie the corresponding units together. For example, the mariners' flinging (*wayyāṭilû*) the cargo overboard in section A (1:5c) corresponds to their flinging (*wayyāṭilulû*) Jonah overboard in section A′ (1:15b). The phrase "cry out to your god/YHWH" links section B (1:6e) with section B′ (1:14a). Finally, the two rounds of dialogue between Jonah and the mariners (sections C and C′) are joined by the contrast between Jonah's confession of his fear of YHWH in 1:9c (*'ănî yārē'*) and the mariners' demonstration of their fear of YHWH in 1:10a (*wayyîrĕ'û ... yir'â gĕdôlâ*).[6]

Throughout the entire unit, in both its dialogue and its narrative, the author deliberately contrasts Jonah and the Gentile mariners. For example, the mariners struggle throughout the unit to stay alive. Jonah, by contrast, resigns himself to death. The mariners display a hunger for revelation by casting lots and questioning Jonah. Jonah, however, is fleeing a revelation and only with reluctance shares what he knows about YHWH and the storm. The mariners pray frequently and fervently, initially to false gods but finally to YHWH (1:14, 16), while Jonah appears not to pray

---

4. For a thorough survey of alternative structural approaches to Jonah 1:4 – 16, see Claude Lictert, "Par terre et par mer! Analyse Rhétorique de Jonas 1," *ETL* 78 (2002): 5 – 24.

5. The basic structure is Fretheim's, but the content labels for each section are my own, based on my discourse analysis and overall understanding of the book's message.

6. Stuart is critical of Fretheim's understanding of the structure of this unit, claiming that all such chiasms are forced and are too elaborate to have been intended by the author (Stuart,

Hosea – Jonah, 457.). Stuart's objections, however, fail to account for the wordplays/repetitions that tie the corresponding units together. He also ignores the crucial interplay between narrative and dialogue, both of which support such a structure. Furthermore, the author of the book of Jonah demonstrates great literary sophistication, and chiastic patterns are one of his favorite devices as evident by their numerous appearances elsewhere in the book. Cf. Trible, *Rhetorical Criticism*, 237 – 44.

at all. By the end of the pre-peak episode, the Gentile mariners seem noble and pious, but Jonah appears stubborn and selfish.

In terms of genre, 1:4b – 2:1b resumes the commission narrative begun in 1:2. Jonah's silent flight interrupted the normal structure of prophetic commissions in which YHWH's selected agent typically raises verbal objections to the commission following its revelation, for Jonah offered no verbal objections. He simply fled in the opposite direction. Though unusual and unexpected, Jonah's response was, nonetheless, a clear objection to the divine commission. At this point, the commission devolves into YHWH's pursuit of Jonah to the very depths in order to conscript him for the mission to Nineveh. While the account of YHWH's pursuit of Jonah does disturb the typical pattern of commission narratives, the text never actually abandons the genre. Rather, it adapts the genre in unexpected and ironic ways.

Since 1:1 – 4a presented the commission and objection stages of the commission narrative, 1:4b – 2:1b proceeds to the stages of divine rebuke and reassurance. Just as Jonah's objection to the commission was nonverbal, so was YHWH's rebuke. God expressed his wrath by means of a fierce storm at sea that sabotaged Jonah's escape. The bulk of the narrative is devoted to the divine rebuke in order to emphasize the severity of Jonah's rebellion and the persistence of the divine call. The unit ends, however, on a note of divine reassurance. The sudden calming of the storm reassured the mariners that YHWH accepted their plea for mercy. YHWH's appointment of the great fish to swallow Jonah reassured the prophet that YHWH had not abandoned him to the grave despite his disobedience and his death wish (2:1b, 2, 7).

Within the framework of the commission narrative, elements of another genre are detectable, a form commonly referred to as a travel narrative, or, more specifically, a maritime travel narrative. Accounts of individuals who survive ordeals at sea as confirmation of divine appointment to some significant task are well-known in antiquity. The Egyptian stories of "The Shipwrecked Sailor"[7] and "The Report of Wen-Amun,"[8] are two examples of narratives relating the harrowing experiences of a protagonist who overcomes numerous obstacles, including a storm at sea, on the way to fulfilling an important task.[9] The New Testament records that both Jesus and Paul survived life-threatening storms at sea, which confirmed their divine appointment to tasks that precluded the possibility of their meeting a premature end in a shipwreck (Matt 8:23 – 27; Mark 4:35 – 40; Luke 8:22 – 25; Acts 27:1 – 28:10).

These accounts share with Jonah 1:4b – 2:1b the elements of a harrowing experience at sea and the confirmation of divine calling. Thus, the nature of this unit, both

---

7. "The Shipwrecked Sailor," trans. Miriam Lichtheim (*COS* 1.39: 83 – 84).

8. "The Report of Wen-Amun," trans. Miriam Lichtheim (*COS* 1.41: 89 – 93).

9. "The Shipwrecked Sailor" dates to sometime in the Mid-

dle Kingdom (2030 – 1640 BC) and "The Report of Wen-Amun" in the third decade of Ramses XI. Thus both predate the book of Jonah by several centuries and could arguably have served as influences. See Lichtheim's introductions to her translations cited above (*COS* 1.39, 83 and 1.41, 89).

as a commission narrative and as a maritime travel narrative, emphasizes YHWH's commitment to the commission and the assurance of its accomplishment by YHWH's chosen agent. The rhetorical significance of combining these genres within the same episode may be to clarify what it means to be chosen by God.

Explanation of the Text

1. The Wrath of YHWH's Severe Mercy (1:4b – 5d)

Jonah 1:4b introduces a new unit with the clause "a great storm ensued on the sea." The main verb ("ensued") is *wayĕhî*, which establishes a new sequence of narrative verbs (*wayyiqtol*) and launches a new episode. The subject of the verb, "a great storm" (*saʿar-gādôl*), is topical and indicates that the storm is the new crisis that ties the six following subunits together.

The Hebrew term *saʿar* frequently designates a divinely induced storm, symbolizing divine wrath (Ps 83:15 – 16; Jer 23:19; 25:32; 30:23; Amos 1:14). Especially relevant for Jonah 1:4 – 2:1 is YHWH's rebuke of prophets who refuse to warn sinners of impending judgment.

> For who of their number has stood in YHWH's council that he might witness and overhear his deliberation? Who among them has given undivided attention to my message and obeyed it? Beware YHWH's gale! A hot blast has shot out and a storm [*saʿar*] is churning. Over the head of the wicked it will explode. YHWH's wrath will not retreat until he has accomplished, until he has established his secret strategy. In days to come you will understand it clearly.
>
> I did not send the prophets, but they ran. I did not speak to them but they prophesied. If only they had stood in my council that they might announce my words to my people and steer them away from their disastrous path and from their evil deeds! (Jer 23:18 – 22)

This text is directed to false prophets who preached even though they had never received a genuine revelation from YHWH. Thus, they lulled Judah into a false sense of security. It speaks just as powerfully, however, to Jonah, who, though given a message, refused to speak it. God did send Jonah and he did run — in the other direction! Therefore, Jonah experienced the same manifestation of divine wrath prescribed for these false prophets — a life-threatening storm. For those who have received revelation and refuse to share it are just as culpable as those who prophesy falsely.

Attention abruptly shifts to the ship's reaction to the storm in 1:4c. As in 1:4a, the grammatical subject moves to the front of the clause to redirect attention from the heavenly origin of the storm to its earthly effects. The author moves in 1:4a – 6g from heaven (flinging of wind), to sea (stirring up of storm), to the ship (threatening disintegration), to the ship's deck (mariners praying and jettisoning cargo), to below the ship's deck (Jonah sleeping soundly). In other words, the narrative descends, pulling the reader down to the depths with Jonah.

The brief mention of the ship's reaction to the storm has long vexed interpreters.[10] The author personifies the ship stating, "As for the ship, it threatened to burst apart" (*wĕhāʾŏnîyâ ḥiššĕbâ*

---

10. Sasson, *Jonah*, 96. Sasson offers a helpful summary of translations and interpretations that have tried to get around the apparently awkward personification of the ship in 1:4c.

lĕhiššābēr). The verb "to think/intend" (*ḥāšab*) elsewhere takes only conscious beings as grammatical subject. A possible reason for the awkward expression is the sound play it creates between the words "threatened" (*ḥiššĕbâ*) and "to burst" (*lĕhiššābēr*), both of which contain a combination of letters whose sounds are reminiscent of the pounding of waves against the planks of the ship (*sh-b, sh-b*).[11]

The personification of the ship is also explicable in terms of a common belief held by ancient Mediterranean seafarers that ships were imbued with the spirit of a guardian deity.[12] Prow figures decorating ancient ships often took the form of these protective spirits. Some ships were decorated with eyes painted on either side of the prow to ward off evil.[13] Attributing personal qualities to ships, therefore, was not unknown in the ancient Mediterranean world. In fact, similar literary examples have been identified in texts from Ugarit, a Phoenician city north of Israel on the Mediterranean coast.[14]

In the case of Jonah 1:4c the personification of the ship may serve to add the vessel to the list of YHWH's accomplices in thwarting Jonah's flight. Thus the ship, as well as the wind and the sea, assist YHWH in sabotaging Jonah's escape. The verb "to think/intend" (*ḥiššĕbâ*) in this context occurs in a form (Piel) that often connotes planning, devising, or conspiring, especially when followed by an infinitive as in Jonah 1:4c.[15]

Ironically, therefore, the ship, Jonah's very means of transportation, turns against him and conspires with YHWH to bring his flight to an abrupt end.

This interpretation finds support in a parallel personification of the sea near the conclusion of the unit. Jonah 1:15c states "and the sea ceased its raging," which employs a noun, "raging" (*zaʿap*), elsewhere used exclusively of persons.[16] Just as the sea's raging is designed to serve YHWH's purposes, so is the ship's threat to burst apart.

Creation's conspiracy against Jonah fills this episode with irony. Jonah had attempted to escape his prophetic task by means of wind, sea, and ship, but rather than cooperate with Jonah, these elements obediently conspire with YHWH to oppose Jonah. Thus creation serves as messenger of divine wrath and model of obedience to the divine call, both roles intended for Jonah. In fact, when one considers this episode in the light of the divine warrior motif in ancient Near Eastern literature in general, a striking difference emerges. In the Canaanite traditions, the sea, deified as Yamm, is an enemy that the Canaanite god Baʿal must subdue before he can establish order and assume his throne.[17] The same is true of the deified sea (Tiamat) and the chief god (Marduk) in the parallel Babylonian myth.[18] In the book of Jonah, however, wind, sea, and even ship are YHWH's willing accomplices in subduing his rebellious prophet. They communicate his wrath, confirm his sovereignty, and contribute to Jonah's return to dry land before YHWH's presence.

The brief mention of the ship in 1:4c serves as a transition to the frenzied activity of the mariners on the ship's deck (1:5a). Sensing both the supernatural character of the storm and the imminent wreck of their ship, the mariners "fear" for their

---

11. Ibid.

12. Aaron Jed Brody, *"Each Man Cried Out to His God:" The Specialized Religion of Canaanite and Phoenician Seafarers* (HSMP 58; Atlanta: Scholars, 1998), 65 – 67.

13. Ibid, 63.

14. For example, one prose text describing a shipwreck states that the ship "died in a torrential rain" (*mtt by gšm ʾdr*). Cf. *KTU* 2.38.

15. *HALOT* (Study Edition), 1:359 – 60.

16. Ibid., 277.

17. "The Baʿlu Myth," trans. Dennis Pardee (*COS* 1.86: 241 – 74). Cf. also Patrick D. Miller Jr., *The Divine Warrior in Early Israel* (Atlanta: Society of Biblical Literature, 1973, 2006), 24 – 48.

18. "Epic of Creation," trans. Benjamin R. Foster (*COS* 1.111: 390 – 402.

lives (*wayyîrĕʾû*). With this clause the author introduces another motif that permeates the episode — the mariners' evolving fear. The fear expressed in 1:5a is characterized by ignorance; the mariners fear the unknown. They have no idea which deity has sent the storm or why. As the plot progresses, however, their fear results less from ignorance and more from revelation and realization. This fear intensifies and shifts from sheer terror to awestruck fear for YHWH's power.

The transformation is marked throughout the episode by the addition of modifiers to the bold statement "they feared." For example, the same wording occurs again in 1:10a, but this time it is followed by an adjective and a direct object — "then the men feared a great fear" (*wayyîrĕʾû hāʾănāšîm yirʾâ gĕdôlâ*) — and yet again in 1:16a with the addition of YHWH as object: "then the men feared, with great fear, YHWH" (*wayyîrĕʾû hāʾănāšîm yirʾâ gĕdôlâ ʾet-yhwh*). Magonet refers to this phenomenon as "the growing phrase" and notes that it plays a key rhetorical role within the unit.[19] Its purpose is to trace the mariners' emerging faith in YHWH in contrast to Jonah's persistent disobedience.

The mariners' fear provokes action. First, they cry out to their various gods for some revelation regarding the storm's cause and consequently its remedy. When the author states "each one cried out to his god," he likely means that those on board cried out to personal gods whom they believed bore special responsibility for their well-being. These were lesser gods, some of whom served no purpose other than the protection of their particular human.[20] Realizing that such personalized deities were incapable of producing such a storm, the mariners were seeking information and intercession. They were asking their gods which cosmic deity was behind the storm and requesting that their personal deities intercede with that god on their behalf.[21]

The mariners followed their desperate prayers with desperate action. They jettisoned as much cargo as possible "to lighten for themselves" (*lĕhāqēl mēʿălêhem*) and increase the ship's buoyancy.[22] The verb "they flung" (*wayyāṭîlû*) derives from the same root used to describe YHWH's "flinging" the wind (1:4a, *hēṭîl*). This verbal cue ties the two actions together and suggests that the mariners' flinging the cargo overboard is an extension of YHWH's initial response to Jonah's flight and a move in the direction of achieving his goal (see comments on 1:5e regarding the "ship's hold"). The scene foreshadows Jonah's eventual fate. Like the ship's cargo, the ship's passenger was finally "flung" overboard (*hēṭîl*, cf. 1:12, 15), which thus completes his descent.

19. Jonathan Magonet, *Form and Meaning: Studies in Literary Techniques in the Book of Jonah* (2nd ed.; Sheffield: Almond, 1983), 31 – 33.

20. Daniel C. Snell, *Religions of the Ancient Near East* (Cambridge: Cambridge University Press, 2011), 27 – 28.

21. Ibid., 28. Based on depictions found on cylinder seals, Snell draws the following conclusion:

> Sometimes the person was led in before a great god, who was seated in regal splendor. The seal owner did not presume to come forward because of his own virtue but was conducted in by the personal god, who was depicted as a god and not a person, as may be seen from the horned headdress. The personal god approached with the same humble attitude as the human toward the great god. Still, the little god walked on the same topographic plane as the other god, and the lesser god had some acquaintance with the great one that would be of benefit to the lowly human.

> In a way, the existence of the personal god is a simplifying element in what must have been for the ancients a confusing mess of gods. You might know which god could help you in a given situation — say, one of sickness — but to approach such an august being directly would be scary. If you had an advocate who knew your problems, in the realm of the gods as in the realm of the city, your way might be eased.

22. Philip Peter Jenson, *Obadiah, Jonah, Micah: A Theological Commentary* (New York: T&T Clark, 2008), 48; Wolff, *Obadiah and Jonah*, 112; Leslie C. Allen, *The Books of Joel, Obadiah, Jonah, and Micah* (NICOT; Grand Rapids: Eerdmans, 1976), 207; James Limburg, *Jonah: A Commentary* (OTL; Louisville: Westminster John Knox, 1993), 49 – 50.

2. The Futility of Ignoring YHWH's Severe Mercy (1:5e – 1:6g)

Jonah 1:5e introduces a noun initial clause (*waw + noun + qatal*) and thus interrupts the plotline to direct attention to a prior event that now becomes relevant to the narrative. By placing "Jonah" at the front of the clause, the author emphasizes the contrast between the frantic activity of the mariners and the complacent passivity of Jonah. The syntax achieves a flashback effect, recalling Jonah's descent into the ship (1:3). He had descended below deck into the ship's cargo hold. The reader now knows where Jonah was while the ship's crew were trying desperately to weather the storm — he was asleep below deck.[23] The English pluperfect captures the idea: "But, as for Jonah, *he had descended* into the bowels of the ship's hold."[24]

The two words at the conclusion of this clause deserve special attention. First, Jonah's descent places him in what the author calls "the bowels" (*yarkĕtê*). The word can refer to the extremity of virtually any space: a building, a mountain range, the furthest point of a cardinal direction (e.g., the far north), or even the earth as a whole.[25] In contexts replete with words and images that suggest death, however, *yarkĕtê* nearly always connotes the underworld, the extremity of mortal experience in the grave. In Isa 14:15 and Ezek 32:21, for example, this *yarkĕtê* and Sheol form a word pair. The expression "the bowels," therefore, may create a double entendre. The deepest part of the ship may serve as an image of Sheol itself, foreshadowing Jonah's near-death experience in the sea.

The final word of the clause, "the ship's hold" (*hassĕpînâ*), occurs only here in the Hebrew Bible. The term is typically understood as a synonym for the standard word for ship (*'ŏnîyâ*). However, the word derives from a verbal root meaning "to cover," which leads Mulzer to conclude that the term refers to an enclosed cargo room below deck of the ship.[26] The author introduces the word here in order to clarify Jonah's location. He is hidden in the cargo room below deck. This detail further underscores Jonah's withdrawal from his calling and from his surroundings. It may also explain why the author juxtaposes a clause describing the mariners' disposal of cargo with one portraying Jonah asleep in the ship's hold. Was it in the process of emptying the ship's hold that the mariners discovered their passenger fast asleep? If so, this might explain the recurrence of the verb "to fling" (*wayyāṭilû*) in 1:5c. As discussed in the comments on the preceding clause, this verb suggests a close relationship between the mariners' flinging the cargo "to the sea" and YHWH's flinging (same verb) the wind "toward the sea." Perhaps the connection is that YHWH exposed Jonah's location on board by means of the mariners' frantic emptying of the cargo hold.

The next clause (1:5f) resumes the plotline with the narrative verb form (*wayyiqtol*) and returns the reader to the moment of the storm. The author thus emphasizes the simultaneity of Jonah's slumber with the chaos unfolding all around him. The author employs two verbs to convey the nature of Jonah's sleep: "he lay down" (*wayyiškab*) and "he fell fast asleep" (*wayyērādam*). The second verb and its related noun (*tardēmâ*) usually speak of a divinely induced slumber that portends one of two experiences: a revelation from God (Gen 15:12; Job 4:13; 33:15; Dan 8:18) or a brush with death (Gen 2:21; Judg 4:21; Ps 76:6 – 7).[27] In Jonah's case the

---

23. Kamp, *Inner Worlds*, 99.
24. Zevit, *The Anterior Construction in Classical Hebrew, 16 – 21.*
25. *HALOT* (Study Edition), 1:439.
26. Martin Mulzer, הניפס" (Jona 1,5) '(gedeckter) Laderaum,'" *BN* 104 (2000): 83 – 94.
27. Magonet, *Form and Meaning, 67 – 69.*

verb "he fell fast asleep" may suggest both experiences, adding to the irony of the prophet's situation.

On the one hand, the verb *wayyērādam* adds to the growing number of allusions to death and the netherworld already hinted at in the text. It may therefore serve to underscore Jonah's proximity to death and foreshadow his near-death experience later in the episode. This impression is reinforced by the striking sound play *wayyērādam* creates with the other verb portending death "to descend" (*wayyēred*; both verbs share the sounds *y-r-d*).[28]

On the other hand, one may also detect in Jonah's slumber a divinely induced sleep in preparation for receiving revelation. Prophets and diviners in ancient Mesopotamia viewed deep sleep as a means of revelation, as is evident in the incubation rites attested throughout the ancient Near East.[29] The Bible attests a similar understanding of deep sleep in revelatory and prophetic contexts (Gen 15:12; 28:16; 1 Sam 26:12 – 25; Job 4:13; 33:15; Zech 4:1). Jonah's sleep may therefore anticipate the renewal of his calling in Jonah 3:1 – 2.[30]

The possibility that Jonah's slumber is preparation for his second calling is supported by the helmsman's exhortation when he discovered Jonah asleep in the bowels of the ship's hold. In disbelief and annoyance at Jonah's complacency, the helmsman said to Jonah, "How can you be sleeping? Up! Cry out to your god!" The helmsman's two commands "Up!" and "Cry out!" (*qûm*, and *qĕrā'*) match exactly the first and last of the commands in YHWH's commission to Jonah (1:2). The helmsman thus echoed YHWH's commission, and Jonah

woke up to the sound of the same two commands from which he had been hiding. Jonah's attempts to escape this call and ignore YHWH's revelation were futile. The commission haunted him even in the bowels of the ship's hold.

3. The Revelation of YHWH's Sovereign, Severe Mercy (1:7 – 9)

Jonah 1:7 introduces the mariners' dialogue as they confer with one another about casting lots. Interestingly, 1:7a echoes 1:5b, contrasting "Each one cried out to his god" with "each one said to his shipmate."[31] Having found the gods unresponsive, the mariners turned to each other and to their collective wisdom regarding their survival.

The imperative "Come!" (*lĕkû*) initiates a sequence of three command verb forms (i.e., imperatives, jussives, or cohortatives), coordinated with the conjunction *waw* ("and"), that constitutes the speech's backbone. This first imperative simply encourages attention to and compliance with the second cohortative command, "Let us cast lots" (*wĕnappîlâ gôrālôt*).[32] The third and final command verb in the sequence, "that we might know" (*wĕnēdĕ'â*), expresses the goal of the second command, like a purpose clause.[33] Syntactically, however, it remains on the main line of the discourse, suggesting that the third command verb is climactic and emphasizes the importance of the mariners' inquiry.

The purpose clause "that we might know" is followed by a verbless clause, which indicates the desired information ("on whose account this evil (has

---

28. Perry, *The Honeymoon Is Over*, 6.

29. Walter Farber, "Witchcraft, Magic, and Divination in Ancient Mesopotamia," in *CANE*, 3:1899.

30. Though the practice of prophetic sleep (often called "incubation") as documented at Mari involved elaborate rituals and sleeping in the sanctuary proper, Husser has observed, "sanctuaries were not the only places where sometimes very

simple forms of incubation were practiced." See Jean Marie Husser, *Dreams and Dream Narratives in the Biblical World* (Sheffield: Sheffield Academic, 1999), 46.

31. Trible, *Rhetorical Criticism*, 138.

32. Merwe, Naudé, and Kroeze, *A Biblical Hebrew Reference Grammar*, 172.

33. Ibid.

befallen) us," *běšellĕmî hārāʿâ hazzōʾt lānû*). Verbless clauses in quoted speech depart from the main line verbs in order to supply vital background information.[34] In this case the clause combines with the climactic command to highlight the mariners' desire to know the deity behind the fierce storm.

The decision to cast lots, therefore, was provoked by two factors. First, the mariners' cries to their gods have proved ineffective. Second, Jonah was not forthcoming with what he knew about their situation because he had withdrawn from his prophetic responsibilities. Given the ineffectiveness of their gods and the unresponsiveness of YHWH's prophet, lots were their only recourse.

Lot-casting was the only form of divination permissible in Israel. The basic procedure involved small stones or other objects marked in such a way as to represent individuals or commodities.[35] The marked lot objects were then cast into a receptacle of some kind.[36] The receptacle was then shaken until one of the marked lot objects fell out, which thus indicated the divinely designated individual or item.[37]

Strawn has argued convincingly that the lot-casting scene is designed to portray the mariners as particularly pious, even from an Israelite point of view. The intent is to portray Jonah negatively by comparison with the mariners.[38] Strawn bases this understanding on two observations. First, lot-casting in the Hebrew Bible is typically associated with Israelite practice.[39] In fact, the word used for "lot" (*gôrāl*) has no cognate in the other Afro-Asiatic languages of Israel's neighbors, which shows that the Hebrew terminology for lot-casting is indigenous to Israel.[40]

Second, the overarching parallelism of the book aligns the mariners' lot-casting with the people of Nineveh's repentance. The repentance described in Jonah 3 is distinctively Israelite in character, combining the elements of fasting, sackcloth, and behavioral change. Fasting in particular was rare in Mesopotamian contexts, and when such a rite was observed, it had no association with repentance.[41] This parallel between Nineveh's repentance and the mariners' lot-casting suggests that just as the repentance of the people of Nineveh is unexpectedly Israelite in character, so also the lot-casting of the mariners is unexpectedly Israelite in character.[42]

The lot-casting scene is a midpoint in the mariners' developing faith. Having given up on their gods, they turned to an Israelite practice that opened the door to YHWH's revelation, eventually leading to their praying, sacrificing, and vowing to YHWH by name. YHWH honored the mariners' piety and satisfied their desire for revelation. He exposed Jonah by lot as the reason for the storm. Though Jonah was reticent to reveal the reason behind the storm, YHWH was eager to do so. In fact, Jonah was finally in a position where he was compelled to serve as YHWH's instrument of revelation.

The mariners barraged Jonah with five probing questions. The series begins with a command form ("please, tell us!" *haggîdâ-nāʾ lānû*), which indicates the transition from narrative discourse to quoted speech. The imperative in this case is

---

34. Tucker, *Jonah*, 27.

35. Brody notes that astragali, sheep's knuckle bones, were sometimes used in the procedure. In fact, astragali were found in the excavation of the Cape Gelidonya shipwreck, which shows that the crew had the requisite lot-casting materials on board. Cf. Brody, *Each Man Cried Out to His God*, 84.

36. John Lindblom, "Lot-Casting in the Old Testament," *VT* 12 (1962): 166–68.

37. Anne Marie Kitz, "The Hebrew Terminology of Lot Casting and Its Ancient Near Eastern Context," *CBQ* 62 (2000): 214.

38. Brent A. Strawn, "Jonah's Sailors and Their Lot Casting: A Rhetorical-Critical Observation," *Bib* 91 (2010): 66–76.

39. Ibid, 70.

40. Ibid, 71.

41. John H. Walton, "Jonah," *EBC*, 8:484.

42. Strawn, "Jonah's Sailors," 72–74.

softened by a Hebrew particle (*nāʾ*), which introduces a polite request rather than an insistent command.[43] Subordinate to the request are the five questions, four of which (the first, second, third, and fifth) are verbless clauses beginning with an interrogative marker. Sentences of this type invert the normal subject-predicate word order of verbless clauses, which highlights the desired information.[44]

First they asked Jonah to identify the person responsible for the disastrous situation ("on whose account this disaster has befallen us"; *baʾăšer lĕmîhārāʿâ hazzōʾt lānû*). This may seem an odd question to ask after the lot had already singled Jonah out as the responsible person. One must remember, however, that the lots only revealed the human target of divine anger. The critical issue as to the identity of the offended deity remained a question. Jonah's response in 1:9c confirmed that it was the identity of the deity the mariners were after, not the human target.[45] In fact, their question is identical in wording to the purpose clause in 1:7e, thus again underscoring the mariners' persistent interest in the identity of the deity responsible.

The book's original audience would likely have understood all five of the mariners' questions to relate to the identification of the offended deity. Jonah's occupation, hometown, country, and race would all have been significant clues as to the particular deity responsible for the storm. In the mariners' worldview, a person served a variety of deities, each associated with a different aspect of that person's life: occupation, city, nation, and family.[46] The barrage of questions was probably motivated by the supposition that Jonah may not even know which deity he offended or why. Therefore, the more personal information they knew, the better their chances of identifying the deity and the offense.

Jonah's response took the last question first. He identified himself as a Hebrew ("I am a Hebrew," *ʿibrî ʾānōkî*). The sentence is a verbless clause, providing the background for the climactic revelation of the divine name that follows. "Hebrew" was the typical designation foreigners applied to Israelites, and thus Israelites often used it as a self-designation when conversing with foreigners. Jonah proceeded to the mariners' first and most pressing question with a second verbless clause: "YHWH, the god[47] of heaven, I fear, who made the sea and dry land." In this case, a participle (*yārēʾ*) serves as predicate, and its direct object "YHWH" occupies first position in the clause. The syntax emphasizes the revelation of YHWH's name, which indicates the climactic nature of Jonah's statement. On this revelation, the whole episode turns.

Jonah's chosen designations for YHWH are rhetorically significant. First, he introduces YHWH as "the god of heaven" (*ʾĕlōhê haššāmayim*), a designation strikingly similar to that of the Phoenician deity associated with the raging sea and especially feared by seafarers, Baʿal Shemêm ("Lord of Heaven").[48]

---

43. Merwe, Naudé, and Kroeze, *A Biblical Hebrew Reference Grammar*, 335.

44. Ellen van Wolde, "The Verbless Clause and Its Textual Function," in *The Verbless Clause in Biblical Hebrew: Linguistic Approaches* (ed. M. O'Connor and Cynthia Miller; Winona Lake, IN: Eisenbrauns, 1999), 330–31.

45. Landes, "Textual 'Information Gaps,'" 279.

46. Snell, *Religions of the Ancient Near East*, 19–28

47. Please note that in the Hebrew text, the designation *ʾĕlōhîm* may either refer to deity in general, or to a non-Israelite

designation for the one true God, the God of Israel. I have distinguished between these uses of the term in this commentary by assuming that any time *ʾĕlōhîm* is qualified by a personal pronoun (i.e., my god, your god, his god) or another noun (i.e., the so-called "construct state," as in the phrase "the god of heaven"), it should be understood as a general reference to deity, "god." By contrast, any time *ʾĕlōhîm* is unqualified, it should be understood as the Gentile designation for the god of Israel, "Elohim."

48. Brody, *"Each Man Cried Out to His God,"* 11 n. 7.

Jonah thus subtly corrected the mariners' misplaced devotion by attributing to YHWH what they would normally have attributed to Ba'al Shemêm.

Jonah proceeded with the relative clause "who made the sea and the dry land." Though it is more common to refer to YHWH as the God "who created earth and sea," the author chose this distinctive wording, "the sea and the dry land," because of the significance of these two environments to Jonah's story. The sea and the dry land are the regions where Jonah and YHWH interact as their conflict unfolds. The story moves from dry land to sea, back to dry land, and finally to very dry land (desert, 4:5 – 8), and YHWH is active in all of these locations.[49] When YHWH and Jonah interact in the inhospitable environments of sea and desert, the tension between them is high. When they interact in the hospitable environment of "dry land," however, the tension between them abates. The phrase reinforces the point that YHWH does not immediately abandon those who are in conflict with him, who flee to the sea or to the desert. Rather, he patiently works toward reconciliation with any who will sincerely engage him.

For the mariners, Jonah's description confirmed the suspicion that they were dealing with a cosmic deity of great power rather than a local deity with limited jurisdiction.[50] Furthermore, the designation identified YHWH as the one who would guide them all safely back to dry land. In this way the author foreshadows the outcome of the current crisis.

4. The Fear Due YHWH's Sovereign, Severe Mercy (1:10 – 12)

The clause "the men feared with a great fear" (*wayyîrĕʾû hāʾănāšîm yirʾâ gĕdôlâ*) resumes the narrative with a mainline *wayyiqtol* verb and creates a significant link with Jonah's claim to fear YHWH. The term "fear" functions as a catch word, serving to juxtapose Jonah's fear and the mariners' fear. Jonah's claim is ironic in light of his defiant flight from YHWH's presence. His version of fear stands in stark contrast to the mariners' evolving fear that leads to greater and greater obedience. This contrast is highlighted by the author's description of the mariners' response to Jonah's revelation. The author excessively modifies the verb that describes the mariners' fear by employing a direct object derived from the same Hebrew root as the verb (*yrʾ*) and appending the adjective "great" (*gĕdôlâ*). The basic verb that describes Jonah's fear pales in comparison to the description of the mariners' intense reverence.

Another notable aspect of the clause is that the author for the first time refers to the mariners simply as "men" (*hāʾănāšîm*). This change of designation may underscore the contrast between the divine and human that is so basic to the profound reverence that came over them. This experience of YHWH's sovereign, severe mercy crystallized for them the creator/creature distinction.

The contrast between Jonah's and the mariners' fear intensifies with the mariners' indicting question: "What have you done?" (*mah-zōʾt ʿāśîtā*). This same question occurs five other times in the Hebrew Bible (Gen 3:13; 12:18; 26:10; 29:25; Exod 14:11) and always expresses moral outrage at what the speaker perceives as foolish behavior. The mariners were shocked that Jonah would dare defy such a powerful, cosmic deity and thus place the entire crew in mortal danger. Their question reflects a comprehension of genuine fear of YHWH, from which Jonah, in his rebellion, has fallen.

Interestingly, the author follows the mariners' question with two causal clauses, explaining

---

49. Perry, *The Honeymoon Is Over*, xxxvi – xxxvii.

50. Walton, *Jonah*, 472.

what prompted such a response. They posed the question "for [*kî*] the men knew that he was fleeing YHWH's presence because [*kî*] he had told them." The two causal clauses embed narrative within the mariners' quoted speech, clarifying the motivation for the question.[51] In this way, the author avoids interrupting with offline background clauses the preceding narrative verb chain that connects the mariners' growing fear with their expression of shock at Jonah's disobedience. By maintaining this close connection, the author further underscores the contrast between the mariners' piety and Jonah's impiety.

The embedded causal clauses effectively disclose to the reader that Jonah's response recorded in 1:9b-d is merely a summary of what he shared. Apparently, his response also included the intent behind this fateful sea voyage — flight from YHWH's presence. The syntax provides another example of the author's strategic use of information gaps. These gaps may create suspense or misdirect the reader to false impressions only to correct them later by additional information.[52] In this particular case, the author stripped Jonah's response down to the two revelations that the author felt were most significant — Jonah's self-identification as one of God's elect people and the revelation of YHWH as the offended deity. Whatever else Jonah may have said on this occasion is omitted so as not to distract from these two central truths. YHWH is the sovereign of all the earth to whom all peoples are accountable, and Jonah belongs to the people through whom YHWH has chosen to reveal himself to the world. Only at the point of the mariners' indicting question did it become relevant that

Jonah also revealed the reason for the sea voyage and for the serious trouble they faced.

Since the mariners do not know YHWH and are unsure how to appease him, they question Jonah again. The form of the mariners' question is particularly pointed: "What must we do with you so that the sea might settle down for us?" The initial verb (*na'ăśeh*) is best understood as an exhortation expressing necessity ("must")[53] followed by a second verb (*wĕyištōq*) expressing purpose.[54] A prepositional phrase (*lāk*) immediately follows the initial verb, identifying Jonah as the object of divine wrath and, therefore, the key to appeasing YHWH's wrath. Their question betrays recognition that some punishment of Jonah is in order. They even offer to serve as the agents of the punishment ("What must *we* do with you?"). The mariners' agency in carrying out a punishment on Jonah becomes important later in the episode, but already the author points in this direction through the wording of their question. The author thus introduces into the story a familiar Old Testament theme — YHWH's use of the nations as agents of his disciplinary action against his own people (cf. Deut 28:33,36; Judg 2:3; 3:1 – 6; Isa 10:5; 28:11 – 13).

The author follows the mariners' question with a motive clause: "for the sea was raging on relentlessly." The motive clause is most likely the author's editorial remark and not part of the mariners' speech, as suggested by the parallel syntax between this verse and 1:10, where the author also followed the mariners' direct speech with an editorial motive clause ("For the men knew that he was fleeing from YHWH's presence because he had told them so").[55] Furthermore, a nearly identical motive clause recurs in 1:13d followed by the prepositional

---

51. Tucker, *Jonah*, 34 – 35.
52. Landes, "Textual 'Information Gaps,'" 273 – 76.
53. Joüon-Muraoka, *Grammar of Biblical Hebrew*, §113m .
54. Tucker, *Jonah*, 36.

55. Contra Sasson, *Jonah*, 123 – 24. Sasson places the motive clause within the quotation on the basis that Jonah employs the phrase in his response.

phrase "against them" (*'ălêhem*), not "against us," which suggests that updates regarding the storm's progress are always authorial asides to the reader. After all, the storm's growing intensity is obvious to everyone on board the ship.

The rhetorical intent of the motive clause is to dramatize YHWH's relentless pursuit of his runaway prophet through the unrelenting nature of the storm. The author expresses the storm's persistence by means of two participles, which together convey consistent intensity (*hôlēk wĕsō'ēr*). The first of these verbs (*hôlēk*) functions as an auxiliary to the second (*wĕsō'ēr*), which thus emphasizes the storm's persistence.[56] The point is that nothing they tried worked. The storm continued to bear down on them, and they were running out of options and time. Since YHWH had revealed that Jonah was the key to survival, the mariners looked to the prophet for guidance as to what punishment YHWH wanted them to administer to Jonah to secure YHWH's favor.

Jonah responded to the mariners' query with a shocking suggestion: "Pick me up, and fling me to the sea so that the sea might settle down for you" (*śā'ûnî wahătîlunî 'el-hayyām wĕyištōq hayyām mē'ălēkem*). A sequence of three command forms, all joined with the conjunction (*waw*), constitutes the main line of Jonah's speech. The first two are imperatives ("Pick me up and fling me," *śā'ûnî wahătîlunî*), but the third is a jussive ("that the sea might settle down," *wĕyištōq hayyām*), expressing the purpose of the preceding command. These are followed by a verbless motive clause expressing the reason for Jonah's radical suggestion ("for I realize, *kî yôdēa' 'ānî*). The inverted word order of this clause (predicate-subject vs. the expected subject-predicate) emphasizes Jonah's acknowledgment of

guilt, perhaps as a means of absolving the mariners of any culpability for his blood.[57]

The procedure Jonah outlines in response to the mariners' raises a couple of important interpretive questions. First, why did Jonah insist on the mariners' participation in his demise at sea? Jonah could have simply jumped overboard and drowned in the sea without involving the mariners in what would arguably be an act of murder.[58] Had Jonah done this, however, the reader might miss the connection between Jonah's fate and that of the jettisoned cargo. What the mariners did to the cargo they also did to Jonah. Their participation strengthens the connection that may be intended to emphasize Jonah's role as YHWH's "instrument" (*kĕlî*), the word used with reference to the jettisoned cargo in 1:5. The same term is sometimes used with reference to YHWH's human agents, frequently in contexts portending judgment (Ps 31:13[12]; Jer 18:4; 19:11; 22:28; 25:34; Hos 8:8).

Jonah becomes a useless vessel in his rebellion, much like the jettisoned cargo that, in the midst of the storm, did nothing but weigh down the ship and endanger the lives of the crew. Jonah slept in the same place where the cargo was stored (1:5), jeopardized the ship and crew as did the cargo, and eventually was jettisoned like the cargo (1:15).

A second reason for the crew's participation may be to reflect the common pattern of divine discipline in which YHWH humbles his people by subjecting them to the nations. In this sense, the mariners may have participated with Jonah in a symbolic act that foreshadowed Israel's (and later Judah's) subjugation to foreign powers. This idea haunts the background of this narrative, and the Assyrian setting likely evoked thoughts of exile and Gentile imperialism among its first readers.[59]

---

56. Tucker, *Jonah*, 37.
57. Ibid., 38 – 39.
58. Perry, *The Honeymoon Is Over*, 7 – 12.

59. This same phenomenon is evident in works even later than Jonah, such as Tobit and Judith.

Finally, Jonah's command to the crew members, "fling me to the sea" (*waḥăṭîlunî ʾel-hayyām*), recalls again YHWH's initial flinging (*hēṭîl*) of the gale. The action eventually came full circle as YHWH's countermove (1:4) had its intended result.

The second interpretive question asks what Jonah was trying to accomplish by this act. If Jonah's objective was simply to spare the crew from suffering for his sin, repentance would have sufficed. Had Jonah confessed his sin to YHWH and repented regarding the commission, the storm presumably would have abated and the mariners would have returned Jonah to dry land. Yet Jonah never seems to entertain this possibility. Perhaps his suggestion to the mariners is his next desperate attempt to avoid his divine calling through death. Perhaps he is inviting YHWH's judgment so that he will not have to embrace his calling.

The reader may find here a first glimpse at Jonah's twisted notion of divine justice. On the one hand, Jonah's sense of justice does not permit him to let the ship's crew suffer for his rebellion. Thus, Jonah confesses his responsibility for the mariners' peril and accepts the consequences of his flight so that the crew might be spared. On the other hand, that same sense of justice also prevents his repentance because he cannot reconcile himself to a commission with which he fundamentally disagrees.[60] Therefore, Jonah expects to die under divine judgment, and he may even have been trying to force YHWH's hand to that end. Perhaps, that is what this flight is intended to accomplish. Jonah knows there is no escaping YHWH. Rather, his flight invites YHWH's judgment as the preferable alternative, Jonah thinks, to YHWH's commission, even if that ultimately means death. Jonah will discover, however, that neither YHWH's judgment nor his salvation is subject to human manipulation.

5. The Futility of Escaping YHWH's Severe Mercy (1:13 – 14)

The narrative resumes with the verb (lit.) "the men dug" (*wayyaḥtĕrû*) with no indication of the mariners' response to Jonah's suggestion. The mariners seem to ignore the proposal as though unwilling to consider, at least at this point, such drastic action as pitching Jonah overboard and leaving him to drown. They do not want the responsibility for taking human life unless it is absolutely necessary. One human solution remains that they have not yet tried, namely rowing back to shore. The mariners take to the oars and strain against the elements in a futile attempt to reach land.

The author's word choice is interesting. The verb "to dig" (*wayyaḥtĕrû*) is not the usual idiom for rowing a ship.[61] Rather, the term refers to digging into the ground or through a wall (cf. Job 24:16; Ezek 8:8; 12:5,7,12).[62] In Amos 9:2 it even refers to digging one's way to Sheol. It is this last occurrence of the term that bears significantly on the author's choice of this verb in Jonah 1:13a. The verb "to dig" suggests a double entendre. Though the mariners are attempting to "row" their way back to dry ground, in reality they are only digging a hole to Sheol into which they will eventually have to cast Jonah.

The reason the crew's efforts to row back to shore are futile is because the storm intensifies in response to their attempt to "dig" through YHWH's wrath. The author repeats the description of the storm from 1:11d, except this time with the addition of a crucial prepositional phrase: "For the sea raged *against them* with growing intensity."

---

60. Fretheim, *The Message of Jonah*, 88 – 89.
61. Some form of the root *šwṭ* "to row" might have been a
more natural choice in this context (cf. Ezek. 27:8, 26).
62. *HALOT*, 365.

YHWH's creational conspiracy permits no human solutions. The elements oppose the mariners until they too join YHWH's conspiracy.

The reader, however, must endure one more delay before the episode at sea climaxes in Jonah's descent to the depths. Having resigned themselves to Jonah's drastic suggestion, the mariners cry out to YHWH before following through on Jonah's drastic suggestion. The shift to direct discourse is marked by the typical quotation formula (*wayyōʾmer*) as well as by a series of deferential particles emphasizing the crew's growing fear for YHWH: "We beg of you" (*ʾānnâ*), "please don't" (*ʾal-nāʾ*). Their petition to YHWH consists of two requests. The first is that YHWH not destroy them simply because Jonah is on board their ship. This interpretation understands the Hebrew phrase *běnepeš hāʾîš hazzeh*, often translated "because of this man's life," to simply mean "this individual," as in the case of the similar but more common idiom *nepeš hāʾādām*.[63]

The mariners' second request is that the action they are about to take not come back to haunt them. Their concern is that the deity, after accepting the sacrifice, might later turn on them and hold them responsible for Jonah's murder. One should keep in mind that these mariners are not accustomed to dealing with a faithful God like YHWH, but with the capricious deities of Canaan and Mesopotamia.[64] Thus they approach this action with great trepidation and misgiving.

This second request concludes with an important motive clause: "For you are YHWH, just as you pleased you have done." With this statement the crew acknowledges YHWH's sovereign freedom — a recurring theme in Jonah. YHWH has orchestrated everything that led to this point. The mariners do the only thing they can in response to YHWH's intervention.

The mariners' prayer in 1:14 is parallel to their more frantic prayer at the onset of the storm (1:5b). It parallels their earlier expression of piety inasmuch as it is categorically the same basic religious activity, but this is where the similarity ends. Everything about this prayer differs from their previous prayers. First, the desperation and uncertainty of the initial prayers to any and every deity they can think of is replaced with the focused invocation of the true God, YHWH. Second, the mere mention of their praying in 1:5b is replaced by the actual content of their prayer in 1:14b-g. No longer are their prayers just so much noise, a din of competing petitions to diverse deities. Their prayers are now directed to the one deity who can save them from their plight.

The crew's invocation also contrasts with Jonah's lack of prayer. The verb describing their praying (*wayyiqrěʾû*)[65] recalls the helmsman's exhortation to Jonah to rise from his slumber and cry out (*qěrāʾ*) to his god (1:6e). The text offers no indication that Jonah heeded this call anymore than he did YHWH's call in 1:2. The mariners, however, do cry out to YHWH, and they do so by name, certain now that they are addressing the correct deity. The contrast between the crew's visible fear and Jonah's confessed fear is now complete.

---

63. H. Seebass, "*nepeš*," *TDOT*, 9:515. Cf. also Sasson, *Jonah*, 133.

64. Glenn Holland, *Gods in the Desert: Religions of the Ancient Near East* (Lanham, MD: Rowman & Littlefield, 2009), 188. Holland states regarding the Mesopotamian worldview, "human beings are subject to the whims of capricious gods, whose actions are motivated by a host of personal reasons, very few of which have to do with the welfare of their human subjects."

65. It is interesting to note that this verb differs from the one used of their praying to their gods in 1:5b, where the verb "to cry out" (*zāʿaq*) is used.

6. The Relenting Wrath of YHWH's Relentless Mercy (1:15a – 2:1b [1:17b])

Having made their petition to YHWH, the crew turn to their somber task. The text marks this transition with a return to narrative verb forms (*wayyiqtol*) in contrast to the polite imperatives of the prayer. In keeping with Jonah's instructions, they lift the prophet up and fling him to the sea. Again the author uses the verb "flung" (*wayṭiluhû*), harkening back to YHWH's "flinging" the gale toward the sea and the crew's "casting" their cargo overboard. YHWH initiated a series of events culminating in this moment.

The sea responds immediately. The author vividly conveys the response by personifying the sea just as he did the ship in 1:4c with the words, "the sea ceased its raging" (*wayyaʿămōd hayyām mizzaʿpô*). The noun "raging" (*zaʿap*) refers elsewhere in the Hebrew Bible exclusively to a *person's* anger.[66] Since the sea serves throughout the episode as the visible manifestation of YHWH's wrath, its personification at the conclusion of the episode conveys the relenting of YHWH's wrath.

With Jonah temporarily out of the picture, the narrative spotlight falls on the ship's crew. Though one might expect all traces of fear to vanish with the storm's departure, the opposite is actually the case. YHWH's relenting of his wrath motivates genuine worship of YHWH. The author repeats one last time the standard expression for the crew's evolving fear with one significant addition: "The men feared with great fear YHWH" (*wayyîrĕʾû*

hāʾănāšîm yirʾâ gĕdôlâ ʾet-yhwh). Finally their fear has a name — YHWH.

The repetition and extension of the author's description of the crew's fear, however, conveys not so much a quantitative increase as a qualitative transformation. The fear that the mariners feel at the end of this episode is qualitatively different from the fear that gripped them at the onset of the storm. The storm no longer threatens them. YHWH's wrath no longer hangs over their heads. Their confusion and sense of helplessness evaporate. What is there left to fear? The mariners are gripped in the end by a profound sense of awe at YHWH's readiness to reveal himself and at his responsiveness to their great need. Never have they encountered a deity so forthcoming regarding his will and so ready to deliver those who turn to him in humble petition.[67]

This fear for YHWH, however, is no mere religious sentiment. It finds tangible expression in the crew's grateful worship. The author describes their worship with surprise as though shocked that these Gentile mariners would offer acceptable worship to YHWH. Both of the verbs describing the crew's worship introduce an object derived from the same root as the verb: "They sacrificed sacrifices to YHWH, and they vowed vows" (*wayyizbĕḥûzebaḥ layhwh wayyidderû nĕdārîm*). Though the result sounds awkward in English, in Hebrew it produces a sound play and expresses surprise at the Gentiles' devotion to YHWH. The mariners' worship does not necessarily mean that they convert to the monotheistic worship of YHWH, but it certainly points in that direction.[68]

---

66. Wolff, *Obadiah and Jonah*, 105.

67. Discerning the will(s) of the gods was a complicated and esoteric endeavor in the ancient Near East. Gods hid clues as to their decrees and decisions regarding the future in the entrails of sacrificial animals, or in heavenly anomalies, and even when these could be read and interpreted the results were not guaranteed. Snell (*Religions of the Ancient Near East*, 98)

states, "The connection between omens and experience, rather, between what was observed to be ominous and what subsequently happened was not always obvious."

68. Commentators differ considerably on the implications of the mariners' worship in 1:16. Wolff, for example, argues for a fictitious full-scale conversion of the mariners to orthodox Yahwism (Wolff, *Obadiah and Jonah*, 122). Stuart, however, in-

A pragmatically minded reader may well wonder how sacrifices could be offered on board a ship. Did mariners normally carry sacrificial animals with them? Were they equipped with an altar and wood and a means of making fire for such religious activities? Brody argues that such rituals were normally performed at harbor sanctuaries, and such could be the case here.[69]

The focus returns to Jonah's fate in 2:1 (1:17). Most treatments of Jonah consider 2:1a (1:17a) to introduce a new episode.[70] Nothing in the discourse itself, however, warrants a break at this point. The story proceeds with a narrative verb form (*wayyiqtol*) and reintroduces YHWH as the main actor. Kamp is more likely correct in placing the beginning of the next episode at 1:17c (2:1c) on the linguistic basis of the reappearance of the verb "Now it happened that …" (*wayĕhî*), which often functions as a new episode marker in Hebrew narrative.[71]

Two other factors argue in favor of retaining 2:1a-b (1:17a-b) as part of the second episode. First, the structure of the episode would be incomplete without YHWH's direct intervention at this point. Just as the preceding episode ended with YHWH's action directed at Jonah when YHWH flung the gale toward the sea, this episode also finds closure with YHWH's action directed at Jonah when YHWH appoints the great fish to swallow his wayward prophet. YHWH's manipulation of creation for Jonah's instruction and redirection frames the scene.

A second consideration favoring retaining 2:1a-b (1:17a-b) as the conclusion to the second episode is the fact that a scene shift does not occur until 2:1c (1:17c) ("Now Jonah was in the fish's belly for three days and three nights"). The first two clauses of 2:1 record events that are still taking place at sea. In fact, Jonah's long descent that began in 1:3 does not hit bottom until the divinely appointed fish swallows him in a manner reminiscent of Sheol (cf. Exod 15:12; Num 16:30 – 32; Job 24:19; Ps 69:16[15]; Prov. 1:12; Jer 51:34). It is only once Jonah is in the fish that the direction of his journey turns back toward YHWH, dry land, and life. Thus, the scene shift at 2:1c is the decisive turning point for the direction of Jonah's journey both geographically and spiritually.

Having turned the reader's attention back to Jonah's fate, the author reintroduces YHWH's intervention because Jonah's fate rests in YHWH's hands. Quite unexpectedly, YHWH appoints a great fish (*dāg gādôl*) to swallow Jonah. The verb form (*wayyiqtol*) links YHWH's action to the preceding series of events and in particular to the mariners' prayer, in which they addressed YHWH by name. The author leaves the impression that the appointment of the great fish is YHWH's answer to the mariners' prayer that they not be responsible for bloodshed.[72] This connection predisposes the reader to view the fish not as an instrument of judgment but as an instrument of salvation. This suspicion will be confirmed in the next episode.

---

sists that the text warrants nothing more than an acknowledgment on the mariners' part that YHWH could do as he pleased and that, in their case, he was pleased to save them from the storm (Stuart, *Hosea – Jonah*, 464). This commentary takes a view somewhere between these two positions. The text falls just short of describing the mariners as converts to monotheistic Yahwism. Nevertheless, YHWH has certainly led them a long way down that road, and the vows they made to YHWH imply a continuing bond with this deity who acted on their behalf when their other gods failed them.

69. Brody, *"Each Man Cried Out to His God,"* 100 – 150.

70. Wolff, *Obadiah and Jonah*, 125; Sasson, *Jonah*, 144; Limburg, *Jonah*, 60; Jenson, *Obadiah, Jonah, Micah*, 60; Allen, *Joel, Obadiah, Jonah, and Micah*, 213.

71. Kamp, *Inner Worlds*, 90.

72. James S. Ackerman, "Satire and Symbolism in the Song of Jonah," in *Traditions in Transformation: Turning Points in Biblical Faith* (ed. Baruch Halpern and Jon D. Levenson; Winona Lake, IN: Eisenbrauns, 1981), 222.

The verb "appointed" (*wayman*) comes from a root pertaining to counting (Qal) or apportioning (Piel).[73] The book of Jonah contains four instances of this verb, all of which pertain to elements of nature YHWH employed to teach Jonah a lesson.[74] The great fish that YHWH graciously provided for Jonah's transportation is parallel to the ship that Jonah paid for out of his own pocket. The ship carried Jonah close to his grave while the fish carried Jonah back to dry land and life.

The verb form, however, also conveys the idea of selecting from a number of options the item best suited for the person or occasion in question. In fact, in most contexts where this verb occurs, a carefully selected agent is required for the accomplishment of an important task. In this case, YHWH has appointed the perfect fish for Jonah — the one best suited to help YHWH make his point. What that point is the reader must wait to discover after the fish expels Jonah. The fish, therefore, has a dual function in the story. On the one hand, it is a means of salvation; on the other hand, it is a means of correction and instruction.[75] This is certainly not the first time YHWH used an odd means of salvation in order to make a point, nor will it be the last (Num 21:6 – 8; 1 Cor 1:18 – 29).

The episode concludes by noting YHWH's purpose in appointing the fish. His purpose is "to swallow Jonah" (*liblōaʿ ʾet-yônâ*). As noted above, the act of swallowing is ordinarily associated with divine judgment in Sheol or with destruction in general. The fish's swallowing Jonah is an act of judgment and perhaps the final leg of Jonah's descent to Sheol. As already noted, however, the syntax has signaled a connection between the appointment of the fish and the mariners' prayer that they be spared from having to shed innocent blood, implying that the fish is an answer to the mariners' prayer and the agent of Jonah's deliverance. How should the reader reconcile these conflicting impressions?

In prophetic literature judgment and salvation are usually not alternatives from which God's people must choose. It is not salvation *or* judgment, but rather, salvation *through* judgment. Divine wrath and judgment become a means of separating YHWH's people from their sin in preparation for a restoration to covenant fellowship with their holy God (cf., e.g., Deut 4:26 – 30; 30:1 – 3; Amos 4:6 – 11). The great fish that YHWH appoints to swallow Jonah, therefore, is the perfect symbol to convey the prophetic principle of salvation not from, but through judgment.

Canonical and Practical Significance

Divine Election, Israel, and the Nations

The ordeal at sea recorded in 1:4a – 2:1b (1:17b) demonstrates that YHWH does not easily give up either on his purposes or his people. He is intent on having his commission fulfilled, and he will not let Jonah escape his role as agent of its fulfillment without a fight. Jonah thus joins the company of others, like Jacob, who wrestled with God over the true meaning of election and calling (Gen 32:24 – 32).

---

73. *HALOT* (Study Edition), 1:599.
74. Sasson, *Jonah*, 148 – 49.

75. Bryan D. Estelle, *Salvation through Judgment and Mercy: The Gospel according to Jonah* (Phillipsburg, NJ: Presbyterian & Reformed, 2005), 66.

Paul summarizes well the point of Jonah 1:4a – 2:1b (1:17b) with his statement in Romans 11:29: "God's gifts and his call are irrevocable" (NIV).

Jonah's resistance to the divine call provokes YHWH's wrath as demonstrated in the fierce storm that sabotages Jonah's attempted escape. YHWH often must display his wrath to convince those he calls that he is serious about their participation in his redemptive work. In Exod 4:10 – 16, for example, Moses' attempt to talk his way out of YHWH's commission eventually provoked YHWH's wrath, at which point Moses conceded and accepted the call.

> Moses said to the LORD, "Pardon your servant, Lord. I have never been eloquent, neither in the past nor since you have spoken to your servant. I am slow of speech and tongue."
>
> The LORD said to him, "Who gave human beings their mouth? Who makes them deaf or mute? Who gives them sight or makes them blind? Is it not I, the LORD? Now go; I will help you speak and will teach you what to say."
>
> But Moses said, "Pardon your servant, Lord. Please send someone else."
>
> Then the LORD's anger burned against Moses and he said, "What about your brother, Aaron the Levite? I know he can speak well. He is already on his way to meet you, and he will be glad to see you. You shall speak to him and put words in his mouth; I will help both of you speak and will teach you what to do. He will speak to the people for you, and it will be as if he were your mouth and as if you were God to him." (NIV)

YHWH's anger at human resistance to his call, however, must not be misinterpreted as the petulance of a deity who throws a temper tantrum when things do not go his way. Rather, YHWH's wrath is a reflex of his passionate love that wants more for us than we want for ourselves. Our participation in YHWH's work is crucial to our spiritual development and our joy. When we refuse his calling for lesser pursuits, YHWH smolders at the shortsightedness, selfishness, and shallowness we have succumbed to in our sin. He burns at the prospect of our forfeiting participation in his joy because we prefer the comfort and familiarity of our old theological constructs and the less demanding life of spiritual mediocrity.

Similarly, one must not think that YHWH's acts of judgment are motivated by sheer vindictiveness. YHWH orchestrated Jonah's ordeal in the sea and in the fish's belly to bring the prophet back to his senses and to challenge his wrongheaded theological assumptions. Divine judgment is a severe mercy designed to restore the wayward to a right relationship with God. It is far too simplistic to think of judgment and salvation as mutually exclusive fates. Moses indicated to Israel that she would undergo both the curses and the blessings of the covenant before finally being restored to God (Deut 30:1 – 10). Jeremiah also makes this point repeatedly to the inhabitants of Judah as he encourages their surrender to Babylon and their submission to exile as the only means of their restoration to covenant relationship with YHWH (Jer 24:1 – 7). As Prov 3:11 – 12 so eloquently states, "My son, do not despise the LORD's discipline, and do not resent his rebuke, because the LORD disciplines those he loves, as a father the son he delights in" (NIV).

Throughout Jonah's voyage at sea, YHWH works through the prophet to reveal himself to the Gentile mariners despite Jonah's withdrawal from the prophetic ministry. Jonah's deep sleep in the remote cargo hold of the ship, his refusal to pray on the mariners' behalf, and his silence during the casting of lots all point to his attempt to withdraw from his prophetic calling. Yet, despite Jonah's passive resistance, YHWH reveals himself through Jonah to the ship's eager crew until they pray, sacrifice, and vow to YHWH by name.

This thematic development points toward two important theological truths that run throughout the Christian canon. The first is the instrumentality of Israel in the outworking of YHWH's global redemptive purposes as expressed especially clearly in the Abrahamic covenant (Gen 12:1 – 3). YHWH insists on mediating his blessings to the world through Abraham's descendents. The difficulty is that Abraham's descendents are fallen just like everyone else, and therefore they suffer from a self-centeredness and parochialism that inhibits their full and willing participation in the broadening mission of God.

The issue, however, is not one of general Israelite prejudice against non-Israelites as Jonah's basically positive interaction with the Gentile crew demonstrates. Rather, the issue is one of divine justice when YHWH's mercy and love are extended to a people who are especially cruel and whose cruelty threatens Israel. Jonah, like many other believers, wrestled with the conflict of interest created between divine justice and divine mercy when YHWH demonstrated the same forbearance toward wicked and dangerous Assyria as he did toward Israel.

Thus, YHWH uses Jonah's flight as an opportunity to demonstrate firm resolve in revealing himself to the nations through Israel. The mariners are a test case of how YHWH will accomplish his purposes even through an imperfect and sometimes resistant people. Furthermore, YHWH's calming of the storm for the mariners' sake foreshadows the more dramatic and scandalous relenting of YHWH in response to Nineveh's repentance; this prepares Jonah for an extension of YHWH's mercy to Israel's bitterest enemy. Most challenging of all is that this extension of mercy must be offered by none other than an Israelite prophet despite what it might mean for his own people.

General and Special Revelation

Jonah's second episode also teaches that YHWH is at work in the world outside of his covenant people to prepare the nations for reception of revelation through his covenant people. YHWH's use of wind, storm, and casting lots speaks to the role of general revelation in YHWH's redemptive purposes. The piety and receptivity of the crew also point in this direction as evidence of the divine image in all humanity.

These mariners displayed a fear and a readiness to respond to revelation that challenged even Jonah's conflicted faith. In this respect the mariners are a model of how Gentiles should have responded to general revelation through creation and through their instincts as creatures made in the divine image, as Paul points out.

> The wrath of God is being revealed from heaven against all the godlessness and wickedness of people who suppress the truth by their wickedness, since what may be known about God is plain to them, because God has made it plain to them. For since the creation of the world God's invisible qualities — his eternal power and divine nature — have been clearly seen, being understood from what has been made, so that people are without excuse.
>
> For although they knew God, they neither glorified him as God nor gave thanks to him, but their thinking became futile and their foolish hearts were darkened. (Rom 1:18 – 21 NIV).

General revelation, however, is not just for unbelievers. The wind, the storm, the lots, and the giant fish also communicate in a profound way to Jonah, who has reservations about YHWH's special revelation. When believers have difficulty accepting the implications of the deep truths of God revealed in Scripture, YHWH often uses creation as confirmation and illustration of what has been revealed in Scripture. As Jesus demonstrated in his teaching, we are surrounded by parables in creation that challenge and stretch many of our assumptions regarding the meaning of special revelation (Matt 6:25 – 31; Luke 12:22 – 29). This is no doubt why creation plays such a prominent role in the book of Jonah as YHWH helps Jonah work through his issues with certain implications of Israel's special revelation that are just beginning to dawn on him. Moberly admirably expresses this point with reference to Jonah:

> When Jonah's problem is that he knows the scriptural words but cannot grasp their true meaning, the book moves the issue onto a different level — crying out not to Scripture but to reason, not to revelation but to natural theology, not to a divine imperative but to analogical wisdom.... The book of Jonah does not question the foundational role of Israel's particular knowledge of God or of the corresponding task of prophecy, nor does it suggest that crying out to natural theology could dispense with the word of YHWH to Moses or Jeremiah. Rather, natural theology plays a subordinate and critical role to enable fresh re-engagement with the given content of revelation when that content has for some reason become problematic.[76]

The Relationship between Judgment and Salvation

Another important aspect of Jonah's ordeal at sea is the way YHWH uses it to grant Jonah a personal experience of judgment and salvation intended to soften the

---

76. R. W. L. Moberly, "Jonah, God's Objectionable Mercy, and the Way of Wisdom," in *Reading Texts, Seeking Wisdom* (ed. David F. Ford and Graham Stanton; Grand Rapids: Eerdmans, 2003), 167.

prophet's attitude toward Nineveh. The emphasis in this episode is clearly on judgment. As suggested in the explanation section, Jonah may well be seeking an experience of judgment as an alternative to carrying out the reprehensible mission to Nineveh. Jonah, however, does not realize what he is asking. YHWH therefore grants him just a taste of genuine divine judgment to bring Jonah to the realization that this is not what he should want either for himself or for Nineveh. God's people should have a healthy enough fear of divine judgment that they would not wish it even on their worst enemy. Ironically, the ship's crew initially demonstrates a healthier fear of divine judgment than Jonah does. Perhaps this too is a way of humbling Jonah by showing him that he could learn a thing or two from Gentiles regarding appropriate fear of YHWH.

Jonah and Jesus: Two Prophets in the Same Boat?

A final observation regarding Jonah's ordeal at sea is that it bears many close similarities to the story of Jesus' calming the sea in the Synoptic Gospels. The two are so similar, in fact, that it is likely that these gospels are deliberately recalling the storm scene from Jonah. The parallels are organized in the table below to facilitate comparison.

Table 3.1: Comparison of Jonah's Ship Scene with Synoptic Gospels' Ship Scene		
Parallel event	**Jonah**	**Jesus**
Escape by sailing in opposite direction[77]	Jonah 1:3	Matt. 8:18
Violent windstorm on the sea	Jonah 1:4a-b	Matt 8:24; Mark 4:37; Luke 8:23
Imminent danger of ship's sinking	Jonah 1:4c	Matt 8:24; Mark 4:37; Luke 8:23
Deep sleep during the storm	Jonah 1:5e-g	Matt 8:24; Mark 4:38; Luke 8:23
Rude awakening by frightened shipmates	Jonah 1:6c-g	Matt 8:25; Mark 4:38; Luke 8:24
Calming of sea by protagonist's action	Jonah 1:15a-c	Matt 8:26; Mark 4:39; Luke 8:24
Shipmates' awestruck fear at divine power	Jonah 1:16a	Matt 8:27; Mark 4:41; Luke 8:25

These seven parallels between the two stories raise questions as to what connection the evangelists saw between Jesus and Jonah and what they were communicating by such a comparison. The deep sleep that comes over both Jonah and Jesus symbolizes death and anticipates the journey that both protagonists make to Sheol and back. For Matthew and Luke, therefore, this gospel episode paves the way for Jesus' discourse on the sign of Jonah later in their accounts (Matt 12:38 – 42; 16:1 – 4; Luke 11:29 – 32) and contributes to their developing theology of the cross.

---

77. Mark Allan Powell, "Echoes of Jonah in the New Testament," *WW* 27 (Spring 2007): 160.

In the case of Mark, who does not include Jesus' discourse on the sign of Jonah, this episode may anticipate more subtle allusions to Jonah in the Gethsemane narrative, where Jesus echoes Jonah when he says "My soul is overwhelmed with sorrow *to the point of death*" (Mark 14:34, NIV, emphasis added; cf. Jonah 4:9).[78] Also, Mark's account in Gethsemane includes an ironic reversal of the storm scene. Whereas Jesus had slept during the disciples' distress at sea, now the disciples sleep during Jesus' distress in the garden. The disciples, therefore, imitate Jonah in their attempt to ignore the revelation of the cross and escape the implications of what Jesus is about to do.

It is not enough, however, to note the similarities between Jonah and Jesus in these two accounts. The evangelists mean to draw a contrast between the two figures as well. In the case of Jonah and Jesus, the main distinction has to do with the motivation behind their sleep. Jonah's sleep and descent to death are motivated by a desire to escape his calling. Jesus' sleep and descent to death, however, are motivated by a desire to embrace his calling. In fact, Jesus' calm confidence that allows him such repose in the middle of a violent storm is due to the fact that he and the Father have already agreed to his death on the cross, which thus precludes the possibility that the storm at sea could result in Jesus' or his disciples' demise.

What one should take away from a comparison of Jonah 1:3 – 16 and the Synoptic accounts of Jesus' calming the storm is a strengthened sense of identity and calling. The questions that the mariners ask Jonah and the question the disciples ask after Jesus calms the sea all focus on the issue of identity. The mariners want to know who Jonah is and who Jonah's god is. In raising these questions they force Jonah to reconsider his own identity as well as the character of his god. Similarly, when the disciples ask "Who is this?" after the sea is calmed (Mark 4:41), they are reassessing their understanding of Jesus' identity and mission. They have just seen evidence that Jesus is divine and therefore Lord of all creation, but his quieting of the symbols of divine wrath also identify him as the human agent through whom YHWH sets wrath aside and reconciles with humanity. Jesus' true identity is only fully revealed at the cross, where he fulfills his divine calling. For Jesus, calling and identity are inextricably linked.

The church's identity is similarly defined by her calling. If believers embrace that calling as Jesus did, they will know who they are and will share in Jesus' joy at accomplishing the Father's will (John 15:10 – 11). If, however, they flee that calling as Jonah did, they will misunderstand their identity and share Jonah's misery (Jonah 4:1, 6, 9).

---

78. Adela Yarbro Collins, *Mark: A Commentary* (Hermeneia; Minneapolis: Fortress, 2007), 676.

Jonah 2:1c – 11b [1:17c – 2:10b]

C. A Prayer of Praise for God's Mercy, Peak episode[1]

Main Idea of the Passage

Jonah realizes that YHWH's judgment is not preferable to the commission after all, and so he cries out to YHWH for deliverance. YHWH retrieves his prophet from the threshold of the netherworld, which inspires Jonah to praise YHWH's mercy with a thanksgiving psalm.

Literary Context

The verb form *wayĕhî*, "now he was," introduces a new section with a new setting. Jonah is now inside the fish, where he breaks into a prayer of thanksgiving for YH-WH's deliverance. The third episode, therefore, consists of an embedded discourse, Jonah's prayer of praise (2:3b – 10), enveloped by a brief narrative frame (2:1c – 3a, 11). This narrative frame situates Jonah's poetic prayer in its prose environment. It also provides an interpretive lens through which the reader is invited to view the prayer. The poetry of the prayer brings the action of the narrative to a pause, allowing both Jonah and the reader to reflect on all that has happened and to consider what it might mean.

The relationship of Jonah's prayer to the surrounding narrative has been the subject of extensive debate. Many scholars view the prayer as a later insertion since the narrative, read without the prayer, remains quite coherent. Furthermore, they argue that the prayer does not fit comfortably within its narrative environment.[2] For

---

1. Note that the Hebrew versification, followed by the English, will only be given in headings in this chapter. The rest of the time, the versification will be that of the Hebrew text.

2. An excellent summary of these arguments and a list of their proponents are included in George M. Landes, "The Kerygma of the Book of Jonah," *Int* 21 (1967): 3 – 4.

example, nothing in the narrative prepares the reader for Jonah's radical change of disposition.[3] Furthermore, the distress Jonah describes in his prayer is not that of being confined in the belly of a fish, but that of drowning in the sea. One also wonders why Jonah is praising YHWH for his deliverance *before* YHWH commands the fish to vomit Jonah back onto dry land. A complaint psalm seems more appropriate to the situation and is certainly more characteristic of Jonah. These issues raise questions as to the propriety of the prayer in its present context.

While the questions regarding the prayer's relationship to the rest of the book are legitimate, many of the incongruities are more perceived than real.[4] Landes, after a thorough analysis of the song in the light of a careful reading of Jonah as a whole, concluded that Jonah's prayer of praise is crucial to both the structure and message of the book.[5] For example, the overarching parallelistic structure of the book necessitates a prayer in Jonah 2:1 – 11 to correspond with the prayer in Jonah 4:1 – 4. In fact, in both halves of the book, the shift to the direct discourse of prayer marks the onset of the peak episode.[6] The table below illustrates the correspondence in terms of the staircase parallelism proposed for the book's structure.

Table 4.1: Peak Episodes in Jonah's Staircase Structure				
	Stage Setting	**Pre-peak Episode**	**Peak Episode**	**Post-peak Episode**
Part 1	1:1 – 4a	1:4b – 2:1b (1:17b)	2:1c – 11 (1:17c – 2:10)	
Part 2	3:1 – 3b	3:3c – 10	4:1 – 4	4:5 – 11

Both of these peak episodes are also crucial to the message of the book because of the insight they give into Jonah's reasoning. These are the only texts in which Jonah explains his interpretation of events. Furthermore, Jonah's prayer culminates in a climactic statement that ties directly into the point that the author (and God) is making: "Deliverance belongs to YHWH" (2:10c). This confession, uttered by Jonah at the moment of his own deliverance, becomes ironic in 4:1 – 4, when he tries to restrict YHWH's deliverance. Once again, Jonah faces the unforeseen implications of his own confession of faith and recoils.

Landes also notes an important correspondence between Jonah 1 and Jonah 2 that further underscores the prayer's coherence in the larger context of the book. Both chapters can be broken down into four parts that parallel each other: a crisis situation, human response to the crisis in the form of prayer, divine response to

---

3. Gerhard von Rad went so far as to suggest that the Jonah of the psalm in Jonah 2 is essentially a different person than the Jonah of the narrative. See Gerhard von Rad, *Der Prophet Jona* (Nürnburg: Laetare-Verlag, 1950), 13.

4. Possible solutions to the incongruities that have led many to view the song as a later addition will be presented and discussed in the explanation section.

5. Landes, "Kerygma," 29 – 31.

6. Longacre and Hwang, "A Text-Linguistic Approach," 342 – 43.

prayer, and human response to deliverance in the form of sacrifices and vows. Landes's scheme is represented by the following table.

Table 4.2: The Parallel Structure of Jonah 1 & 2[7]	
Jonah 1 (Focus on the Mariners)	**Jonah 2 (Focus on Jonah)**
1. Crisis situation: storm at sea (1:4)	1. Crisis situation: drowning at sea (2:4)
2. Response to crisis: prayer (1:14)	2. Jonah's response to crisis: prayer (2:2)
3. YHWH's response: deliverance from storm (1:15c)	3. YHWH's response: deliverance from Sheol (2:1, 7c)
4. Response to deliverance: sacrifice and vows (1:16)	4. Response to deliverance: pledge to sacrifice and pay vows (2:10)

Landes also draws a similar parallel between Jonah 3 and 4, demonstrating that the book is organized symmetrically.[8] The implication of this insight for understanding the structure of the narrative is that, in addition to the parallelism that exists between the two halves of the book, parallelism also exists between the episodes in each of the book's halves. The former could be called "external parallelism" since it crosses the literary axis dividing the two halves and embraces the entire narrative. The latter could be called "internal parallelism" since it operates within each discreet half of the book. The interrelationship of these two kinds of parallelism can be visualized according to the following diagram.

Figure 4.1: Internal and External Parallelism in Jonah

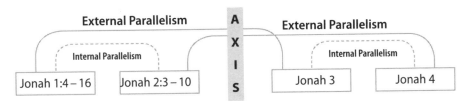

The diagram above illustrates that Jonah's prayer in chapter 2 constitutes a hinge text in the sense that it both looks back, reinforcing 1:4 – 16, and looks ahead, anticipating 4:1 – 4. The narrative pauses at this point to provide a catharsis of Jonah's and the reader's emotions in Jonah's first direct address to God, which thus brings closure to Jonah 1. The prophet who would not renounce (*qĕrā'*) Nineveh for YHWH and would not cry out (*qĕrā'*) to YHWH for the mariners finally does voluntarily cry out (*qārā'tî*) to YHWH on his own behalf. Yet, Jonah's prayer also pauses the narrative in order to lay the thematic groundwork for what follows, which casts significant clues that prepare the reader to interpret correctly the complex plot line and dialogue in the remainder of the book.

7. Landes, "Kerygma," 26.   8. Ibid.

A final observation with respect to literary context is that the fish's belly is a new and unique environment in the narrative. Thus far the narrative has moved from dry land to ship to the depths of the sea — a geographical movement that, in the Semitic worldview, symbolizes transition from the orderly world of human habitation to the disorderly and inhospitable realm of chaos and death. The fish, however, functions as a means of deliverance and transportation from the murky depths back to the orderly realm of dry land. In this respect, the fish is the antithesis of the ship, which carried Jonah from the orderly realm of dry land out to the chaotic, deadly sea.

Correspondingly, Jonah's disposition and activity in the fish is the antithesis of his disposition and activity on the ship. Whereas Jonah pays out of his own pocket for passage on the ship, the journey in the fish back to land and life is free, courtesy of YHWH. Whereas Jonah sleeps deeply in the innards (*yarkĕtê*) of the ship, in the belly (*mēʿeh*) of the fish he is alert. Whereas Jonah is reticent and prayerless on board the ship, inside the fish he is effusive with praise. This contrast implies that the ship is a negative, transitional environment belonging to Jonah's rebellious flight. It carries Jonah away from YHWH's presence and, therefore, away from the well-ordered realm of human habitation and divine-human communion. The fish, however, is an instrument of YHWH's salvation and a symbol of his free, undeserved grace. It is a positive, transitional environment that carries Jonah back to active fellowship with the divine presence and therefore back to the well-ordered realm of human habitation. This important contrast should impact the way one reads the peak episode of the book's first main section.

The position this unit occupies in the larger structure of the book is illustrated in the following outline.

I. From Silent Resistance to Jubilant Acceptance: The Compelling Nature of God's Mercy (1:1 – 2:11 [2:10], Macro Unit 1)

  A. A Silent Escape from God's Mercy (1:1 – 4a, Stage setting)

  B. The Relentless Pursuit of God's Mercy (1:4b – 2:1a [1:17a], Pre-peak episode)

  C. A Prayer of Praise for God's Mercy (2:1c – 2:11 [1:17c – 2:10], Peak episode)

    1. Jonah's reversal regarding his preference for judgment over obedience (2:1c – 7b [1:17c – 2:6b])

    2. Jonah's partial and prideful response to grace (2:7c – 11b [6c – 10b])

II. From Compliant Acceptance to Angry Resentment: The Offense of God's Mercy (3:1 – 4:11, Macro Unit 2)

Translation and Outline

Jonah 2:1c–11b

C. A Prayer of Praise for God's Mercy (2:1c-11b [1:17c-2:10b])

1. Jonah's reversal regarding his preference for judgment over obedience (2:1c-7b [1:17c-2:6b])

2:1c   Now Jonah was in the fish's belly for three days and three nights,

    a. Recognition of YHWH's salvation through judgment (2:1c-3a [1:17c-2:2a])

2:2   and Jonah prayed to YHWH, his god, from the fish's womb
2:3a   and said,
2:3b   I cried out, because of my distress, to YHWH, and he answered me;

    b. Recognition of God's responsiveness to distress (2:3b [2:2b])

2:3c   ⬆ from Sheol's belly I screamed for help, you heeded my voice.
2:4a   You had cast me down to the deep, into the heart of the sea,

    c. Recognition of God's use of severe, but merciful, discipline (2:4 [2:3])

2:4b   ⬆ where the river swirled about me.
2:4c | All your breakers and waves passed over me.
2:5a   As for me, I said,

    d. Recognition of appeal to YHWH as the only hope (2:5 [2:4])

2:5b   ⬆ I have been banished from your sight;
2:5c | nevertheless, I will try again to gaze toward your holy temple!
2:6a   The waters had enclosed me, threatening my life;

    e. Recognition of the severity of his separation from God (2:6a-7b [2:5a-6b])

2:6b   ⬆ the deep had enveloped me;
2:6c | reeds had wrapped around my head.
2:7a   To the base of the mountains I had descended,
2:7b   ⬆ to the land whose bars would trap me forever.

2:7c   Then you restored from the pit my life, YHWH, my God.

2. Jonah's partial and prideful response to grace (2:7c-2:11b [2:6c-10b])
    a. Jonah's testimony to divine mercy(2:7c [2:6c])

2:8a   ⬇ Just when I had felt myself succumbing to death,

    b. Jonah's misplaced emphasis (2:8a-b [2:7a-b])

2:8b   YHWH I had remembered.
2:8c   My petition had reached you;

    c. Jonah's relief over the effectiveness of his prayer (2:8c-d [2:7c-d])

2:8d   ⬆ (it had reached) your holy temple.
2:9   Devotees of useless idols forsake their experience of mercy,

    d. Jonah's confidence in his own piety (2:9-10b [2:8-9b])

2:10a   ⬆ but, as for me, with a grateful voice I will sacrifice to you;
2:10b | what I have vowed I will pay.
2:10c   Deliverance belongs to YHWH!

    e. Jonah's declaration of YHWH's sovereignty in salvation (2:10c [2:9c])
    f. Jonah's experience of a humbling salvation (2:11 [2:10])

2:11a   Then YHWH spoke to the fish,
2:11b   and it vomited Jonah on to the dry ground.

Structure and Literary Form

The basic genre of commission narrative continues to shape the development of the story in 2:1c (1:17c) as the commission progresses to the sign phase. Miraculous signs or symbolic acts frequently accompany divine commissions as both confirmation and clarification of the assigned task.[9] Jonah's three-day-and-three-night so-

---

9. Habel, "The Form and Significance of the Call Narratives," 301.

journ in the fish's belly fulfills this function in the case of Jonah's commission. The prophet underwent an experience of judgment (drowning at sea) and deliverance (being swallowed by a fish), which should have prepared him to accept and execute the task YHWH assigned to him. YHWH used the ordeal to soften Jonah's attitude toward his commission by reminding him of his own need for divine mercy and by reminding him of both the terror of divine judgment and the exultation of salvation from that judgment.

Of particular significance in this regard is Habel's contention that the sign/symbolic act in commission narratives was specifically designed to assure the appointee that he was truly receiving a word from YHWH and, thereby, becoming a mediator of that word.[10] The symbolic act, therefore, reminded Jonah of the vocation he has been attempting to escape — the prophetic office. The fish's compliance with YHWH's appointment provides a model for Jonah.

Jonah's prayer, however, interrupts the commission narrative at 2:3. The narrative pauses to linger over Jonah's first direct address to YHWH, which serves as a bridge from the rebellious Jonah of chapter 1 to the compliant Jonah of chapter 3. The prayer conforms to the poetic language of the psalms and thus introduces a different genre. In fact, it is precisely this shift to poetry that marks the prayer as the peak episode of the first main section of the book.[11] This peak unit, therefore, consists of a poem framed by a brief narrative introduction (2:1c – 2) and a brief narrative conclusion (2:11). The introduction describes the setting, and the conclusion segues back to the main narrative.

Since this third episode consists of a poem set within a narrative frame, the method of analysis must account for this shift in genre. As the translation display in the preceding section demonstrates, the basic unit of analysis for Hebrew poetry is different from that for Hebrew prose. Whereas prose is analyzed at the clause level, poetry is analyzed at the colon level. A colon (pl. cola) is a line of poetry that may consist of anywhere from zero to three clauses.[12] It is typically brief, and it is usually combined with at least one other poetic line. Related lines may exhibit a close semantic, grammatical, rhythmic, or phonetic relationship.[13]

The relationship between poetic cola is usually referred to as parallelism because the cola tend to correspond with each other in length, meaning, or grammatical structure, thus forming pairs (bicola), triads (tricola), and quatrains (tetracola). Not all cola, however, exist in such a relationship; on rare occasions, a colon may stand

---

10. Ibid.

11. Longacre and Hwang, "A Text-Linguistic Approach," 343.

12. A colon with zero clauses is simply a colon without a verb or predicate whether explicit or implicit. Such a colon would, therefore, be a sentence fragment and entirely dependent on its parallel colon for its completion.

13. This definition of a poetic colon is based largely on the works of Adele Berlin, *The Dynamics of Biblical Parallelism* (rev. ed.; Grand Rapids: Eerdmans, 2008), 3, and M. O'Connor, *Hebrew Verse Structure* (Winona Lake, IN: Eisenbrauns, 1980, 1997), 86 – 87.

alone (a monocolon). The text display reflects these relationships by means of in-
dentation and arrows. For example, 2:8c – 10c consists of a bicolon followed by a
tricolon followed by a monocolon. This combination is diagrammed as follows with
the individual cola labeled by letter [e.g., A) ... B) ... etc.]:

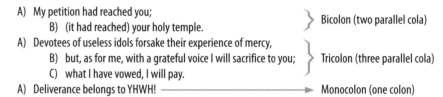

Generally speaking, this analysis follows the division of verses into cola suggested
by the traditional system of Hebrew accents. These accents divide each verse into
two or more sections of comparable length on the basis of syntactical breaks and
semantic correspondence.[14] Since, however, these divisions were not always made on
a linguistic basis, O'Connor's system of defining cola by linguistic constraints serves
as a check to ensure that the divisions are as close as possible to those intended by
the poet.[15]

Two additional aspects of Hebrew poetry are important for the following analysis. First, as a rule, when cola are in a parallel relationship with each other, the second
colon is semantically or grammatically dependent on the first.[16] This has been represented in the translation display by indenting the dependent cola and connecting
them with arrow to their governing cola. Second, parallel cola express vertical grammar as well as the typical horizontal grammar. In other words, close grammatical
relationships exist between parallel cola as well as between the words within each
colon.[17] A good example of this phenomenon is 2:7a-b (2:6a-b), a bicolon in which
the cola are connected by a shared verb as indicated by the verb's ellipsis in the second colon.

A) To the base of the mountains I had descended,
  ↑ B) to the land whose bars would trap me forever

The vertical nature of the cola's grammatical relationship is even more evident
when the bicolon is envisioned as follows.

14. For an excellent introduction to this system of accents, their history, and their significance for interpretation of the Hebrew Bible see Israel Yeivin, *Introduction to the Tiberian Masorah* (trans. E. J. Revell; Atlanta: Scholars Press, 1980), 157 – 264.

15. O'Connor, *Hebrew Verse Structure*, 54 – 86. An excellent and fairly accessible summary of O'Connor's work is available in William L. Holladay, "*Hebrew Verse Structure* Revisited (I):

Which Words 'Count'?," *JBL* 118 (1999): 19 – 32; idem, "*Hebrew Verse Structure* Revisited (II): Conjoint Cola, and Further Suggestions," *JBL* 118 (1999): 401 – 16.

16. Nicholas P. Lunn, *Word-Order Variation in Biblical Hebrew Poetry* (Milton Keynes, UK: Paternoster, 2006), 22.

17. David Toshio Tsumura, "Vertical Grammar of Parallelism in Hebrew Poetry," *JBL* 128 (2009): 167 – 181.

A) To the base of the mountains

       I had descended,

B) to the land whose bars would trap me forever.[18]

With these basics of Hebrew poetry in place, a structural analysis of the entire unit is now possible. As one would expect of poetry, Jonah's prayer is artfully composed and displays sophisticated rhetorical and structural devices. Many scholars have noted the skillful use of repetitions and inversions within the poem, and on this basis, some scholars have proposed various concentric or chiastic structures for the prayer.[19] Many of these proposals are insightful and have contributed significantly to the understanding of the poem's structure.

Two aspects of the poem, however, deserve more attention than they have traditionally received. The first has to do with the prayer's place within the larger narrative. Most studies of the poem's structure analyze its organization in isolation from the narrative context. This yields some fruit with respect to internal structures but tends to skew the picture of the poem's structure as a whole. It also reinforces the misconception that the prayer has been imposed on the narrative.

The second has to do with the presence of grammatical signals within the poem as structural indicators. While it is inevitable and even desirable that analyses of artistic compositions, such as the poem in Jonah 2, employ a reader's instincts and impressions, recent studies of the linguistic nature of poetry offer confirmation and clarification of such impressions by means of the explicit marking of boundaries. These two aspects of Jonah's prayer play a key role in this structural analysis.

As others have noted, Jonah 2 employs inversion or chiasm extensively. In fact, Jonah's prayer divides into two stanzas, each of which has a chiastic structure. These two chiasms interlock at 2:7c — a juncture marked by the rare occurrence of a monocolon. Furthermore, the monocolon at 2:7c not only serves as the juncture for the interlocking chiasms, but it also serves as a tie in for the narrative frame that surrounds the poem. It does this by employing the same title for God (YHWH, his god/YHWH, my god, 2:2, 7c) that is otherwise unique to the narrative frame. Jonah 2:7c thus draws 2:1c – 3a and 2:11a-b into the chiasm as its outermost panels. The poem also concludes with a monocolon at the precise point of the climax of Jonah's prayer, where he utters the confession that becomes the preoccupation of the rest of

18. Ibid, 171 – 73. The phenomenon of a shared verb in a bicolon expressed only in one of the two cola, called gapping or ellipsis, has long been recognized by scholars of Hebrew poetry. Tsumura is the first, however, that I know of who has associated gapping with the larger phenomenon of "vertical grammar."

19. Duane L. Christensen, "Andrzej Panufnik and the Structure of the Book of Jonah: Icons, Music and Literary Art," *JETS* 28 (1985): 138; Sasson, *Jonah*, 167; F. M. Cross, "The Prosody of Lamentations 1 and the Psalm of Jonah," in *From Epic to Canon: History and Literature in Ancient Israel* (Baltimore, MD: Johns Hopkins University Press, 1998), 99 – 134.

the book: "Deliverance belongs to YHWH." Monocola, therefore, play an important structural role by marking the high points of the prayer.[20]

The diagram below (Figure 4.2) illustrates this arrangement, using letters with superscript "F" to represent sections belonging to the narrative frame, letters with

Figure 4.2: Poetic Structure of Jonah 2

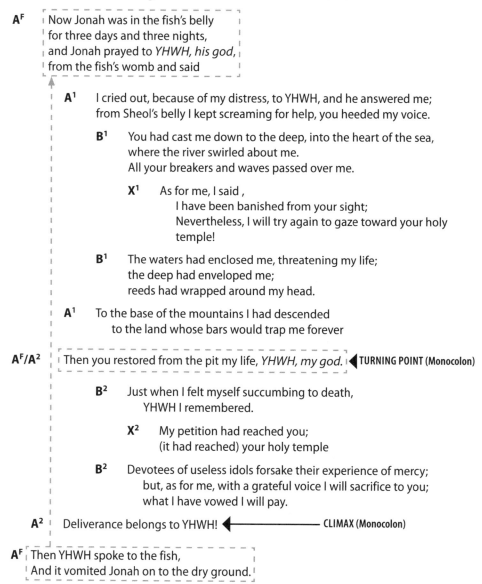

A^F Now Jonah was in the fish's belly
for three days and three nights,
and Jonah prayed to *YHWH, his god*,
from the fish's womb and said

    A¹ I cried out, because of my distress, to YHWH, and he answered me;
from Sheol's belly I kept screaming for help, you heeded my voice.

        B¹ You had cast me down to the deep, into the heart of the sea,
where the river swirled about me.
All your breakers and waves passed over me.

           X¹ As for me, I said ,
I have been banished from your sight;
Nevertheless, I will try again to gaze toward your holy temple!

        B¹ The waters had enclosed me, threatening my life;
the deep had enveloped me;
reeds had wrapped around my head.

    A¹ To the base of the mountains I had descended
to the land whose bars would trap me forever

A^F/A² Then you restored from the pit my life, *YHWH, my god.* ◀ **TURNING POINT (Monocolon)**

        B² Just when I felt myself succumbing to death,
YHWH I remembered.

           X² My petition had reached you;
(it had reached) your holy temple

        B² Devotees of useless idols forsake their experience of mercy;
but, as for me, with a grateful voice I will sacrifice to you;
what I have vowed I will pay.

    A² Deliverance belongs to YHWH! ◀——————— **CLIMAX (Monocolon)**

A^F Then YHWH spoke to the fish,
And it vomited Jonah on to the dry ground.

---

20. Watson, *Classical Hebrew Poetry*, 170.

superscript "1" to represent sections belonging to the first stanza, and letters with superscript "2" to represent sections belonging to the second stanza. What is particularly noteworthy in the diagram is that the central monocolon (2:7c) serves a dual role in the poem (as indicated by its dual label A^F/A^2). It simultaneously corresponds to the narrative frame [2:1c – 2:3; 2:11a-b (A^F)] and serves as the opening line of the second stanza [2:7c (A^2)]. Thematically, this structure binds together the opening, closing, and center of this poem around the single theme of YHWH's ability and willingness to deliver from death. Furthermore, the correlation of the two monocola that mark the boundaries of the second stanza (2:7c and 2:10c) underscore the related theme of YHWH's freedom to deliver anyone from any circumstance by his grace.

Understanding the structure is one prerequisite to an accurate reading of the poem. Another prerequisite is an understanding of the poem's genre. Jonah's prayer conforms to a well-known class of psalms called thanksgiving psalms. These psalms are recognizable by the basic elements they share in common. Common elements include (1) an introductory summary, (2) a description of a crisis from which YHWH delivered the psalmist, (3) a record of the psalmist's appeal for help, (4) a description of the deliverance YHWH provided, and (5) a vow to offer thank offerings as soon as the psalmist can return to the temple.[21] The following table (Table 4.3) arranges these elements as they occur in Jonah's prayer.

Table 4.3: Elements of a Thanksgiving Psalm	
Element	**Occurrence**
1. Introductory Summary	Jonah 2:3b-c "I cried out, because of my distress, to YHWH, and he answered." (2:3b)
2. Recollection of the Crisis	Jonah 2:4a – 7b "The waters had enclosed me, threatening my life; the deep had enveloped me; reeds had wrapped around my head." (2:6a-c)
3. Cry out for Help	Jonah 2:3b-c, 8b-d "YHWH I had remembered. My petition had reached you; (it had reached) your holy temple." (2:8b-d)
4. Description of Deliverance	Jonah 2:7c "Then you restored from the pit my life."
5. Vows	Jonah 2:10a-b "As for me, with a grateful voice I will sacrifice to you; what I have vowed I will pay." (2:10a-b)
6. Praise	Jonah 2:10c "Deliverance belongs to YHWH!"

---

21. Claus Westermann, *Praise and Lament in the Psalms* (trans. Keith R. Crimm and Richard N. Soulen; Atlanta: John Knox, 1981), 102 – 4. Westermann prefers the designation "declarative psalm of praise of the individual," but for this study the more conventional, descriptive, and concise designation "thanksgiving psalm" is retained.

The identification of Jonah's prayer as a thanksgiving psalm is significant with regard to the book's message in at least three respects. First, the fact that Jonah's prayer from the fish is a thanksgiving psalm heightens the irony of its contrast with his second prayer (4:2 – 4), which takes the form of a complaint against the very mercy that he praises while in the fish's belly.

Second, the prayer's emphasis on Jonah's personal experience of a crisis in judgment, followed by an extraordinary act of salvation, places it within the subcategory that Hauge labels an "I-psalm." Hauge argues that "I-psalms" document an intensely personal journey from Sheol to YHWH's temple (or vice versa). These poles represent the extremes of Israel's spiritual experience.[22] Jonah is suspended between these two extremes in this prayer.

Third, the genre of the psalm seems incongruent with Jonah's situation. One might expect Jonah to pray a lament while in the belly of the fish. In fact, a penitential lament would fit the context admirably, indicating that YHWH's disciplinary action affected the desired change in the wayward prophet. Yet, instead, Jonah offered a thanksgiving prayer. Notably absent are any admissions of guilt or promises of repentance. These are surprising omissions when one considers all that transpired between YHWH and Jonah in the preceding episodes.

Explanation of the Text

1. Jonah's Reversal regarding His Preference of Judgment over Obedience (2:1c [1:17c]-2:7b [6b])

a. Recognition of YHWH's Salvation through Judgment (2:1c – 2 [1:17c – 2:1])

The author opens the third episode with the verb *wayĕhî*, which indicates a new episode and a new setting — the fish's belly (cf. 1:1, 4b). The notation that Jonah spends three days and three nights inside of the fish employs a prevalent ancient Near Eastern motif. As Bauer pointed out, journeys are frequently portrayed in Scripture as transpiring over a three-day period — a time frame associated with an indefinitely long period.[23] Landes took

Bauer's observation a step further, suggesting that the time period "three days" or "three days and three nights" relates particularly to the time required for one to journey from the realm of life to Sheol or vice versa.

Landes based this association on multiple occurrences of the phrase in both biblical and extrabiblical texts. For example, in the Sumerian myth "The Descent of Inanna," the goddess Inanna travels to the netherworld to retrieve her consort, Damuzi — a journey requiring three days and three nights.[24] This ancient Sumerian reference to the time period reflects a general understanding in the Mesopotamian world that Sheol is far removed from the realm of life.

22. Martin Ravndal Hauge, *Between Sheol and Temple: Motif, Structure, and Function in the I-Psalms* (Sheffield: Sheffield Academic, 1995), 67 – 110.

23. H. B. Bauer, "Drei Tage," *Bib* 39 (1958): 354 – 58.

24. George M. Landes, "The 'Three Days and Three Nights' Motif in Jonah 2:1," *JBL* 86 (1967): 446 – 50.

Landes's suggestion finds support in a number of biblical texts in which a journey of three days brings a person close to death or restores a person back to life. Genesis 22:4, for example, indicates that Abraham's journey to Mount Moriah, where he would sacrifice Isaac to YHWH, was a journey of three days.[25] Similarly, the Israelites wander without water in the desert for three days before YHWH provides potable water (Exod 15:22). Movement from death back to life also requires a journey of three days, as indicated by Hosea 6:1 – 2:

> Come, let us return to the LORD.
> He has torn us to pieces
> > but he will heal us;
> he has injured us
> > but he will bind up our wounds.
> After two days he will revive us,
> > *on the third day* he will restore us,
> > that we may live in his presence.
> > > > (NIV, emphasis added)

The three days and three nights of Jonah's sojourn within the fish may, therefore, be understood as indicating a journey from death back to life, as several references from the prayer indicate (2:3c, 7a – 8a). The use of the motif emphasizes that Jonah was at death's door, and that even from that remote place, YHWH heard his cry and responded with salvation.

During this journey from death back to life, Jonah expresses gratitude and praise for YHWH's mercy. This prayer represents Jonah's first address

to YHWH in the book. Even in the midst of the fierce storm when the entire crew was praying, Jonah slept instead of prayed. Even after the helmsman rebuked Jonah and called him to prayer, the text gives no indication that Jonah obeyed. Once he is in the fish's belly, however, Jonah finally prays.

The author marks this climactic moment by introducing for the first time the technical word for prayer (*yitpallēl*). All preceding instances of prayer have been designated by other terms ["crying out" (*zā'aq*) or "invoking"(*qārā'*)]. In fact, the only other time *yitpallēl* occurs in the book is in 4:2, where Jonah utters his complaint to YHWH.

For all of its orthodoxy and beauty, however, this prayer reveals some of the great defects in Jonah's character.[26] For example, conspicuously absent is any admission of guilt or request for forgiveness, though the preceding narrative indicates that such is certainly needed.[27] Furthermore, Jonah's prayer includes an indictment against "devotees of useless idols" who "forsake their experience of mercy," which Jonah uses as a foil for his own piety and devotion (2:9 – 10). These shortcomings of the prayer's content hint at the shallowness of Jonah's "repentance" that shapes the remainder of the narrative.

Also of interest in 2:2 is the author's designation for "god." He states that "Jonah prayed to YHWH, his god" (*'el-yhwh 'ĕlōhāyw*). This is the first time the author has employed this designation for YHWH, and its occurrence here recalls the mariners' praying in the preceding episode, where

---

25. Genesis Rabbah LVI:I actually cry outs to Jonah 2:2, in addition to a host of other biblical references, as commentary on the significance of the third day of Genesis 22:4. Rabbinic tradition was well aware of the ancient symbolism of a three-day journey. See Neusner, *Habakkuk, Jonah, and Obadiah in Talmud and Midrash*, 74.

26. Balentine notes that prayer is often used in Hebrew narrative as a tool for characterization. In particular it is used to lampoon a character with mixed motives or devious intent.

Balentine points to Jonah's prayer as a parade example of this technique. See Samuel Balentine, *Prayer in the Hebrew Bible: The Drama of Divine-Human Dialogue* (Minneapolis: Fortress, 1993), 71 – 80.

27. Thanksgiving psalms may have indications of past guilt and forgiveness as part of the basis for their praise (cf., e.g., Ps 32:1, 5). These would be found in the "recollection of the crisis" and "description of deliverance" sections of a thanksgiving psalm.

the author noted "each one cried out to his *god*" (*el 'ĕlōhāyw*). The contrast between Jonah and the mariners, therefore, continues even into this episode, where Jonah's hesitancy to pray is highlighted by this reminder of how out-of-sync Jonah is with his former shipmates. They were praying to their gods long before Jonah started praying to YHWH, his God (1:5b). In fact, the mariners began praying to Jonah's god even before Jonah did (1:14a). Nonetheless, the author states "Jonah prayed … to his god" (2:2) as a reminder to the reader that YHWH continued to be Jonah's god even after everything the prophet did to rebuff him.[28]

A final and unexpected rhetorical flourish concludes 2:2 and sets the stage for Jonah's poetic prayer. The author indicates that the point of origin for Jonah's prayer is "from the fish's womb" (*mimmĕ'ê haddāgâ*). This designation for Jonah's location differs from the previous designation in one small, but significant detail. In 2:1c the author indicates that Jonah remained three days and three nights "in the fish's belly" (*bimĕ'ê haddāg*), using the masculine form of the noun for "fish." In 2:2, however, the author locates Jonah in "the fish's womb," using the feminine form of the noun for "fish."[29] This change is the motivation behind the shift in the translation from the gender neutral "fish's belly" in 2:1c to the gender specific "fish's womb" in 2:2.

An intriguing explanation for the switch of gender in the second occurrence of the noun "fish" is

that this may be the author's way of clarifying the nature of the fish as an instrument of salvation through judgment. In the previous episode when the fish swallowed Jonah, the nature of the fish was ambiguous (2:1a-b). As an answer to the mariners' prayer, the fish could be viewed as Jonah's rescue from drowning. The fish's act of swallowing Jonah, however, suggests judgment since the verb "swallow" (*bala'*) elsewhere in the Old Testament is associated with destruction. In 2:2, however, YHWH's saving intent grows clearer through the author's choice of the feminine form of the noun "fish." The combination of this feminine form with a word rich in maternal connotations (*mē'eh*) suggests life and a new beginning.[30] Contrary to both Jonah's and the reader's initial expectations, the fish was an agent of life rather than of death, as Jonah's prayer confesses (2:3).

Another possible effect of the author's shift to the feminine form of the noun "fish" (*haddāgâ*) is that it underscores the parallel between the fish and the ship (*'ŏnîyâ*, also a feminine noun). The ship carried Jonah away from YHWH's presence and into the deadly realm of the sea. The fish, by contrast, carried Jonah from a watery grave back to the realm of life.

b. Recognition of God's Responsiveness to Distress (2:3 [2:2])

The prayer proper begins in 2:3 with the verb "and he said" (*wayyōmer*), marking the transition

---

28. Stuart, *Hosea – Jonah*, 475.

29. The feminine form of the Hebrew noun for fish usually denotes a school of fish whereas the masculine form denotes a single fish (cf. Clines, *Concise Dictionary*, 75). The context clearly prohibits the meaning "school of fish." The rabbis explained the peculiarity by positing that Jonah was swallowed by a masculine fish and was regurgitated while still in the sea, only to be swallowed again by a pregnant feminine fish! In this way the rabbis ingeniously account for both the feminine form's normal meaning and its peculiar use in this context. Cf.

E. Levine, *The Aramaic Version of Jonah* (2nd ed.; New York: Sepher-Hermon, 1978), 71 – 72.

30. As Trible helpfully points out, "the appearance of the feminine form *dāgâ* after the term *mē'eh*, which designates an internal organ, suggests female imagery: 'from the womb of the fish.' When Jonah prays to Yahweh from within the 'mother' fish, Jonah appropriately moves from death to life." See Phyllis Trible, "The Book of Jonah" (*NIB*; Nashville: Abingdon, 1996), 7:505.

from narrative to direct speech (expository discourse). The prayer begins with a statement that summarizes the entire salvation experience (2:3b-c). Thus, Jonah immediately embeds an oral narrative that launches the prayer off of the main line. As a result, the initial verb is a *qatal* form ("I cried out," *qārā'tî*) instead of the expected verbless clause.[31]

The verb is followed by a prepositional phrase, describing the circumstances that prompted the initial cry for help. Literally the phrase is "from my distress" (*miṣṣārâ lî*). The Hebrew preposition *min*, however, can have a causal force, and since "distress" is not a location but a state of being, a causal nuance makes good sense in this context.[32] The colon clarifies that Jonah's distress in drowning motivated the cry for help, to which YHWH responded. Thus, the prayer contained in Jonah 2 is actually the second of two prayers Jonah uttered. The first was a petition for YHWH's intervention that he might be delivered from a certain death. The second was Jonah's response of thanksgiving for YHWH's attentiveness to that initial petition.

YHWH's response is closely linked to the initial cry for help as indicated by the narrative verb form "and he answered me" (*wayya'ănēnî*). The verbs bracketing the first colon (*qārā'tî … wayya'ănēnî*), therefore, present a complete summary of Jonah's salvation experience. Jonah 2:3c then repeats this summary, specifying the nature and severity of the trouble: "from Sheol's belly I screamed for help, you

heeded my voice." The prayer's first colon is strikingly similar to Pss 18:6 and 120:1:

Many of the lines in Jonah's prayer bear close resemblance to expressions from Israel's prayer book, portraying Jonah as well-acquainted with his spiritual heritage. This ultimately proves ironic in the context of the book, for while Jonah was readily able to quote beautiful truths from the psalms, he appears not to have grasped their implications.

Jonah's situation comes into sharper focus as he identifies the location from which he cries to YHWH: "Sheol's belly." This colorful designation for the ocean depths where Jonah expected to find his final resting place evokes the image of Sheol as an entity with a rapacious appetite that indiscriminately swallows everyone (Prov 30:15 – 16). Jonah exaggerates his encounter with death, speaking as if he has already entered the icy chambers of the abyss. The point of such hyperbole is that Jonah wonders if he might be too far gone. He was so close to death that he couldn't even tell whether he was still alive or not, whether he was still within YHWH's reach. YHWH heard the cry emitted even from the grave, and he extended his arm to retrieve his prophet from the depths of the netherworld (cf. Pss 30:3; 49:15; 86:13; 116:1 – 6).

Whereas the preceding colon placed the verb first and followed it with the prepositional phrase, 2:3c reverses that sequence. The second line of a bicolon often exhibits different word order than

Table 4.4: Comparison of Jonah 2:3a with Psalm 120:1 & Psalm 18:6		
Psalm 120:1	**Jonah 2:3b-c (2b-c)**	**Psalm 18:6**
"To YHWH, in my distress, I cried out, and he answered me.	I cried out, because of my distress, to YHWH, and he answered me. From Sheol's belly I screamed for help, you heeded my voice	In my distress I cried out to YHWH, and my God I summoned. He heard from his temple my voice; my scream (he heard) with his own ears

31. Tucker, *Jonah*, 50 – 51.
32. Bill T. Arnold and John H. Choi, *A Guide to Biblical*

Hebrew Syntax (New York: Cambridge University Press, 2003), 117.

the first as a means of differentiation and specification. In this case, the clause's initial prepositional phrase "from Sheol's belly" (*mibbeṭen šĕʾôl*) specifies the nature and severity of the "distress" in the preceding colon. The phrase "Sheol's belly" may refer to the fish's belly, which Jonah may have initially believed would be his grave.

The verb that describes Jonah's desperate screams is *šiwwaʿtî*. The second colon returns to the *qatal* form rather than continuing the narrative sequence of the preceding verb (*wayyaʿănēnî*). This is likely due to the fact that the second colon repeats, rather than advances, the summary of Jonah's salvation experience already expressed in the first. It would appear from this scream that YHWH successfully shook Jonah out of his complacency and reticence through this experience of salvation through judgment.

This colon, like the previous one, concludes with a statement of YHWH's attentiveness and responsiveness. Jonah 2:3c differs, however, from 2:3b in that it addresses YHWH directly in the second person. This shift reflects another aspect of Hebrew parallelism: difference within similarity. The second line of a bicolon will often show small alterations in word order, person and gender of the pronouns, or verb tense in order to establish a sense of progression or intensification. In this case, the psalm moves from speaking about YHWH to speaking to YHWH, from reporting salvation to expressing gratitude for salvation. Jonah finds himself counting on the attentiveness of the god he has been ignoring and rebuffing. The experience understandably provokes praise.

c. Recognition of God's Use of Severe, but Merciful, Discipline (2:4a-c [2:3a-c])

With 2:4 Jonah begins recalling the details of his salvation experience. The experience begins, however, not with salvation but with judgment. YHWH employed severe disciplinary measures to save Jonah not only from his external circumstances, but also from his reckless rebellion. In the exercise of prayer Jonah begins to understand what YHWH has been doing. YHWH has given Jonah what he asked for in order to show him that judgment is not, after all, preferable to submission to the divine commission.

In 2:4a-b Jonah flashes back to his experience of drowning: "You had cast me down to the deep, into the heart of the sea, where the river swirled about me." Though the colon begins with the typical narrative verb form (*wayyiqtol*), which is normally rendered by a simple past tense, the pluperfect is preferable in this context because Jonah is recalling events prior to the deliverance he just summarized in 2:3. In fact, all of the events recorded in 2:4a – 6e form part of the flashback of Jonah's recollection of his drowning. The pluperfect is an unusual value for the narrative verb form, but it is possible in certain circumstances.[33]

Jonah had come to realize that though the mariners served as agents, YHWH was actually the one who threw him into the sea. Thus Jonah states explicitly what the author implied in Jonah 1 through the repetition of the verb "to fling" (*hēṭîl*; 1:4a, 5c, 12c, 15b).

At this point the poem abounds with images of death and Sheol. Terms like "the deep," "the heart

---

33. Collins helpfully outlines the criteria for interpreting a narrative verb form (*wayyiqtol*) as a pluperfect on text-linguistic grounds. The first criterion is that a *wayyiqtol* may have pluperfect force when some repeated element in the clause explicitly points back to a previous event. The second is when the logic of the referent described requires that an event presented by a *wayyiqtol* actually took place prior to the event portrayed by the preceding verb. The third is when the verb begins a section or a paragraph. In the case of Jonah 2:3, arguably all three of these criteria are met. See C. John Collins, "The *Wayyiqtol* as 'Pluperfect': When and Why," *TynBul* 46.1 (1995): 127 – 28.

of the sea," and "the river" all have associations with the netherworld in Hebrew thought. The reason for these associations has to do with the ancient Near Eastern understanding of the universe. From a Semitic point of view, the world is surrounded by water, a cosmic sea kept at bay by a solid dome that YHWH has placed around the earth in order to make a habitable space for humans and land animals. This sea is often envisioned as split into two bodies of water by the dome or expanse, and it is referred to as "the waters above" and "the waters below" (cf. Gen 1:6). The waters below were a boundary separating the realm of life from the realm of death. Thus, sinking in the sea serves as a common image for near-death experiences.

YHWH's purpose in sending Jonah into the heart of the sea, to the threshold of Sheol, was to revive his appreciation for mercy and to convince him that the divine calling is preferable to divine judgment (i.e., death). YHWH accomplished this by giving Jonah a taste of strict justice as indicated by the imagery of 2:4b:

A) "You had cast me down to the deep, into the heart of the sea
B) where the river swirled about me."

The B-colon clarifies the goal and intent of the action described in the A-colon. YHWH was bringing Jonah down to the "river" (*nāhār*). Jonah described the experience of being caught in the undertow of the stormy sea in terms of undergoing a river ordeal. In Mesopotamian thought a river flowed through the bottom of the sea and served as the threshold to the underworld. This river was the location where souls were judged to determine guilt or innocence.[34] Trial by river ordeal was a common phenomenon in the ancient Near East in which the accused was plunged into the river, and his fate was determined by whether or not he could withstand the rushing waters.[35] What Jonah describes in 2:4 is reminiscent of such a trial.

In 2:4c a third colon combines with the previous two to heighten the sense of helplessness and despondence Jonah felt as the raging sea overwhelmed him. Jonah adds to the description of the river ordeal the image of billows and waves sweeping over him. Jonah quotes from the second colon of Ps 42:8 (7):

A) "Deep to deep is calling with the noise of your torrents;
B) all your breakers and waves, over me they pass."

Jonah was inundated by the sea. His cries for help appeared to be drowned out by the din of the pounding surf, and his attempts to remain afloat were foiled by the mounting waves. Repeatedly, Jonah found himself plunged back to the depths. This vivid description of Jonah's near-death experience serves as a dark backdrop against which the account of YHWH's deliverance stands out in bold relief.

d. Recognition to Cry Out to YHWH as the Only Hope (2:5a-c [2:4a-c])

In 2:5b-c Jonah expresses desperate determination as he resolves to persist in prayer until YHWH answers. The precise nuance of Jonah's statement in 2:5c has been a matter of some debate. Many translations understand the colon to be a confident assertion that YHWH will deliver Jonah: "Nevertheless, I will again gaze at your holy temple."[36]

---

34. In Mesopotamian lore, this was known as the River Hubur, which one had to cross in order to enter the netherworld. Its crossing was perilous, constituting a river ordeal. See J. Scurlock, "Death and Afterlife in Ancient Mesopotamian Thought," *CANE*, 3:1886.

35. P. Kyle McCarter, "The River Ordeal in Israelite Literature," *HTR* 66 (1973): 403.

36. So renders the KJV, ESV, NASB (Update), NIV, and NKJV.

Such confidence, however, seems out of place at this point in the prayer since Jonah is still relating his experience of drowning.

Instead of expressing confidence in YHWH's future deliverance, the phrase "I will again gaze toward your holy temple" indicates Jonah's commitment to persist in prayer.[37] The psalms frequently employ similar phraseology with reference to prayer, especially to prayer uttered at a great distance from Zion (Pss 18:4 – 6 [3 – 5]; 28:2; 134:2; 138:2). In fact the idea of facing and praying toward the temple finds its roots in Solomon's dedicatory prayer at the celebration of the temple's completion in 1 Kgs 8:48 – 51. The notion is especially relevant in the context of banishment or exile (Dan 6:11 [10]). Furthermore, the context of Jonah's prayer itself suggests that Jonah's petition for help was directed toward and reached YHWH's temple (2:8c-d).

Another consideration that bears on the interpretation of this phrase is the force of the verb "to repeat, do again" (*'ôsîp*). The verb occurs in a form (the imperfect) that is capable of expressing attempted action.[38] Such a connotation fits the context in Jonah's prayer admirably and yields the sense "Nevertheless, I will *try* again to gaze toward your holy temple." The idea, therefore, is that despite the fact that Jonah was banished from YHWH's presence and had no right to cry out to him for mercy, he attempted to fix his attention on YHWH's dwelling place and pray for deliverance on the basis of YHWH's mercy.

e. Recognition of the Severity of His Separation from God (2:6a – 7b [2:5a – 6b])

Jonah's prayer returns to the dark imagery of Sheol as the prophet comes to grips with the true severity of his separation from YHWH. The prayer's chiastic structure is particularly evident in 2:6a – 7b, as many of the motifs and images of 2:4a-b recur. Particularly prominent in this section of the poem are images of enclosure and shutting up — all indications of permanent separation from YHWH.

> A) The waters had enclosed me, threatening my life;
> B) the deep had enveloped me;
> C) reeds had wrapped around my head.

This tricolon in 2:6 moves further down the descent to Sheol with each colon. A set of three words in particular marks the descent: "waters" (*mayim*), "the deep" (*tĕhôm*), and "reeds" (*sûp*). This triad closely approximates that found in 2:4a-b: "the deep" (*mĕṣûlâ*), "the heart of the sea" (*lēbab yammîm*), and "the river" (*nāhār*). Of particular significance is the correspondence between "the river" and "reeds." Reeds are river plants that are not normally associated with the sea, and their presence in 2:6c has puzzled many commentators.[39] If, however, the reeds are related to the mention of the river in 2:4b, their presence makes sense. The descent documented in both 2:4a-b and 2:6a-c wind up at the same place — the river, where judgment by river ordeal takes place to confirm Jonah's guilt and the propriety of his being confined in Sheol. The mention of the reeds enhances the imagery of the river ordeal as Jonah finds himself bound and yanked down by the entangling river plants.

Another triad further stresses the dire consequences of Jonah's separation from YHWH: "enclosed" (*'ăpāpûnî*), "enveloped" (*yĕsôbĕbēnî*), and "wrapped" (*ḥābûš*). Taken together these verbs give the impression that Jonah is being wrapped in

---

37. Landes, "Kerygma," 21.

38. P. P. Saydon, "The Conative Imperfect in Hebrew," *VT* 12 (1962): 124 – 26.

39. For example, Wolff, *Obadiah and Jonah*, 136, and Sasson, *Jonah*, 185.

grave clothes and buried in a tomb. The last colon in particular portrays Jonah being wrapped in reeds as though he were being prepared for burial. Jonah had wanted death, so YHWH gave him a near-death experience. As the prayer has already revealed, however (2:3), upon experiencing the descent to Sheol, Jonah quickly sought YHWH's mercy.

The first stanza of Jonah's psalm concludes with a particularly well-crafted bicolon in 2:7a-b.

A) To the bases of the mountains I had descended;

    B) to the land whose bars would trap me forever.

The first colon of 2:7a displays marked word order.[40] The verb, which normally occupies first position, has been placed last in order to emphasize the destination of Jonah's descent. Also of significance is the fact that the cola share the verb "I had descended," which is explicit in colon A and implied in colon B (a phenomenon known as "gapping").[41] Bicola displaying marked word order in colon A and gapping in colon B mark the conclusion of major sections of a poem. Thus, the bicolon in 2:7a-b brings closure to stanza 1 of Jonah's prayer.[42]

Since the phrases "to the base of the mountains" and "to the land" are the focus of 2:7a-b, they play a climactic role at this critical juncture of the poem. Jonah's descent finally hits bottom. He finds himself at "the base of the mountains." This statement refers to the two subterranean mountains that support the earth in Semitic conceptions of the world.[43] Scripture normally refers to them as the "pillars of the earth" (1 Sam 2:8; Job 9:6; Ps 75:4 [3]). Most significant for Jonah's prayer is the fact that these mountains flank the threshold of Sheol, and their bases are tantamount to the doorway to the grave.

Jonah's descent to the very bottom of these subterranean mountains brings the poem to its lowest point, the location most remote from YHWH's presence represented by the temple, which rests on the opposite extremity — the sacred mountain (cf., e.g., Isa 2:2). In Israel, the sacred mountain is represented by Zion. Thus, the mountains to which Jonah descended are the inverse, the negative, of the sacred mountain where Jonah previously stood in YHWH's presence. Jonah had just completed an "anti-pilgrimage" to the "anti-temple" of Sheol. Instead of a psalm of ascent sung by pilgrims during their climb to the summit of Zion, Jonah sings a psalm of descent in anticipation of death and separation from YHWH.

A similar dynamic is at work in 2:7b with reference to the phrase "to the land." The context of the poem suggests that this designation refers to the netherworld. The irony is that normally the term "land" (*'ereṣ*) in the Old Testament refers to Israel's inheritance, Canaan, where YHWH dwelt in perpetuity with his people. Jonah, however, is not entering this land, but rather its antithesis — the land of exile, away from YHWH's presence.

2. Jonah's Partial and Prideful Response to Grace (2:7c – 2:11b [2:6c – 10b])

a. Jonah's Testimony to Divine Mercy (2:7c [2:6c])

The second stanza of the poem opens with a monocolon. Monocola are relatively rare in Hebrew poetry and often mark significant transitions within a poem. Such is the case with Jonah 2:7c, which serves as the turning point for the entire

40. Lunn, *Word-Order Variation*, 71 – 82.
41. Ibid, 18.
42. Ibid, 187.

43. Michael D. Coogan, *A Brief Introduction to the Old Testament: The Hebrew Bible in its Context* (New York: Oxford University, 2012), 29.

prayer. Just as Jonah's descent was abruptly interrupted as he reached the threshold of the grave, so the direction of the poem abruptly changes. The declaration of 2:7c is unexpected: "Then you restored from the pit my life, YHWH, my god." The matter-of-fact statement betrays the ease with which YHWH closes the distance between himself and his imperiled prophet.

Jonah first felt YHWH's saving grip on his ebbing life in what he calls "the pit" (*šaḥat*). In Hebrew the term "pit" derives from a verb meaning "to ruin, destroy, annihilate" and thus has connotations of a corpse's decomposition, the final return to dust.[44] By using this term, Jonah shows how certain he was that death was imminent. Nonetheless, at the last minute, YHWH reached down and retrieved Jonah from the abyss.

Due to its association with destruction and annihilation, "pit" (*šaḥat*) is a common designation for the grave or Sheol in the Old Testament, especially in the poetry of the psalms. In fact, "pit" and "Sheol" often occur together as a parallel word pair. Psalm 16:10 provides an example.

A) For you would never abandon me to Sheol
   B) nor allow your devotee to see the pit
      (*šaḥat*).

Jonah 2:7c echoes Ps 103:4 as it recalls one of YHWH's signature demonstrations of grace immortalized in Israel's praises: "Bless, O my soul, YHWH … who redeems from the pit your life."

Jonah identifies his rescuer at the end of the monocolon as "YHWH, my god" (*yhwh ʾĕlōhāy*). This designation recalls the opening of the narrative frame in 2:2, where the author stated, "Jonah prayed to YHWH, his god" (*yhwh ʾĕlōhāyw*), which thus ties the climax and pivot of the poem to the surrounding narrative. In theological terms, the designation recalls Israel's covenant formula, "I will be your God, and you will be my people" (Gen 17:7 – 8; Exod 6:7; Lev 26:12), which shows Jonah's reliance on the Abrahamic and Sinai covenants as his framework for understanding YHWH. In the wake of his deliverance, Jonah enthusiastically reaffirms YHWH as his god.

b. Jonah's Misplaced Emphasis (2:8a-b [2:7a-b])

The bicolon in 2:8 displays an interesting reversal of syntactic and semantic dependence. Whereas in the other bicola and tricola the first colon functions as the head on which subsequent cola are dependent, in 2:8a-b the reverse is true.

A) Just when I had felt myself succumbing
      to death,
B) YHWH I had remembered.

This reversal serves two rhetorical purposes in the prayer. First, it further highlights the preceding monocolon as the turning point of the poem. Second, it reinforces the general change of direction characteristic of the poem's second stanza. Preoccupation with descent to the netherworld is now replaced with a reorientation toward YHWH and his temple.

The first colon (2:8a) focuses on the timeliness of Jonah's reorientation to YHWH. He has remembered YHWH's mercy just in time. The second colon (2:8b) then emphasizes Jonah's remembrance of YHWH. It is at this point that the reader first begins to suspect that Jonah's response to YHWH's gracious deliverance is not all that it should be. Jonah's emphasis on his remembrance of YHWH is the first clue that his focus is still misplaced.

Two aspects of the statement "YHWH I had remembered" in the context of Jonah's prayer are problematic. First, the poem's abundant use of aquatic imagery and its numerous references to en-

---

44. *HALOT* (Study Edition), 2:1470 – 71.

gulfing waters and drowning recall the flood narrative of Genesis 6 – 9.[45] As a survivor of a deluge of primordial waters, Jonah functions as a Noah figure. Anderson has convincingly argued that the flood narrative is structured as a palistrophe (an extended chiasm), the centerpiece of which is the statement "Then God remembered Noah" (Gen 8:1).[46] In the light of this comparison, Jonah's statement seems ironic because it is an inversion of the flood narrative's key phrase. Jonah's emphasis is misplaced. The salient point is not that he remembered YHWH, but that YHWH remembered him.

Second, in the context of prayer the faithful nearly always confess that YHWH remembered them rather than vice versa.[47] The only exception to this pattern is in Ps 119:55, where the psalmist asserts, "In the night, Lord, I remember your name, that I may keep your law" (Ps 119:55 NIV). This statement, however, occurs in the context of a Torah psalm, expressing praise for how God's word keeps the psalmist innocent in the midst of a compromised culture, not in the midst of a thanksgiving psalm for undeserved salvation.

Statements regarding a person's or Israel's remembrance of God typically take the form of exhortations consisting primarily of commands.[48] Thus, Jonah's statement "YHWH I had remembered" seems out of place both in the context of his prayer and in the context of the narrative as a whole.

c. Jonah's Relief over the Effectiveness of His Prayer (2:8c-d [2:7c-d])

The next bicolon continues the theme of Jonah's misplaced emphasis. Jonah expressed relief that his prayer reached YHWH's ears from such a great distance. In fact, Jonah's prayer traveled the span from Sheol to YHWH's temple. Jonah's statement, however, is ambiguous with respect to whether the effectiveness of his prayer is due to YHWH's mercy or to his own correct piety.

Two factors argue that Jonah's focus is the latter. First, Jonah's prayer is void of any acknowledgment of wrongdoing on his part. It is completely lacking in confession and penitence.[49] His prayer acknowledges only that he was in danger; it never delves into the real reason for the circumstances from which he seeks deliverance. Second, the preceding bicolon and the following tricolon betray Jonah's emphasis on his piety. The context suggests, therefore, that the intervening bicolon has a similar emphasis. These issues foreshadow and contribute to Jonah's conflict with YHWH in chapter 4.

Jonah 2:8d concludes with the phrase "your holy temple," corresponding to the identical phrase in 2:5c. In both cases, the word "temple" stands at the center of a chiasm. Thus, in the overarching structure of the poem, these two cola are aligned (see X^1 and X^2 in figure 4.3). In this alignment 2:8d responds to 2:5c. In 2:5c Jonah committed himself to prayer by fixing his gaze on YHWH's temple. In 2:8d Jonah reports the results of that action — the prayer successfully reached its destination. Jonah's strong temple orientation displayed in the very structure of his prayer indicates a one-sided cultic emphasis that potentially falls short of true repentance. It is to that cultic emphasis that the poem turns in its closing stanzas.

d. Jonah's Confidence in His Own Piety (2:9 – 10b [2:8 – 9b])

Another abrupt shift occurs in the prayer at 2:9, where Jonah suddenly introduces an idol polemic

45. Eric W. Hesse and Isaac W. Kikawada, "Jonah and Genesis 1 – 11," 5.

46. B. W. Anderson, "From Analysis to Synthesis: The Interpretation of Gen 1 – 11," *JBL* 97 (1978): 38.

47. Judg 16:28; 1 Sam 1:11, 19; 2 Kgs 20:3 (Isa 38:3); 2 Chr 6:42; Pss 25:7; 106:4; Jer 15:15; Lam 5:1.

48. Deut 8:18; Judg 8:34; Neh 4:8 [14]; Jer 51:50.

49. Ackerman, "Satire and Symbolism," 224.

Table 4.5: Comparison of Jonah 2:9 – 10 with Psalm 31:7 – 8	
Jonah 2:9 – 10b (8 – 9b)	**Ps 31:7 – 8**
A) Devotees of useless idols forsake their experience of mercy, B) but, as for me, with a grateful voice I will sacrifice to you; C) what I have vowed I will pay.	A) I despise[50] those who adhere to useless idols, B) but as for me, I trust YHWH. A) I will rejoice ecstatically over your mercy B) because you noticed my affliction. C) You understood my personal distress.

in order to contrast his piety with that of idolaters. He expresses his disdain for idolatry in terms reminiscent of Psalm 31:7 – 8 [6 – 7] but with a few notable differences. The two passages are compared side by side above.

Jonah 2:9 – 10b (8 – 9b) softens the edge of the polemic in Ps 31:7a by omitting the initial "I despise," though the sentiment is the same. The words "devotees" (Jonah 2:9a) and "those who adhere to" (Ps 31:7a) derive from the same Hebrew verb (*šāmar*), though Jonah employs an otherwise unattested intensified form (*mĕšammĕrîm* [Piel]) in order to convey persistent allegiance ("devotees").[51]

Both passages mention YHWH's mercy (*ḥesed*), and both modify this noun with a possessive pronoun. In the case of Ps 31:8a, the term clearly refers to YHWH's mercy ("your mercy," *ḥasdekā*). In Jonah's prayer, however, the term is ambiguous because it is modified by a third person plural pronoun, "their *ḥesed*" (*ḥasdām*). The question arises as to whether Jonah is referring to YHWH's mercy

expressed toward individuals ("their experience of divine mercy") or the faithfulness of the worshipers themselves ("their loyalty"). A number of factors argue in favor of the former. First, if Jonah is relying on Ps 31:8a, it is difficult to explain why he would change a clear reference to YHWH's mercy so appropriate to his prayer to an obscure reference to the fickle devotion of idolaters.

Second, the view that Jonah is referring to the loyalty (or lack thereof) of human worshipers depends on Glueck's understanding of *ḥesed* as a virtue to which one is obliged by covenant.[52] A number of scholars, however, have refuted the connection between the word *ḥesed* and covenant obligation by arguing that *ḥesed* actually refers to attitudes and actions that go above and beyond the call of duty.[53] The term in the Old Testament thus never refers to human actions toward God, though it can refer to charitable acts toward one's fellow humans.[54]

The third and final consideration is that the

---

50. NRSV, NJB, and TEV all translate this verb as "you hate" on the basis of a variant reading found in one Hebrew manuscript (DeRossi, IV, 23), the Septuagint, the Vulgate, and the Peshitta. This reading is certainly possible, but the MT makes good sense as it stands, and I have retained it in my translation for the purposes of this discussion. Cf. Peter C. Craigie, *Psalms 1 – 50* (WBC 19; Waco, TX: Word, 1983), 258.

51. Jenni, *Das hebräische Pi'el*, 223. It is also possible that Jonah is employing a cultic use of the Piel as Levine argues for verbs related to priestly activities in Leviticus and Numbers. Apparently, actions expressed in the Qal when associated with other contexts frequently change to the Piel when applied to

a religio-cultic context. See Baruch A. Levine, "The Hebrew 'Piel' in Religio-Cultic Usage" (paper presented at the annual meeting of the SBL, Boston, MA, November 22, 1999), 3 – 4.

52. Nelson Glueck, *The Word "Hesed" in Old Testament Usage* (trans. A. Gottschalk; Giessen: Töpelmann, 1927; English trans., Cincinnati: Hebrew Union College, 1967).

53. Michael V. Fox, "Jeremiah 2:2 and the 'Desert Ideal,'" *CBQ* 35 (1973): 443; Katherine Doob Sakenfeld, *The Meaning of Hesed in the Hebrew Bible* (HSS 17; Missoula, MT: Scholars, 1978); Edgar Kellenberger, *ḥesed wā'emet als Ausdruck einer Glaubenserfahrung* (ATANT 69; Zürich: Theologische Verlag, 1982).

54. Fox, "Desert Ideal," 443.

term *ḥesed* can refer to a proof of mercy, a display of mercy, or an experience of mercy.[55] The idea, therefore, in Jonah 2:9 is that those who persist in their devotion to useless idols quickly forget the mercy YHWH has shown to them. By contrast, Jonah promises to remember YHWH's saving mercy and to commemorate it by sacrifices and vows.

Since this is what Jonah 2:9 likely means, then to whom is Jonah referring? Who are these "devotees of useless idols" who "forsake mercy"? The narrative context of the prayer suggests that Jonah is referring to none other than the mariners of chapter 1. In support of this conclusion is the fact that Jonah's mention of sacrifices and vows recalls 1:16, where the same two words occur with reference to the mariners' worship of YHWH. These mariners and Jonah both experienced an act of divine mercy. The mariners experienced the sudden cessation of the storm, and Jonah was delivered from drowning by means of the great fish. In his prayer, Jonah contrasts the mariners' response to YHWH's mercy with his own. Jonah expresses doubt about whether the mariners' encounter with YHWH resulted in any permanent change of religious allegiance. Jonah, it would seem, suspected that YHWH's salvation would result in nothing more than their adding YHWH to the long list of deities that they already served. More likely, they would forget altogether about YHWH once they were safe on land.

Jonah insists, however, that his own experience of divine mercy will result in orthodox and lasting piety, particularly in the cultic forms of sacrifices and vows. The reader again encounters a great irony in Jonah's prayer. Since he was thrown overboard before the mariners' sacrificed and vowed to YHWH, Jonah was unaware that the mariners had already done everything that he promised to do.

Compounding this irony is the fact that while Jonah promises to offer sacrifices and pay what he has vowed, he makes no mention of submitting himself to the divine commission. This is not to say that Jonah remains completely unreformed in his attitude about YHWH's commission. As Jonah 3 demonstrates, the prophet does in fact go to Nineveh without objection. Rather, the absence of any confession of wrongdoing or commitment to repentance demonstrates again Jonah's misplaced emphasis. His acts of piety are not irrelevant. They, however, are not enough, in and of themselves, to ensure the change of disposition that Jonah needs — a fact underscored later by YHWH's confrontation with Jonah in chapter 4.

That confession and repentance are not foremost in Jonah's mind when he prays suggests that the prophet stands in need of further education at YHWH's merciful hand. The sacrifices, vows, and even the pilgrimage to Nineveh will all be meaningless without Jonah's progress toward conformity to YHWH's merciful character.

e. Jonah's Declaration of YHWH's Sovereignty in Salvation (2:10c [2:9c])

Jonah's prayer concludes with a monocolon that dramatically declares, "Deliverance belongs to YHWH." This confession abruptly follows Jonah's promise to commemorate YHWH's salvation with sacrifice and payment of vows. Presumably, the monocolon explains the basis for Jonah's promise of piety. His sacrifices and payment of vows are due to the fact that YHWH deals in salvation.

Jonah's expression is unique to his prayer, although others in Scripture voice similar sentiments. The monocolon consists of two Hebrew words. The first is the typical word for victory, deliverance, or salvation, which appears here in a special lengthened form found only in poetry and

---

55. *HALOT* (Study Edition), 1:337.

only in three other texts (*yĕšûʿātâ* [cf. Pss 3:3; 80:3; Isa 62:1]).[56] While the lengthened form carries no difference in meaning from its shorter and more common counterpart (*yĕšûʿâ*), its extra syllable does serve to add a beat to an already brief poetic colon.

The second element in the monocolon is the prepositional phrase "to YHWH" (*layhwh*). The preposition in this context expresses possession: thus, "deliverance belongs to YHWH." The implication is that YHWH is sovereign in salvation. It is his enterprise; therefore, neither YHWH's judgment nor his salvation is subject to human manipulation. Jonah had already attempted to manipulate divine judgment by fleeing YHWH's presence. His goal, it seems, was to provoke YHWH to either banish him or take his life, which would preclude his mission to Nineveh. YHWH, however, did not deal with Jonah according to strict justice, but according to his mercy. Jonah miscalculated and wound up saved rather than condemned.

The experience convinced Jonah for a while that divine judgment is not preferable to the divine commission. Jonah, nonetheless, again attempts to manipulate YHWH's judgment and salvation in chapter 4, which indicates that he was not fully prepared to accept the implications of this bold confession.

f. Jonah's Experience of a Humbling Salvation (2:11a-b [2:10a-b])

Jonah 2:11a returns to the narrative mainline with the *wayyiqtol* verb form, followed by a shift to YHWH as subject and to the author as speaker. These two clauses conclude the narrative frame surrounding the poem and record YHWH's response to Jonah's speech and the fish's response to YHWH's speech. The fish responds by vomiting Jonah onto dry land.

The statement "YHWH spoke to the fish" translates an unusual use of the verb "to say" (*wayyōʾmer*). This verb typically introduces quoted speech while the verb "to speak" (*dābar*) reports the act of speaking as a narrated event.[57] In 2:11a, however, "YHWH said …" does not introduce YHWH's actual utterance to the fish. This may be yet another example of information gapping, a favorite technique of this particular author. If that is the case, then the author creates suspense regarding what YHWH said to the fish. The reader, like Jonah, is on the outside of this exchange. The reader only knows that whatever YHWH said to the fish, it compelled the fish to spew Jonah out.

YHWH's choice to have the fish "vomit" (*wayyāqēʾ*) Jonah onto dry ground was likely intended to humble the prophet who, though grateful for YHWH's salvation, retained a dangerous pride (2:9 – 10b). In the Old Testament the image of vomit is consistently negative. It can signify divine judgment, as when YHWH warns that covenant infidelity can sicken the land to the point that it will vomit out its inhabitants (Lev 18:25 – 28; 20:22). In a similar vein, it describes those who are drunk on YHWH's judgment until they vomit (Isa 19:14; 28:8; Jer 25:27). Most relevant for the present context is the use of the image as a symbol of humiliation. Jeremiah 48:26 offers the best example of this imagery: "Make her drunk, for she has defied the LORD. Let Moab wallow in her vomit; let her be an object of ridicule" (NIV). The reader can easily imagine Jonah in a similar, humiliating situation when he hit the ground, covered in the fish's vomit. YHWH's chosen means of salvation appears to take aim at this prophet's misplaced pride.

---

56. "Salvation" (*yĕšûʿâ*) is one of several feminine nouns that takes a – *tâ* suffix in poetic contexts. See GKC, 251.

57. Cynthia Miller, *The Representation of Speech in Biblical Hebrew Narrative: A Linguistic Analysis* (HSMP 55; Winona Lake, IN: Eisenbrauns, 2003), 137 – 38.

Canonical and Practical Significance

The Sign of Jonah and the Centrality of the Resurrection

The book of Jonah's third episode presents what is perhaps the book's most significant canonical connection — Jonah's three-day-and-three-night sojourn in the belly of the fish. According to Matthew's gospel, Jesus chose Jonah 2:1c (1:17c) as a prophetic sign of his resurrection from the dead in response to his critics' demand for more evidence of his ministry's legitimacy (Matt 12:39). The sign resurfaces in Matt 16:4 and Luke 11:29 – 30, but without specific reference either to the three days and three nights of Jonah 2:1c or to Jesus' resurrection. In fact, Luke's gospel relates the sign of Jonah not to Jesus' resurrection but to Nineveh's responsiveness to Jonah's preaching as a contrast to the Pharisees' rejection of Jesus' preaching. The current discussion, therefore, will focus primarily on Matt 12:39, with secondary reference to 16:4. Luke 11:29 – 30 will be treated in connection with the section on Jonah 3:3c – 10e.

Jesus' first mention of the sign of Jonah in Matthew's gospel occurs in the context of the Pharisees' accusation that Jesus exorcises demons by the power of Beelzebub rather than by the power of God. Jesus issued a severe warning regarding their blasphemy of the Spirit's power — a sin for which God offers no forgiveness (Matt 12:24 – 34). Jesus' stern warning provoked some Pharisees to request a sign as evidence that Jesus had sufficient authority to rebuke them in this manner.

> Then some of the Pharisees and teachers of the law said to him, "Teacher, we want to see a sign from you."
> He answered, "A wicked and adulterous generation asks for a sign! But none will be given it except the sign of the prophet Jonah. For as Jonah was three days and three nights in the belly of a huge fish, so the Son of Man will be three days and three nights in the heart of the earth. The men of Nineveh will stand up at the judgment with this generation and condemn it; for they repented at the preaching of Jonah, and now something greater than Jonah is here. (Matt 12:38 – 41 NIV)

The context suggests that Jesus' sign of Jonah was primarily a proclamation of judgment on the Pharisees' inability to recognize the significance of the signs Jesus had already performed. Yet another sign was not the answer to the Pharisees' problem. Jesus warned the Pharisees that their resistance to the available signs would eventually lead to their rejection of the ultimate sign, his resurrection from the dead. Only one sign remained, but the Pharisees were too hardened to understand its significance. Their hardened state led Jesus to contrast them with the people of Nineveh, who responded so readily to Jonah's preaching.

Jesus' appropriation of Jonah 2:1c (1:17c) is difficult to understand without some knowledge of the development of this text in Jewish tradition. Jewish tradition predating Jesus' ministry already recognized the symbolic significance of Jonah's near-death experience.[58] For example, 3 Macc 6:8 (1st century BC) records Eleazar's prayer for the deliverance of the Jewish people from Ptolemy IV Philopater. At the conclusion of his rehearsal of all of God's saving acts on behalf of his people, Eleazar mentions Jonah's deliverance from the belly of the sea monster: "And Jonah, wasting away in the belly of a huge, sea-born monster, you, Father, watched over and restored unharmed to all his family" (NRSV).

Eleazar's prayer demonstrates that Jonah's deliverance from the sea by fish was already considered paradigmatic of God's deliverance of his people from death. Of particular interest in this text is Eleazar's mention of how God returned Jonah to his family. The book of Jonah makes no mention of the prophet's family (aside from his father's name), nor of his being returned to them. Eleazar was apparently alluding to a Jewish tradition preserved in *The Lives of the Prophets* (1st century AD). According to this text (10:4 – 7), Jonah was none other than the widow's son whom Elijah raised from the dead.[59] Ginzberg notes that the identification of Jonah with the resurrected widow's son was a widespread tradition that eventually found written expression in this portion of *The Lives of the Prophets*.[60] On the basis of this tradition, therefore, the conclusion of Eleazar's prayer conflates the Jonah story with 1 Kgs 17:23: "Elijah picked up the child and carried him down from the room into the house. He gave him to his mother and said, 'Look, your son is alive!'" (NIV). Jonah, therefore, was often associated with resurrection, not only because of his near-death experience at sea, but also because of the tradition that identified him with the widow's son whom Elijah raised from the dead.

Of particular significance is Jesus' appeal to Jonah as *a sign* pointing toward Jesus' resurrection. A Jewish homily that circulated sometime between the first century BC and the second century AD, preserved in Armenian translation, refers to Jonah's expulsion from the fish as a "sign of rebirth."[61] This same terminology resurfaces in the rabbinic work *Pirqe Rabbi Eliezer* with reference to the mariners' witnessing Jonah's deliverance:

> The sailors saw all the signs, the miracles, and the great wonders which the Holy One, blessed be He, did unto Jonah, and they stood and they cast away everyone his God, as it is said, "They that regard lying vanities forsake their own shame."[62]

The word Eliezer uses for "signs," 'ôtôt, is the term one typically finds in commis-

---

58. Simon Chow, *The Sign of Jonah Reconsidered: A Study of its Meaning in the Gospel Traditions* (ConBNT 27; Stockholm: Almqvist & Wicksell, 1995), 43.

59. *Lives of the Prophets* (trans. D. R. A. Hare) OTP, 2:392 – 93.

60. Louis Ginzberg, *The Legends of the Jews*, vol. 4 (trans.

Boaz Cohen; Philadelphia: Jewish Publication Society, 1913), 197.

61. Chow, *The Sign of Jonah Reconsidered*, 36.

62. *Pirqe Rabbi Eliezer* (trans. Gerald Friedlander; New York: The Bloch Publishing Company, 1916), 72.

sion narratives related to the confirmatory sign YHWH bestows on his chosen agents (Exod 3:12; Judg 6:17). Thus early Jewish tradition apparently recognized Jonah as a sign in keeping with the story's nature as a commission narrative. This term entered into the NT via the LXX's preferred Greek equivalent for the word, *sēmeion* (σημεῖον), the very term Matthew applies to the Jonah sign.[63]

The sign of Jonah underscores Jesus' resurrection as the decisive sign of his divine commission. As Paul argued in 1 Corinthians 15, the entire gospel hinges on the resurrection. Therefore, the church must never waiver from her commitment to the centrality of this truth.

The Exodus Motif and Jonah's Calling

In addition to the famous sign of Jonah, the book's third episode picks up other biblical themes that are often overshadowed by Jesus' allusion to Jonah's journey in the fish. A particularly striking example is the relationship of Jonah's prayer to Exod 14 – 15. Much of the vocabulary and imagery Jonah employs in his thanksgiving psalm echo the Song of Moses and the surrounding narrative relating Israel's escape from Egyptian bondage. Hunter, for example, lists nineteen key words shared by Jonah 2 and Exod 14 – 15, suggesting a deliberate allusion to the exodus narrative.[64]

Of particular interest is Jonah 2:6 – 7, which is particularly dense with references to the exodus and the Song of Moses, such as the enveloping depths/heart of the sea (Exod 15:5, 8), reeds (15:4), cosmic mountain(s)/Sinai (15:17), and land/inheritance (15:12 – 13). Furthermore, the text arranges these references in the same order as Israel's movement from Egypt to the Promised Land.

Table 4.6: Allusions to the Exodus in Jonah 2:6 – 7	
Movement in the Exodus	**Movement in Jonah 2:6 – 7**
1. The Sea of Reeds (*yam sûp*)	1. Sea … reeds (*yam … sûp*)
2. Your own mountain (*har*, i.e., Sinai)	2. Base of the mountains (*hārîm*)
3. The Promised Land/Canaan (*'ereṣ /kĕna'an*)	3. The Land of No Return (*'ereṣ*)

By means of these parallels, the poem describes Jonah's descent to Sheol as the antithesis of Israel's exodus. Instead of moving from the Sea of Reeds to the Mountain of God (Sinai) to the Land of Promise, Jonah moved from the sea with its reeds, to the bases of the cosmic mountains, to the Land of No Return (Exod 15:4).[65]

---

63. Chow, *The Sign of Jonah Reconsidered*, 36.

64. A. G. Hunter, "Jonah from the Whale: Exodus Motifs in Jonah 2," *The Elusive Prophet: The Prophet As a Historical Person, Literary Character, and Anonymous Artist* (ed. Johannes C. Moore; Leiden: Brill, 2001), 145.

65. The word used to describe YHWH's tossing the Egyptian army into the sea (*yārâ*) differs from that used to describe Jonah's being tossed into the sea (*hēṭil*), but this in no way detracts from the close conceptual parallel.

The description of Jonah's descent to Sheol in terms reminiscent of the exodus may be intended to underscore the fact that Jonah's rebellion is inconsistent with Israel's defining narrative. Israel's experience of salvation was not an end in and of itself, but a means to an end. YHWH was redeeming a people for his glory, through whom the nations might come to know him (Isa 42:6; 49:1 – 6). In accepting YHWH's salvation, Israel was also accepting YHWH's mission. The two are inseparable.

Thus, when Jonah ran away from his calling, he denied the implications of Israel's defining story (Exod 19:6). When Jonah cried out for salvation, however, he experienced something much like the exodus — a deliverance from sea to dry land for the purpose of revealing YHWH to the nations. The language and imagery of Jonah's prayer indicate that the prophet's salvation experience reminded him of that defining narrative and was intended to prepare him to reenter YHWH's service. Jonah's salvation was followed immediately by a renewal of the divine commission (3:1 – 3) precisely because salvation always entails acceptance of YHWH's calling.

YHWH's Sovereignty in Salvation

The climactic confession in Jonah's prayer is that "deliverance belongs to YHWH." A nearly identical confession appears in Ps 3:9 (8) in the context of David's prayer for deliverance from his enemies. He states, "To YHWH belongs deliverance." These two statements reflect the general Old Testament belief that YHWH alone can offer genuine salvation, and that he alone may determine its timing, mode, and objects. Yet despite this confession, God's people have sometimes attempted to place their own conditions and limitations on it. The Jerusalem Council in Acts 15 provides one example of the early church's struggle with this very issue. Jewish Christians were considering whether circumcision, dietary restrictions, and the observance of a particular liturgical calendar should be made conditions of salvation and fellowship for Gentile converts.

The apostle John reasserts and expands on the confession of Ps 3:8 and Jonah 2:10 in Rev 7:10 in the context of a heavenly vision. John suddenly finds himself in the midst of an innumerable multitude from every nation, tribe, people, and language. Everyone in this international gathering wears white and holds palm branches as they cry out in unison, "Salvation belongs to our God, who sits on the throne, and to the Lamb." John's allusion to this Old Testament confession clarifies its meaning in two respects. First, John underscores God's sovereignty in salvation by adding the relative clause, "who sits on the throne." The emphasis falls on God's exclusive right to offer salvation and to set its terms and its limits. Second, John adds to the end of the statement "and to the Lamb," which indicates that the Father shares his sovereignty over salvation with the Son.

Jonah's grateful admission that true deliverance comes only from YHWH entails implications that the prophet did not understand until after his mission to Nineveh. YHWH's sovereignty over salvation means that YHWH may offer deliverance to whomever he chooses. Jonah had no right to object to or restrict that salvation, especially since he himself was a beneficiary of YHWH's merciful deliverance.

The Humbling Nature of Salvation

The book's third episode ends with a saving act that has stripped Jonah of his pride. The image of Jonah vomited up on dry land reminds the reader that YHWH's salvation has a humbling effect. YHWH's chosen means of salvation always challenges our pride, so much so, in fact, that many find it difficult to accept. Paul argued this point extensively in 1 Cor 1:18 – 29.

> For the message of the cross is foolishness to those who are perishing, but to us who are being saved it is the power of God. For it is written:
>
> > "I will destroy the wisdom of the wise;
> > the intelligence of the intelligent I will frustrate."
>
> Where is the wise person? Where is the teacher of the law? Where is the philosopher of this age? Has not God made foolish the wisdom of the world? For since in the wisdom of God the world through its wisdom did not know him, God was pleased through the foolishness of what was preached to save those who believe.
>
> Jews demand signs and Greeks look for wisdom, but we preach Christ crucified: a stumbling block to Jews and foolishness to Gentiles, but to those whom God has called, both Jews and Greeks, Christ the power of God and the wisdom of God. For the foolishness of God is wiser than human wisdom, and the weakness of God is stronger than human strength.
>
> Brothers and sisters, think of what you were when you were called. Not many of you were wise by human standards; not many were influential; not many were of noble birth. But God chose the foolish things of the world to shame the wise; God chose the weak things of the world to shame the strong. God chose the lowly things of this world and the despised things — and the things that are not — to nullify the things that are, so that no one may boast before him. (NIV)

Jonah's favorable comparison of himself to idolaters (2:9 – 10b) is reminiscent of the Pharisee's prayer in Jesus' parable (Luke 18:10 – 14). He thanks God for his moral superiority to others, such as the tax collector who prays nearby. The tax collector, however, is humbled by a profound recognition of his sin and of his need for divine mercy. Jesus declared that the tax collector's prayer was accepted by God rather than the Pharisee's precisely because it originated from a humble heart. As the Scriptures say, "God opposes the proud but shows favor to the humble" (Prov 3:34 [LXX]; 1 Pet 5:5; Jas 4:6 [NIV]).

Piety and Repentance

The humbling nature of YHWH's salvation raises the related issue of repentance. Pride presents a significant obstacle to genuine repentance, and it appears to play a role in Jonah's struggle to embrace his calling. The cultic emphasis in Jonah's prayer combined with the absence of confession or of a request for forgiveness raises questions regarding the nature of Jonah's repentance. Samuel's instructions regarding the role of cultic worship may be just as applicable to Jonah as they were to Saul.

> But Samuel replied:
>
> "Does the LORD delight in burnt offerings and sacrifices
>> as much as in obeying the LORD?
> To obey is better than sacrifice,
>> and to heed is better than the fat of rams.
> For rebellion is like the sin of divination,
>> and arrogance like the evil of idolatry. (1 Sam 15:22 – 23a, NIV)

Judging by Samuel's criteria, Jonah, by reason of his pride, was already guilty of the very sin he condemned so vehemently: idolatry (2:9 – 10 [8 – 9]).

II. From Compliant Acceptance to Angry Resentment: *The Offense of God's Mercy*

Jonah 3:1 – 3b

A. A Second Chance at Compliance with God's Mercy (Stage setting)

Main Idea of the Passage

YHWH mercifully offers Jonah a second chance to submit to the commission to go to Nineveh. Outwardly, Jonah complies, but his attitude toward the mission remains fundamentally unchanged.

Literary Context

The words of Jonah 3:1 – 3b have a familiar ring. They are, in fact, an almost verbatim repetition of the divine call issued in 1:1 – 2. Jonah 3:1 – 3b leaves the reader with a sense of literary déjà vu, creating the impression of a new beginning. The story starts over, granting both Jonah and Nineveh a second chance. Having witnessed YHWH's commission and Jonah's response before, the reader may experience a little anxious suspense, wondering whether the repetition marks a vicious cycle of sin or a spiral of spiritual progress.

With the reissuing of YHWH's call, the author clearly marks the second main section of the book and initiates the parallelism that characterizes the story's primary structure. The parallelism, however, is not exact, and often repetition serves merely to highlight differences between a book's two main sections. Some of these differences are subtle, such as the slight rewording of parts of YHWH's commission; others are more obvious, such as Jonah's compliance to YHWH's second call in contrast to his rebellion against the first. Nearly all of the differences, however, are rhetorically significant and guide the reader toward an understanding of the book's message.

Like its corresponding section in part 1, 3:1 – 3b is a stage-setting text that serves to reorient the reader after the excitement of the first three episodes.[1] The stage set-

---

1. Longacre and Hwang, "A Text-Linguistic Approach," 342.

ting here is no more informative than the one that opens the book. The reader is uncertain of where the fish deposits Jonah, having only the vague reference from 2:11 that Jonah is now back on "dry ground" (*hayyabbāšâ*). In the literary world of Jonah, however, the designation of dry land may reveal more than it appears to at first.

The first main section of the book traced Jonah's journey from dry land to the depths of the primordial sea, the threshold of Sheol, and back again to dry land. Now that Jonah is back on dry land, communion with YHWH resumes. Jonah is restored to the realm of life and order. The events that transpire on dry land reflect the orderliness of that environment, just as the events that transpired at sea reflect the morbidity and chaos of that environment. Jonah and the reader are in a peaceful, orderly place as the divine word invades the prophet's consciousness again.

The advantage of such a hazy literary setting is that it offers no distractions to the divine word that erupts on the scene. The text's singular focus is YHWH's commissioning word. The outline below demonstrates where this unit falls in the larger context of the book's second main section.

I. From Silent Resistance to Jubilant Acceptance: The Compelling Nature of God's Mercy (1:1 – 2:11 [2:10], Macro Unit 1)

II. From Compliant Acceptance to Angry Resentment: The Offense of God's Mercy (3:1 – 4:11, Macro Unit 2)

➡ **A. A Second Chance at Compliance with God's Mercy (3:1 – 3b, Stage setting)**
   1. The commission: a second chance to learn the scope of God's scandalous mercy (3:1 – 2)
   2. The compliance: a concession to God's mercy (3:3a – b)
   B. Responsiveness to and the Responsiveness of God's Mercy (3:3c – 10, Pre-peak episode)
   C. Resentment at God's Mercy (4:1 – 4, Peak episode)
   D. An Object Lesson on the Divine Mercy and Divine Justice (4:5 – 11, Post-peak episode)

Translation and Outline

(See the next page.)

Structure and Literary Form

As noted above, Jonah 2:2 – 10c interrupted the commission narrative with the insertion of a thanksgiving prayer. The commission had left off at the sign or symbolic act represented by the three-day-and-three-night journey in the fish. Jonah 3:1a resumes the commission narrative, but not at the point one would expect. Rather

Jonah 3:1–3b

3:1a	Yahweh's word came to Jonah again:
3:2a	Up!
3:2b	Go to Nineveh, that great metropolis,
3:2c	and proclaim to them the proclamation
3:2d	that I am about to speak to you.
3:3a	So Jonah got up
3:3b	and went to Nineveh as Yahweh commanded.

A. A Second Chance at Compliance with God's Mercy (3:1–3b, Stage setting)

1. The commission: a second chance to learn the scope of God's scandalous mercy (3:1a-2d)
   a. YHWH's merciful repetition of the commission (3:1a-2b)
   b. YHWH's clarification of the commission (3:2c-d)

2. The Compliance: A Concession to God's Mercy (3:3a-b)
   a. Jonah's new direction (3:3a-b)
   b. Jonah's new director (3:3b)

than simply picking up with the clarification of the commission where the narrative left off, the author returns to the beginning of the commission. YHWH reissues the command and the entire sequence starts over from the beginning.

This time the commission narrative proceeds in typical fashion. YHWH issues the divine command, and Jonah obeys in terms that match the wording of the commission. One departure from the typical commission narrative form, however, stands out. Jonah offers no verbal objections to the call. Just as his initial objection was silent (1:3), so now his compliance is silent. The omission is odd for two reasons. First, an agent's verbal objection to the divine call is a stable, standard feature of commission narratives.[2] Second, it is unusual that a prophet who was initially so opposed to the divine commission would so tacitly comply the second time around.

A consideration of the larger context reveals, however, that Jonah's verbal objection to the commission is not actually missing. Rather, the author has deliberately displaced it, moving Jonah's objection to the second peak episode of the book (4:1 – 4). The change of location gives this element of the commission narrative special prominence.

Evident, therefore, in the book's fourth episode is the author's penchant for manipulating the genre with which he is working for rhetorical purposes.[3] A number of examples have already appeared, but this displacement is particularly crucial to the book's logic. Jonah 3:1a – 3b creates the impression that Jonah is completely reformed. Were it not for the subtle hints in the more self-centered sections of Jonah's prayer, readers would likely assume that they have just witnessed a classic example of complete repentance. The larger narrative, however, raises suspicions that Jonah's compliance, while an improvement over his previous flight is superficial. The author will later confirm these suspicions in the peak episode (4:1 – 4), where readers

---

2. Habel, "The Form and Significance of the Call Narratives," 301.

3. Ben Zvi perceptively notes, "Genre manipulation is a common rhetorical device in prophetic literature. The differ- ence (in the book of Jonah) is the level at which genre is manipulated. Here it is manipulated at the highest possible level, that of the prophetic book itself." See Ehud ben Zvi, "Atypicality and the Meta-Prophetic Character," 89 n. 11.

finally hear what they have been waiting for — Jonah's verbal objection to YHWH's commission.

In terms of structure, 3:1a – 3b divides into two parts. The first part is YHWH's repetition of the call issued in 1:1 – 2. The repetition, however, is not exact. A couple of subtle but telling differences are evident. These differences constitute the clarification portion of the commission narrative. The second part records Jonah's compliance to the commission by utilizing YHWH's own words as an indication of Jonah's external obedience. The boundary between the unit's two sections is marked by the transition from YHWH's quoted speech in 3:1a – 2d to the resumption of narrative in 3:3a-b.

Explanation of the Text

1. The Commission: A Second Chance to Learn the Scope of God's Scandalous Mercy (3:1a – 2)

a. YHWH's Merciful Repetition of the Commission (3:1a – 2b)

When YHWH reissues his call to Jonah in 3:1a, the same prophetic word formula occurs as that found in 1:1a: "YHWH's word came to Jonah...." What catches the reader's attention, however, is the word "again" (šēnît). This term stands out for the simple reason that it is the first departure from the wording of the introduction to the original commission (1:1a).

The phrase "YHWH's word came ... *again*" is not unique to the book of Jonah. One finds this term appended to the prophetic word formula on four other occasions (Jer 1:13; 13:3; 33:1; Hag 2:20). In these other cases, however, YHWH's second word is an addendum to a previous revelation, a clarification, reassurance, or extension of an immediately preceding oracle. Only in Jonah does this terminology signify a second opportunity to render obedience to the divine command.[4] In fact, Jonah is unique among the prophets in his receiving a second chance to obey YHWH's command.[5] Prophets were typically judged more quickly and severely precisely because of their special calling and privileged access to revelation (Num 22:22 – 35; 1 Kgs 13:20 – 25; Jer 23:23 – 40; James 3:1).

In Jonah's case, however, YHWH makes an exception for two important reasons. First, judgment is what Jonah had initially wanted. Rather than fulfill his commission, Jonah invited YHWH's judgment as a means of escape from the mission to Nineveh. Believing that he could calculate and manipulate divine retribution, Jonah counted on YHWH's swift justice meted out to other prophets as his way out. YHWH did not oblige but proved to Jonah that neither his judgment nor his mercy can be manipulated. Second, YHWH shows Jonah mercy because this is the quality he wishes to grow in this judgment-obsessed prophet.

---

4. Limburg (*Jonah*, 75) is likely correct in concluding that the modifier "again" or "a second time" (šēnît) indicates a repetition of the original commission especially in light of the nearly identical wording. For an alternative, though less likely, interpretation see Sasson, *Jonah*, 225 – 26; Trible, "Jonah," 7:511.

5. Jenson, *Obadiah, Jonah, Micah*, 70.

b. YHWH's Clarification of the Commission (3:2c-d)

The next notable aspect of YHWH's repetition of the commission is the clause "proclaim to them the proclamation" (*wiqĕrā' 'ēleyhā 'et-haqqĕrî'â*). With this utterance, YHWH introduces a number of interesting variations to the original command. First, he changes the preposition following the command from "against" (*'al*) to "to" (*'el*). This alteration changes the nuance of the command from "condemn [them]" (1:2c) to "proclaim to them" (3:2c).[6]

This slight alteration makes the second command more neutral than the first. It lacks the confrontational and condemning connotations evident in 1:2 and may introduce an element of ambiguity. YHWH hints at two possible outcomes. The alteration may, therefore, serve as a foreshadowing of the clemency that YHWH will show Nineveh.

The next thing the reader notices about the restated commission is that it lacks the motive clause of 1:2d. Previously, YHWH followed the command with its basis: "because their evil has ascended before me." The second time, however, YHWH replaces the basis with the content of the proclamation: "Proclaim to them *the proclamation that I am about to speak to you.*" The absence of the motive clause does not mean that the underlying reason for the commission has changed. Rather, it indicates that the emphasis has shifted from the reason for the commission to divine control of the message and the messenger. YHWH does not give Jonah a free hand to craft the message.

The noun "proclamation" (*qĕrî'â*) occurs only here in the Hebrew Bible and was likely chosen for the sound play it creates with the preceding verb, "proclaim" (*qārā'*). This clause is one of many examples of the author's penchant for pairing verbs and nouns based on the same root. The construction is especially common at structurally or thematically significant points in the book (see the Introduction, pp. 39 – 40). In this context, the cognate construction joins with other rhetorical features to mark the book's central turning point.

2. The Compliance: A Concession to God's Mercy (3:3a-b)

a. Jonah's New Direction (3:3a-b)

As in 1:3a, Jonah rises in keeping with YHWH's initial command, "Up!" In 1:3, however, Jonah "got up" only to "go down." The anticipated symmetry of command followed by obedience was broken. This time, however, Jonah rises to fulfill the commission. The symmetry is restored. The prophet has a new direction and heads east in obedience to YHWH's command.

b. Jonah's New Director (3:3b)

The report of Jonah's obedience concludes with the usual note of divine approval for actions that conform to YHWH's command: "according to YHWH's word" (*kidbar yhwy*). The reader has waited a long time to hear these words. They were expected in 1:3 but were delayed by Jonah's flight. After the second commission, however, Jonah rejects self-directed flight in favor of a God-directed journey.

---

6. While it is true that in biblical Hebrew the prepositions (*'al*) and (*'el*) sometimes interchange with no appreciable change in meaning, this does not mean that they lost their semantic distinction. Furthermore, the phenomenon is more common in Samuel, Kings, Jeremiah, and Ezekiel than in Jonah or elsewhere in the Hebrew Bible. Therefore, unless sufficient evidence suggests otherwise, the normal semantic distinctions will be assumed for Jonah. For helpful discussions see BDB, 41, and Gary A. Rendsburg, "Some False Leads in the Identification of Late Biblical Hebrew Texts: The Cases of Genesis 24 and 1 Samuel 2:27 – 36," *JBL* 121 (2002): 36 n. 65.

Canonical and Practical Significance

Jonah, Peter, and the God of Second Chances

In Matthew 16:17 Jesus refers to Peter as "Simon son of Jonah," which suggests some connection between the apostle and the prophetic protagonist of the book of Jonah. Bible scholars remain uncertain, however, as to what connection Jesus had in mind.[7] Though some have suggested that "Jonah" is simply an abbreviated form of "John," the name normally assigned to Peter's biological father (John 1:42; 21:15 – 17), Gundry has effectively refuted this view. He argues persuasively that Jesus likely created a pun based on the name of Peter's father in order to call to mind the renegade OT prophet.[8]

One possible connection is that Jesus is referring to Peter's flight from his calling, which parallels Jonah's flight from his. Peter's threefold denial of Jesus is the culmination of a persistent rejection of Jesus' call to follow him to the cross. This rejection first surfaces in Matthew 16:22, where Peter rebukes Jesus for predicting that his ministry will end in his crucifixion — the same context in which Jesus refers to Peter as the "son of Jonah." Just like Jonah, Peter receives a second chance to submit to Jesus' commission to follow the way of the cross (John 21:15 – 19). Jonah and Peter alike are witnesses to the God of second chances.

Peter also parallels Jonah in that he was the first of the apostles to cross the Jew/Gentile boundary with the gospel (Acts 10). Like Jonah, Peter was initially resistant to God's call to enter the realm of the ceremonially unclean Gentiles. In fact, Peter had to see the vision of the blanket containing both clean and unclean animals three times before he was prepared to follow God's call to Cornelius's house (Acts 10:16).

Perhaps the greatest serendipity of all was the location where Peter received the vision. He was at Joppa on the roof of Simon the tanner's house (Acts 10:5 – 6). At the very port where Jonah fled the commission to go to Nineveh, Peter receives the commission to open the door of the church to the Gentiles. Jonah and Peter both share the distinction of breaking new ground in God's saving work.

Those who have been scandalized by the inclusiveness of God's mercy and have fled from sharing that mercy can take heart from Jonah's and Peter's shared experience. YHWH is a God of second chances, who patiently waits for his servants to embrace the call of his scandalous, inclusive mercy.

---

7. Powell, "Echoes of Jonah," 158.

8. Robert H. Gundry, *Matthew: A Commentary on His Handbook for a Mixed Church under Persecution* (2nd ed.; Grand Rapids: Eerdmans, 1994), 332 – 33. For the opposing view see R. T. France, *The Gospel of Matthew* (NICNT; Grand Rapids: Eerdmans, 2007), 620.

CHAPTER 5

Jonah 3:3c – 10

B. Responsiveness to and the Responsiveness of God's Mercy

Main Idea of the Passage

Despite the sinfulness of human agents, YHWH communicates his mercy, inspires repentance in the wickedest of sinners, and relents from his wrath.

Literary Context

Jonah 3:3c – 10e mirrors 1:4b – 2:1b [1:17b] in both structure and content. Both units contain important sequences of quoted speech (Jonah 1, dialogue between Jonah and sailors; Jonah 3, Jonah's announcement and the king's pronouncement). Both units recount how Gentiles respond favorably to YHWH. Finally, both units demonstrate how YHWH averts a crisis of judgment by relenting from his wrath. These correspondences reflect the parallelism that supports the structure of the entire book. The connections also invite the reader to interpret one episode in light of the other.

There are also important correlations between 3:3c – 10e and 2:1c – 11 [1:17c – 2:10]. Both sections feature a three-day journey. They both portray animals assisting in acts of repentance. Finally, both demonstrate YHWH's mercy toward those who are undeserving. These correspondences connect Jonah's experience of YHWH's mercy with Nineveh's experience of YHWH's mercy.

The alignment of chapters 2 and 3 is designed to make the point that a person like Jonah, who has received divine mercy, is in no position to begrudge its extension to others. Of course, as Jonah 4 demonstrates, Jonah fails to grasp this implication of his own experience. His deep-seated dislike for Assyria dilutes Jonah's experience of YHWH's mercy, preventing him from sharing YHWH's gracious disposition toward Nineveh. Thus, 3:3c – 10e also functions as an important literary bridge between

Jonah's two prayers. The events recounted in this episode explain why Jonah shifts from a prayer of thanksgiving (Jonah 2) to a prayer of complaint about the injustice of YHWH's saving mercy (4:1 – 4).

II. From Compliant Acceptance to Angry Resentment: The Offense of God's Mercy (3:1 – 4:11, Macro Unit 2)

   A. A Second Chance at Compliance with God's Mercy (3:1 – 3b, Stage setting)

→ **B. Responsiveness to and the Responsiveness of God's Mercy (3:3c – 10, Pre-peak episode)**

      1. The motives and methods of God's mercy (3:3c – 6)

      2. The goals of God's mercy (3:7 – 10)

   C. Resentment of God's Mercy (4:1 – 4, Peak episode)

   D. An Object Lesson on the Justice of Divine Mercy (4:5 – 11, Post-peak episode)

Translation and Outline

(See the next page.)

Structure and Literary Form

Jonah 3:3c – 10 divides into two sections, corresponding to the two formal announcements that punctuate the narrative with quoted speech. The first is Jonah's oracle of doom against Nineveh (3:4c). Though brief, this oracle serves as the center of gravity for the first subunit (3:3c – 6). Everything preceding the oracle sets the stage for Jonah's proclamation, and everything following it is a direct result of that oracle's impact. The emphasis in the first subunit is YHWH's method in communicating his concern for Nineveh. A description unfolds in narrative form of how YHWH operates through his human agents to deliver his word and spark citywide reform. This subunit displays the rhythm of announcement and response. Jonah delivers an announcement of doom, and Nineveh responds with repentance.

The second subunit (3:7 – 10) revolves around the king's edict for a citywide fast, the donning of sackcloth, prayer, and repentance from violence. The same pattern found in the preceding subunit organizes this one as well. Its content centers on the royal pronouncement, and it follows the rhythm of announcement and response. The king announces a citywide fast and requires the cessation of violence, and YHWH responds by graciously rescinding destruction.

In terms of form, 3:3c – 10 presents the reader with an interesting array of genres, including a prophetic oracle of doom against a foreign nation, a royal pronouncement,

Jonah 3:3c–103

B. Responsiveness to and the Responsiveness of God's Mercy (3:3b–10, Pre-peak episode)

1. The Motives and Methods of God's Mercy (3:3c-6)

3:3c	Now Nineveh was a great metropolis belonging to God.	a. God's sovereignty over Nineveh (3:3c)
3:3d	(It was) a three-day journey.	b. God's assessment of Nineveh (3:3d)
3:4a	Jonah had just begun making his way into the city, a single day's journey,	c. God's use of sinful human agents (3:4a-c)
3:4b	when he announced,	i. Jonah's minimal commitment (3:4a-b)
3:4c	Forty days until Nineveh is overturned.	ii. Jonah's meager message (3:4c)
3:5a	Then the men of Nineveh trusted God	d. God's dismantling of human hierarchies (3:5a-3:6)
3:5b	and announced a fast	i. The leveling effect of trust and repentance (3:5a-c)
3:5c	and wore sackcloth from the greatest of them to the least of them.	
3:6a	The message reached the king of Nineveh,	ii. God's humbling of the mighty through convicting
3:6b	and he arose from his throne	power of the word (3:6)
3:6c	and disrobed	
3:6d	and clothed himself with sackcloth	
3:6e	and sat upon the dust.	

2. The Goals of God's Mercy (3:7a-10)

3:7a	Then he issued a proclamation	a. A reclamation of politics for noble purposes (3:7a-b)
3:7b	and said in Nineveh by royal authority with the help of his officials,	b. The participation of all creation in redemption (3:7c)
3:7c	Both man and beast, both herds and flocks must taste nothing.	c. A restoration of sensitivity to and sorrow over sin (3:7d-8a)
3:7d	They must not graze.	
3:7d	They must not drink water.	
3:8a	They must cover themselves with sackcloth, both man and beast.	
3:8b	They must cry out to God earnestly.	d. A reform of integrity in prayer (3:8b)
3:8c	They must repent, each one, of his wicked behavior and the violence	e. A recommitment to genuine repentance (3:8c)
3:8d	that he performs with his own hands.	
3:9a	Who knows?	
3:9b	God may change his mind	
3:9c	and relent	
3:9d	and recover from his intense anger	f. A renewal of the knowledge of God's character (3:9a-c)
3:9e	so that we will not perish.	g. A recovery from divine wrath (3:9d)
3:10a	Then God saw their deeds,	h. A recovery from human fear of judgment and death (3:9e)
3:10b	that they repented of their wicked behavior.	i. The reconciliation of God to his creatures (3:10a-10e)
3:10c	So he relented concerning the disaster	i. God's recognition of repentance (3:10a-b)
3:10d	that he threatened to perform against them,	ii. God's reversal of the announcement of judgment (3:10c-e)
3:10e	and he did not do it.	

a prophetic account detailing Jonah's fulfillment of his commission, and an impressive conversion story. The interpreter's task is to discover how these genres interact so as to present a coherent narrative.

Up to this point, the book of Jonah has been shaped primarily by the genre "commission narrative." Once Jonah has accepted and obeys that commission, however, the commission narrative genre recedes into the background. It resurfaces in Jonah 4, when the reader finally hears Jonah's displaced verbal objection to the divine call, but it factors little in shaping the content and message of 3:3c – 10. The primary genre in the current episode is the prophetic account (see Introduction, pp. 36 – 37).

The other genres that appear in this episode play a supporting role to the prophetic account. Jonah's oracle of doom provides a foil for YHWH's demonstration of mercy; the king's royal edict demonstrates an exemplary use of political power for the purposes of ethical reform; and the story of Nineveh's conversion from violence sets the stage for YHWH's merciful rescinding of disaster.

Explanation of the Text

1. The Motives and Methods of God's Mercy (3:3c – 6)

a. God's Sovereignty over Nineveh (3:3c)

The narrative briefly pauses at the beginning of this unit as the author focuses on Nineveh. This focus is indicated by the placement of "Nineveh," the grammatical subject, in first position of the clause: "*Nineveh* was a great metropolis" (*wĕnînĕwēh hāyĕtâ ʿîr-gĕdôlâ*).

For the third time in the book, Nineveh is described as a great city. As noted in the comments on 1:2, where this description first occurs, the language echoes Sennacherib's effusive praise for his capital city. On YHWH's lips (1:2; 3:2) the description is a counterclaim to responsibility for the city's greatness. YHWH, not Sennacherib, is the reason for Nineveh's greatness.

The author underscores this point in 3:3c by adding the description: "Now Nineveh was a great metropolis *belonging to God*" (*lēʾlōhîm*). The prepositional phrase *lēʾlōhîm* (lit., "to God") has been interpreted in a wide variety of ways.[1] The most convincing interpretation is Sasson's suggestion that the preposition conveys possession or sover-

eignty.[2] The author makes the bold affirmation that Nineveh is not Sennacherib's city, nor Ishtar's city, but YHWH's city. Fundamentally, this is the reason for YHWH's interest in Nineveh. Of course, every city is under God's dominion. The implications of this truth, however, may not have been entirely grasped by Israel. Therefore, the truth bears repeating, especially in a context where its implications are emphasized.

The author is intentional in the use of the designation "God" (*ʾĕlōhîm*) rather than the divine name "YHWH." When narrating the story, the author refers to God as YHWH, unless God's interaction with Gentiles is in view.[3] In these cases, the author shifts to the designation "God" (*ʾĕlōhîm*). Jonah 3:3c is the first occasion the author has had to refer to Israel's deity in relation to Gentiles. Previous uses of the term *ʾĕlōhîm* (1:5, 6, 9; 2:2, 7) have either been with reference to deity in general ("a god" or "gods") or, if with reference to the God of Israel, have been modified by a possessive pronoun (1:6e, "your god," 2:2 "his god," 2:7 "my god"), indicating that it is not being used as a title or name.

Jonah 3:3c is, therefore, significant as the first

---

1. The most popular options are (1) that the phrase indicates Nineveh's function as a polytheistic cult center ("a great city to the gods"), (2) that the phrase functions as a superlative ("the greatest city"), and (3) that it expresses a dative of advantage ("an important city for God's purposes"). For a full discussion see Donald J. Wiseman, "Jonah's Nineveh," *TynBul* 30 (1979): 29 – 51; D. Winston Thomas, "A Consideration of Some Unusual Ways of Expressing the Superlative in Hebrew,"

VT 3 (1953): 209 – 24; and Stuart, *Hosea – Jonah*, 487.

2. Sasson, *Jonah*, 229.

3. Elizabeth Goldstein, "On the Use of the Name of God in the Book of Jonah," in *Milk and Honey: Essays on Ancient Israel and the Bible in Appreciation of the Judaic Studies Program at UCSD* (ed. Sarah Malena and David Miano; Winona Lake, IN: Eisenbrauns, 2007), 76.

example of the author's practice of always using "God" (*ʾĕlōhîm*) with reference to Israel's deity when discussing God's relationship with Gentiles. The practice underscores one of the book's main theological points. God's mercy is as broad as is his sovereignty. Though Jonah readily acknowledged God's sovereignty over all the earth (1:9), he struggled with the equally universal scope of God's mercy, once he realized that not even Assyria, Israel's dreaded enemy, was excluded.

b. God's Assessment of Nineveh (3:3d)

The author proceeds to describe Nineveh with the clause "(It was) a three-day journey." Interpreters continue to struggle to understand the precise meaning of this awkward and somewhat esoteric phrase. The traditional understanding that the expression refers to the city's great size makes the most sense in context. The description appears to be an exaggeration of Nineveh's breadth. The author's purpose for employing such an exaggeration, however, may be to indicate the city's condition in relation to its size. Nineveh's great size was matched by its great wickedness, ultimately leading to a great, cataclysmic disaster.

The reference to "three-day journey" recalls Jonah's journey in the fish's belly and evokes again images of death and destruction.[4] The phrase "three-day journey," therefore, may be intended to indicate the city's proximity to destruction. Nineveh symbolically bordered on the netherworld because of the unrestrained cruelty of her people. The expression, therefore, serves as YHWH's assessment of Nineveh's precarious condition.

c. God's Use of Sinful Human Agents (3:4)

Jonah 3:4a resumes the narrative with a sequence of three *wayyiqtol* verbs, all of which have Jonah as their subject (lit.): "Jonah began ... he announced and said" (*wayyāḥel yônâ ... wayyiqrāʾ wayyōʾmar*). The first of these is followed by an infinitive clause "to enter" (*lābôʾ*) and an appositive "a single day's journey" (*mahălak yôm ʾeḥād*), placing particular emphasis on Jonah's entrance into the city.

When the verb "he had ... begun" (*wayyāḥel*) is succeeded by an infinitive, the construction usually conveys the onset of a process, emphasizing its duration (cf. Num 25:1; Judg 16:22; 2 Chr 3:1 – 2). In this case, the combination of clauses "he began to enter ... and proclaimed and said ..." places the timing of Jonah's pronouncement immediately upon his arrival. A comparable English idiom would be "Jonah had *just* begun making his way into the city, a single day's journey, when he proclaimed and said...."[5]

A second indication of timing follows with the appositive "a single day's journey" (*mahălak yôm ʾeḥād*). Using the exaggerated scale of Nineveh's three-day breadth, the author emphasizes the limited distance Jonah traveled when he issued his fateful announcement. Jonah's one-day journey contrasts markedly with the description of Nineveh as a three-day journey (*mahălak šĕlōšet yāmîm*). Given this estimate of the time required to traverse the city, Jonah didn't even reach the city's center.[6] The author's emphasis on the timing and location of the oracle's delivery suggests Jonah's reticence to canvas the city. This impression is later

---

4. Landes, "The 'Three Days and Three Nights' Motif," 449.

5. Sasson, *Jonah*, 231.

6. For well-researched estimations of the layout of cities, see Stephen Lumsden, "The Production of Space at Nineveh," *Nineveh: Papers of the XLIXe Rencontre Assyirologique Interna-tionale* (ed. Dominique Collon and Andrew George; London:

British School of Archeology in Iraq, 2005), 1:191, and Julian Reade, "The Ishtar Temple at Nineveh," *Nineveh: Papers of the XLIXe Rencontre Assyriologique Internationale* (ed. Dominique Collon and Andrew George; London: British School of Archeology in Iraq, 2005), 2:348.

confirmed by the phrase "the message reached the king" (*wayyiggaʿ haddābār ʾel-melek*, 3:6), which indicates the king's second-hand knowledge of the oracle by virtue of the citizens' reaction.[7]

The narrative pauses for the quotation of Jonah's oracle; note the direct discourse marker "and he said" (*wayyōʾmar*). The announcement itself is remarkably terse, consisting of a temporal phrase followed by a verbless clause (noun + participle): "Forty days until Nineveh is overturned" (*ʿôd ʾarbāʿîm yôm wĕninĕwēh nehpāket*). The initial temporal phrase stands outside of the sentence structure as indicated by its separation from the clause by the *waw* conjunction prefixed to "Nineveh."[8] This placement suggests that the temporal phrase is the focus of the oracle, emphasizing the amount of time Nineveh has to respond.[9] This appears to be the one indication of hope for Nineveh, and it may have served as the motivation for the people's efforts to forestall the portended disaster.

Aspects of Jonah's delivery of the oracle underscore the prophet's ambivalence toward his task. For example, indications of the message's divine origin are conspicuously absent. Prophets were normally careful about validating their oracles by punctuating them with statements like "thus says YHWH" (*kōh ʾāmar yhwh*) or "YHWH's oracle" (*nĕʾum yhwh*). Jonah, however, has included no such marks of validation.[10] Their absence is not likely due to the fact that Jonah addressed an audience unacquainted with YHWH. Moses addressed a similar audience and yet was careful to indicate his message's divine origin (Exod 4:22; 5:1; 7:17; 8:1, 20 [5, 24]; 9:1, 13; 10:3).

It is also odd that the oracle includes no indication of the grounds for the judgment, especially in light of the fact that YHWH indicated the reason in the original commission (1:2). Furthermore, Jonah gives no indication of what action might be taken in order to avert the predicted fate. Both of these elements are typical features of doom oracles against a foreign nation.[11] These omissions raise the suspicions that Jonah's obedience is not all that it appears to be and that he may not have repeated the divine message exactly as he received it.

Two aspects of Jonah's proclamation require further explanation. The first is the forty-day time frame. Jonah's first readers would have likely recognized the symbolism of a forty-day period. Two episodes from the Pentateuch are suggestive of the number's significance: the flood narrative (Gen 6 – 9) and Moses' intercession for Israel after her sin with the golden calf (Exod 34:28; Deut 9:28 – 25). Both passages occur in the context of a judgment involving a forty-day period. Furthermore, in both passages a great population (human and animal) are in jeopardy.

Jonah's oracle recalls the flood narrative in order to remind readers of the universal scope of YHWH's moral governance. The statement of humanity's depraved condition in Gen 6:5 serves as an apt summary of Nineveh's moral state at the time of Jonah's proclamation and confirms the basis of YHWH's threatened action. By recalling the flood narrative, Jonah's oracle revisits a time when Israel did not exist and YHWH dealt directly with all humanity. The allusion serves as a reminder that Israel's story begins, not with Israel, but with God, the creator of all, who formed a covenant with all humanity (Gen 6:18; 9:9 – 17). It also serves as a reminder of the goal of YHWH's covenant with

---

7. Sasson, *Jonah*, 247.

8. Tucker, *Jonah*, 70.

9. Waltke and O'Connor, *Introduction to Biblical Hebrew Syntax*, 76 – 77.

10. Trible, "Jonah," 7:511.

11. Sweeney, *Isaiah 1 – 39*, 23 – 24.

Israel — universal blessing administered by God's elect people (Gen 12:1 – 3; Isa 49:1 – 6).

The allusion to Moses' intercession for Israel when YHWH is about to exterminate the entire nation for their idolatry with the golden calf suggests that the forty-day period affords the opportunity for supplication. Moses remained prostrate before YHWH for the entire duration of the time span, receiving neither food nor water as he pleaded with YHWH on Israel's behalf (Exod 34:28; Deut 9:9). From an Israelite perspective, this role belongs to Jonah. He is the prophet and, like Moses, should intercede on behalf of those whom YHWH has threatened to judge. Jonah, however, does not do this. He will eventually pray, but his prayer is a complaint that YHWH has failed to destroy Nineveh, not a petition that God might spare Nineveh. The citizens of Nineveh had to petition God for themselves, and, as indicated in the royal pronouncement, they, like Moses, deprive themselves and their animals of food and water during their supplications.

Considered together, the allusions to the flood and to Moses' intercession for Israel suggested by the forty-day period of Jonah's oracle present to the citizens of Nineveh two possible fates.[12] On the one hand, in the event that they fail to heed God's warning and continue in their great wickedness, the forty-day period would symbolize doom as in the flood. On the other hand, in the event they respond to God's warning with repentance, the forty days would symbolize the possibility of a rescinding of annihilation as in the case of Moses' intercession of Israel at Sinai.

The next aspect to consider in Jonah's doom oracle is the intriguing verb he uses to describe Nineveh's projected destruction. Jonah warned that the city "will be overturned" (*nehpāket*).[13] The verb "overturn" (*hāpak*) recalls the destruction of Sodom and Gomorrah as the historical precedent for God's response to extreme wickedness and, by association with this context, clearly conveys the possibility of annihilation (Gen 19:21, 25, 29).

The verb "overturn" (*hāpak*), however, also carries the sense "to change/reform," which opens the possibility of the alternate interpretation: "Forty days until Nineveh is reformed."[14] It is possible, therefore, that Jonah's oracle contained ambiguity. Like the forty-day time frame, the verb portending Nineveh's destruction suggested two possible fates: destruction by a physical overturning of the city, or reformation by an ethical overturning of the citizen's behavior.[15]

Ambiguity is not unknown in Israelite prophecy, and it was occasionally used to ensnare those who had turned their hearts against God (cf. Judg 18:6; 1 Kgs 22:15).[16] In these other examples, the ambiguity is primarily directed to the recipient of the prophecy as a means of exposing recalcitrance toward God. In Jonah 3:4c, however, the ambiguity appears to be aimed at the prophet himself, in order to expose Jonah's bitterness toward Assyria.

If this is the word YHWH used when he gave this message to Jonah in 3:2d, Jonah may have

---

12. Erik Eynikel, "One Day, Three Days, and Forty Days in the Book of Jonah," *One Text, A Thousand Methods: Studies in Memory of Sjef van Tilborg* (ed. Sjef van Tilborg, Ulrich Berges, and Patrick Chatellion Counet; Leiden: Brill, 2004), 76.

13. Arnold and Choi, *Guide to Biblical Hebrew Syntax*, 81.

14. *HALOT* 1 (Study Edition), 253.

15. Eynikel, "One Day, Three Days, and Forty Days," 75.

16. Daniel I. Block, "What Has Delphi to Do with Samaria? Ambiguity and Delusion in Israelite Prophecy," *Writing and Ancient Near Eastern Society: Papers in Honour of Alan R. Millard* (ed. Piotr Bienkowski, Christopher Mee, and Elizabeth Slater; London: T&T Clark, 2005), 189 – 216. Block notes the lack of a messenger formula or an oracular formula in the two ambiguous oracles he examines. Interestingly, Jonah's oracle also lacks these indications of the message's divine origin.

made his journey to Nineveh under the impression that Nineveh's destruction was inevitable. The impression, however, was not created by YHWH, but by Jonah's own deep desire to see Assyria destroyed. Jonah's impression of the second commission, therefore, may have differed from his impression of the first. The first time YHWH commissioned Jonah, the prophet suspected that the reason for condemning Nineveh was to grant an opportunity for repentance (cf. 4:1 – 4). The second commission, however, may have diminished these concerns largely because of Jonah's association of the verb "overturn" with the destruction of Sodom and Gomorrah. If the purpose of the mission was simply to announce Nineveh's certain doom, then Jonah could reconcile himself to the unpleasant task of prophesying in Assyria. The stage is thus set for Jonah's furious response to Nineveh's repentance and YHWH's clemency.

d. God's Dismantling of Human Hierarchies (3:5 – 6)

The plotline resumes in 3:5 with a series of ten narrative verbs (3:5 – 7b). The first three have the "men of Nineveh" as their subject. Attention shifts abruptly from Jonah, who plays no further role in the scene, and focuses on the citizens' remarkable response to God's warning. Despite the shortcomings of the prophet and of his delivery of the message, the oracle's effects were immediate and impressive: "The men of Nineveh trusted God."

The verb that describes the audience's response to Jonah, "they trusted God" (*wayya'ămînû … bĕ'lōhîm*) recalls the exemplary faith of Abraham, who similarly "believed God," with the result that YHWH regarded him as just (Gen 15:6). The idiom conveys a trust that relies on what another has said

and leads the one trusting to act accordingly.[17] The allusion to Gen 15:6 reminds readers that Abraham exemplified the kind of faith that pleases God prior to the covenant of circumcision; this suggests that such faith is possible on the part of Gentiles and that such faith existed prior to the creation of Israel. The reader's thoughts are directed once again back to Genesis and back to the universal scope of God's plans for his covenant people.

While the text does not go so far as to say that the citizens of Nineveh converted to the monotheistic worship of YHWH, it certainly points in the direction of the Gentiles' inclusion in God's covenant. Furthermore, the text hints that YHWH was working toward this goal very early in redemptive history. In fact, nothing can account for Nineveh's surprising receptivity other than God's preparation for this moment. Whether through omens,[18] or through the waning of Assyrian power, or through a sensitizing of conscience, or a combination of these factors, God apparently had been laying the foundation for the groundswell of repentance that erupted in response to Jonah's announcement. Not wanting to distract from the wonder of such thorough and widespread repentance, however, the author spends no time speculating about the reasons.

God launches the reform among the common people, "the men" of the city. From this humble beginning, God brings about mass contrition with fasting (*ṣôm*) and the donning of sackcloth (*wayyilbĕšû śaqqîm*). The rituals extended "from the greatest to the least" (*miggĕdôlām wĕ'ad-qĕṭannām*). A remarkable effect of the citywide fast is that it removed all external indications of status. Everyone was humbled and clothed with sackcloth. God affected an "overturning" of Nineveh's hierarchy.

---

17. *HALOT* (Study Edition), 1:64.

18. Stuart, *Hosea – Jonah*, 490 – 91. Stuart offers a long list of reasons why Nineveh in the early eighth century might have been so receptive to a prophet like Jonah, all of them related in one way or another to the disastrous reign of Ashshur Dan III (773 – 756 BC).

This emphasis is confirmed in the next paragraph, when Jonah's message "reached" (*wayyigga' ... 'el*) the king of Nineveh (3:6a). A shift occurs in the narrative as attention moves from the citizens to their leader. The initial narrative verb in the new paragraph, however, has "the message" (*haddābār*) as its subject rather than the king. The author highlights the agency of the message itself before proceeding to the royal response for two possible reasons. First, the author may be reinforcing that Jonah was no longer participating in Nineveh's reform. The message reached the king independently of the prophet, whose single-day venture into the city was over. Second, the author may be highlighting YHWH's oversight of the message. YHWH ensured that his message reached the king even without Jonah's full cooperation.

The verb in this clause combines with a preposition (*wayyigga' ... 'el*) to form an idiom that means "to extend to, reach, or touch (in a tactile sense)."[19] The author gives the impression that the king joined the fast after the citizens had already initiated it. This would represent a significant departure from the norm since the king usually initiated such religious activities in the ancient Near East.[20] His contribution is a royal proclamation institutionalizing the spontaneous moral reform.

The designation "the king of Nineveh" is unprecedented in both biblical and Mesopotamian literature. One would expect the monarch to be called "the king of Assyria," as encountered elsewhere in the Old Testament (2 Kgs 15:19 – 29; 16:7 – 18; 17:24 – 27; Isa 7:17 – 20, etc.). Typically, such unexpected expressions in the book of Jonah serve the author's rhetorical purpose. Such is the case with the phrase "king of Nineveh."[21]

The odd expression has two significant rhetorical effects. First, the designation undermines Assyrian imperialistic rhetoric by treating the ruler as king of a mere city-state. In keeping with his emphasis on the humbling effects of God's salvation and God's dismantling of human hierarchies, the author minimizes the king's stature, importance, and realm of influence. The author gives him a designation befitting a client king or vassal, emphasizing his subordination to his overlord, God, to whom Nineveh belongs.[22] A similar phenomenon occurs in passages like 1 Kgs 21:1 (cf. 2 Kgs 1:3), where Ahab is disparagingly called "king of Samaria" as a means of diminishing his significance and asserting his subordination to YHWH despite his autonomous behavior. Perhaps the best example of this technique is Isa 7:8 – 9a.

> For the head of Aram is Damascus,
>   and the head of Damascus is only Rezin.
> Within sixty-five years
>   Ephraim will be too shattered to be a people.
> The head of Ephraim is Samaria,
>   and the head of Samaria is only Remaliah's
>   son. (NIV)

---

19. Sasson, *Jonah*, 248.

20. Throughout Mesopotamia, kings served not only as the chief political figure but also as the chief religious functionary as well assuming such titles as *sanga*, meaning "chief accountant of the temple" and *en* meaning high priest. See Karen Rhea Nemet-Nejat, *Daily Life in Ancient Mesopotamia* (Peabody, MA: Hendrickson, 2002), 217.

21. Attempts to explain this phrase on historical/philological grounds, while informative and often ingenious, are still speculative and unconvincing. For a recent example of such an attempt as well as a review of other explanations, see Paul Ferguson, "Who Was the 'King of Nineveh' in Jonah 3:6?" *TynBul* 47 (1996): 301 – 14.

22. Esarhaddon's vassal treaties are instructive with regard to how Assyrians referred to vassals in these documents. For example, Ramataya is referred to as "city-ruler of Urakaza-banu," while Esarhaddon refers to himself as "king of the world." Such texts emphasized the insignificance of the vassal's kingdom compared to that of the overlord. See James Maxwell Miller and John H. Hayes, *A History of Ancient Israel and Judah* (Louisville: Westminster John Knox, 1986), 373.

YHWH offered Ahaz perspective regarding the threats of Ephraim and Aram, two kingdoms that had joined forces against Ahaz. In each case YHWH referred to the respective kingdoms first by nation, then by capital city, and finally by the individual king. The effect was to whittle the threat down to size and to make these two "smoldering firebrands" appear less formidable. In the light of YHWH's sovereignty these two kings are merely men enthroned over cities and answerable to God, the ruler of all creation.

The second rhetorical effect is that the designation "king of Nineveh" recalls the title "king of Sodom" and thus reinforces the association between Nineveh and Sodom, already established by Jonah's oracle. Sodom's fate was a real possibility for Nineveh as God moved in judgment against this wicked city. Once again, the author recalls stories from Genesis relating YHWH's dealings with humanity before Israel entered the picture, thus reminding his readers of the universal scope of YHWH's redemptive activity.

In response to the news of Jonah's proclamation and the growing response among his subjects, the king of Nineveh humbled himself in four steps, marked by a series of four narrative verb forms (*wayyāqom/wayyaʿăbēr/wayěkas/wayyēšeb*). First he rose from this throne, relinquishing the trappings of his royal authority. Next he removed his robe, signifying his wealth and prestige, and replaced it with sackcloth. Finally, he joined the rest of Nineveh in the dust, adding his pleas for mercy

to theirs. At the end of this process, the king was indistinguishable from the people. God's dismantling of human power structures was complete. The inversion of Nineveh's hierarchy is highlighted by the inverted structure by which the author describes the king's penitence:

  A   he arose from his throne
    B   he removed his robe
    B´   he donned sackcloth
  A´   he sat in the dust[23]

2. The Goals of God's Mercy (3:7 – 10)

The king moves beyond personal repentance and issues a pronouncement demanding citywide participation in repentance and prayer to God. Significantly, the pronouncement climaxes with the addition of a new element to the ritual acts mentioned so far — renouncing wickedness and violence. This marks a clear break from the typical Assyrian practice of diverting divine wrath by the manipulative means of ritual or divination.[24] Other Assyrian pronouncements exist that call for public mourning and fasting for the sake of appeasing an angry deity, but calls for ethical change are rare in the vast collection of Assyrian royal pronouncements.[25]

The placement of the king's pronouncement in Jonah 3 is curious. The author includes it after the acts of contrition, which indicates that it followed sequentially the citizens' response to Jonah's oracle.[26] One wonders why the pronouncement

---

23. Trible, *Rhetorical Criticism*, 183.

24. John H. Walton, *Ancient Near Eastern Thought and the Old Testament* (Grand Rapids: Baker, 2006), 248.

25. Ibid., 246 – 48; Wiseman, "Jonah's Nineveh," 51.

26. Sasson, *Jonah*, 247. I disagree with the judgment of Wolff and Heimerdinger, who argue that the royal pronouncement has been temporally displaced and that the narrative verb forms (*wayyiqtol*) in 3:6 – 9 should be understood as pluperfects. First, it would be unprecedented for such a lengthy sequence of narrative verbs to take on such an unusual nuance without some kind of formal syntactical marking. Second, their justification for this conclusion is based on a misunderstanding of the rhetorical significance of 3:5c "from the greatest of them to the least of them." They take this to be an indication of sequence when in fact it is simply an indication of the scope of Nineveh's response and of the leveling effect of Jonah's prophecy. See Wolff, *Obadiah and Jonah*, 145; Heimerdinger, *Topic, Focus, and Foreground*, 87.

is necessary if repentance is already in progress. Three observations are pertinent regarding the pronouncement's function within the episode. First, the pronouncement comes after repentance has already begun in order to emphasize that the royal proclamation is not the impetus for the demonstrations of contrition. This distinction belongs solely to YHWH's word through Jonah.

Second, the pronouncement enhances Nineveh's repentance by adding two elements not mentioned before. The king adds, "They must repent, each one, of his wicked behavior and the violence that he performs with his own hands." It was appropriate that this aspect of the repentance had to wait until the royal pronouncement, since maintaining justice and peace fell within the responsibilities of the king. The other addition is the requirement that animals participate in the acts of contrition. The extent of the repentance is taken to the extreme in the royal pronouncement and emphasizes the thoroughness of Nineveh's response to God.

The third observation is that the pronouncement functioned as assurance that the repentance was recognized by God as a communal act of the city. The declaration of judgment was directed to the city; thus, it was appropriate that the penitents respond officially as a city. The king's power was the best instrument for such a response. Furthermore, the pronouncement ensured that any who had not yet joined the effort would do so once it became a matter of official state policy.

The pronouncement's wording is significant at a number of points. It is introduced by an extended indication of quoted speech: "He ... said in Nineveh by royal authority with the help of his of-ficials...." This lengthy preface raises the question as to precisely where the pronouncement itself begins.[27] Typically, when Hebrew introduces a quotation with three different indicators of direct speech ("He *cried out* and *spoke ... saying*"), the quote begins immediately after the third indicator, "saying" (*lēʾmōr*).[28] Such is the case here.

The verb "he issued a proclamation" (*wayyazʿēq*, Hiphil) is from the same root as the verb that describes the mariners' frantic appeals (*wayyizʿāqû*, Qal) in 1:5b. This link serves to connect the two episodes. The mariners foreshadow the citizens of Nineveh in terms of exemplary piety, and the author invites comparison by means of this verbal echo.

The phrases "by royal authority" (*miṭṭaʿam hammelek*) and "with the help of his officials" (*ûgĕdôlāyw*) indicate that the statement bears the full weight of the municipal government. The word for "authority" (*ṭaʿam*) anticipates the king's prohibition of food by means of a pun with the verb "to taste" (*ṭāʿam*), which occurs later in the pronouncement. In fact, the two words appear to derive from the same root.

The initial words of the pronouncement are shocking to modern ears. This royal edict is addressed to both humans and animals! In fact, the term for animals is further modified by "herds and flocks" — all domesticated animals that would be present in the city. The same phrase recurs in 3:8 following the verb "cover oneself" (*wĕyitkassû*). Thus it is emphasized that even animals must participate in the fast.

The king's inclusion of animals in the penitential rites has long puzzled readers of Jonah. It makes lit-

---

27. The decree could be understood to begin with the words "in Nineveh," with the two verbs "he announced and said" (*wayyazʿēq wayyōʾmer*) introducing the quotation.(Sasson, *Jonah*, 253). The quotation could begin immediately after the proper noun Nineveh (W. Rudolph, *Joel-Amos-Obadjah-Jonah* [KAT 13.2; Gütersloh: Gerd Mohn, 1971], 323 – 71). Or, the quotation could begin immediately after the infinitive "saying," following the introduction of the king and his officials as the speakers (Miller, *The Representation of Speech*, 196 – 97).

28. Miller, *The Representation of Speech*, 196 – 97.

tle sense to impose this pronouncement on animals that are not morally responsible. The participation of animals in Nineveh's repentance, however, should be viewed in light of the larger role that creation plays throughout the book. Jonah was saved from drowning by a fish that Yahweh commanded to vomit the prophet onto shore (2:11). Similarly, the wind, the plant, and the worm all functioned as Yahweh's compliant appointees in chapter 4. All of this serves to underscore the biting irony that non-human creation is more responsive to God than his own people (cf., e.g., Isa 1:1 – 3).[29] Throughout the book, animals serve as both agents of God's salvation and models of compliance to his will.[30]

The inclusion of the animals in the fast may recall the flood narrative, in which animals along with humans were spared by God's mercy. Indeed, not only do animals share in the deliverance in the biblical account (Gen 6 – 9), but in the Akkadian flood story (Atra-Ḥasis), as well.[31]

The pronouncement is divided into two balanced parts; note the repeated mention of the addressees "both man and beast" (vv. 7c, 8a). The first part consists of prohibitions from food and water expressed in a string of prohibitions (lit., "Let them not taste … let them not graze … let them not drink"). This fast was extreme and exceeded typical fasting practices. It is comparable only to Moses' forty-day deprivation on top of Mount Sinai (Deut 9:9, 18), when he pleaded to God for Israel's survival.

The second part of the pronouncement balances the first with a string of three positive commands ("They must cover themselves with sackcloth … cry out to God … [and] repent"). The king's second injunctive that everyone, man and beast alike, "must cry out to God earnestly" (*wĕyiqrĕʾû ʾel-ʾĕlōhîm bĕḥāzĕqâ*) recalls the helmsman's exhortation to Jonah, "cry out to your god" (*qĕrāʾ ʾel-ʾĕlōheykā*). This verbal correlation emphasizes the parallel roles that each of these characters plays. Each is the leader of his community, and each one issues a command to pray. It further underscores a contrast between Jonah and the Gentiles that began in Jonah 1. The objects of the king's command were responsive to his exhortation to "cry out." Jonah, however, was apparently unresponsive to the helmsman's exhortation.

The king's final command leaves the realm of ritual and enters the realm of ethical transformation. It is ironic to hear the prophetic ideal of ethical repentance expressed so eloquently by an Assyrian king, especially one contemporary with the wicked reign of Jeroboam II (cf. 1 Kgs 14:24; Amos 5:24).

The declaration's postscript offers a rationale for the preceding commands. It begins with the rhetorical question "who knows" (*mî-yôdēaʿ*), which acknowledges the divine freedom to relent or to proceed with the planned disaster. This text joins with other Old Testament passages in acknowledging divine freedom and, therefore, the uncertainty of outcomes in petitions for clemency.[32] The rhetorical question arises in most cases out of an

---

29. Fretheim, *The Message of Jonah*, 111.

30. Yael Shemesh, "'And Many Beasts' (Jonah 4:11): The Function and Status of Animals in the Book of Jonah," *JHS* 10 (2010): 5 – 8. Shemesh helpfully categorizes various roles that animals play in biblical narratives and then applies these categories to the book of Jonah. The results are illuminating and bring order to an otherwise unwieldy and confusing subject. Among the categories Shemesh names are agent of salvation, didactic model, and fellow petitioner for divine mercy, all of

which are relevant to the uses of animals in Jonah.

31. "Atra-Ḥasis," trans. Benjamin R. Foster (*COS* 1.130, 450 – 452), note esp. ii 30 – ii 40.

32. James Crenshaw, "The Expression *mî yôdēaʿ* in the Hebrew Bible," *VT* 36 (1986): 276. According to Crenshaw, out of a total of ten occurrences of the rhetorical question, in only five is the possibility of changing God's plan entertained. Furthermore, in only two of these (Jonah 3:9; Esth 4:14) does the change actually occur.

understanding of the interplay between divine mercy, which predisposes God to forgive, and divine justice, which frees God from any obligation to forgive in response to repentance.[33]

Jonah 3:9, however, is unique in that this text is the only one of the ten occurrences of this rhetorical question in which the speaker is a Gentile. Furthermore, it is one of only two occurrences where the desired change in God's plan actually occurs. The point is that the king is careful not to misrepresent these acts of repentance as requiring God to relent from judgment. It is an admission that, if any change occurs, it will be on the basis of God's gratuitous mercy. Quite out of character for an Assyrian king, this monarch renounces manipulative motives and embraces repentance for its own sake, regardless of the outcome. The helmsman in 1:6 employed a similar expression after his exhortation to Jonah: "Perhaps the deity will consider our plight." The key word is "perhaps" (*'ûlay*), which likewise hinted at God's freedom.

The structure of the postscript parallels that of the two parts of the pronouncement by attributing three actions to God that mirror the three prohibitions and the three commands imposed on the city. The king says, "[He] may change his mind and relent and recover from his intense anger." The first of these verbs "he may change his mind" (*yāšûb*) matches the one the king used in 3:8c with reference to the citizens' repentance, suggesting a close relationship between the citizens' reform and God's relenting. Though repentance in no way guarantees divine mercy, it does stand in close relationship to divine mercy in two respects. First, demonstrations of divine mercy frequently inspire repentance. In this case, God's warning through Jonah demonstrated his hesitancy to punish Nineveh without due warning and opportunity for repentance.

Second, God has proven that, in his mercy, he is responsive to repentance, especially when that repentance is characterized by humility.

The second of these closely paired verbs, "he may relent" (*wĕniḥam*), occurs frequently in contexts where God plans one course of action but then alters his plan in response to human behavior (Gen 6:6; Exod 32:14; Judg 2:18; 1 Sam 15:11, 35; 2 Sam 24:16). As these passages demonstrate, the change can either be in the direction of mercy or in the direction of judgment, depending on the situation.

The third action is God's recovery from his fierce anger (*wĕšāb mēḥărôn 'appô*). The verb here is the same as the one in 3:9b, though in a slightly different form. This time it is followed by the prepositional phrase "from his intense anger." The king expresses the hope that as Nineveh turns (*yāšubû*) from her wickedness (3:8c), God will turn (*yāšûb*) from his wrath. The postscript closes with the desired outcome: "so that we will not perish."

Jonah 3:10 resumes the narrative with a sequence of two *wayyiqtol* verbs, both of which have God as their subject "God saw ... and he relented" (*wayyar' hā'ĕlōhîm ... wayyinnāḥem hā'ĕlōhîm*). The initial verb is followed by both a direct object and an object clause, "their deeds, that they repented of their wicked behavior" (*ma'ăśêhem*). The author thus places special emphasis on the people's ethical reform. God was attentive to the people's efforts to change their behavior and hopefully their fate. Significantly, the author omits any mention of the fasting and the sackcloth. It was not their rituals that caught God's attention but their ethical transformation (cf. Joel 2:13). Nineveh's repentance extended to attitudes and actions. By contrast, Jonah's repentance focused on sacrifices and vows (2:10).

---

33. Ibid, 275.

The prepositional phrase "of their wicked behavior" (*middarkām hārāʿâ*) is significant because it contains the word "evil," which continues to punctuate the narrative. It recalls the motive clause following YHWH's initial commission: "because their evil has ascended before me" (1:2d). The evil that prompted this entire venture was abandoned in repentance.

God responded to Nineveh's repentance by relenting from the disaster he had threatened. The word "disaster" (*hārāʿâ*) is the same Hebrew word the author used in the preceding clause with reference to the evil from which Nineveh turned. It is also the word the author used to describe the terrible storm at sea that threatened the lives of the ship's crew. Here it occurs with reference to the disaster from which God turned. God's actions reflect Nineveh's action in a remarkable way. They repented of their "evil," and God relented concerning the "evil" that he had planned for them.

God's dealings with humanity should never be reduced to simplistic retributive formulas. The author emphasizes this with respect to God's threatened judgment. He states God "relented concerning the disaster *that he threatened*." The last phrase in that sentence (*ʾăšer-dibber*) stresses God's freedom with respect to the prophetic word. God's pronouncements through his prophets do not obligate him to courses of action from which he cannot turn.

The unit closes with a restatement of God's relenting from his wrath: "and he did not do it" (*wĕlōʾ ʿāśâ*). The narrative expresses God's clemency both positively and negatively, thus conforming to the wording of the royal decree ("God may change his mind, and relent [*wĕniḥam*] ... so that we will not perish" [*wĕlōʾ nōʾbēd*]). Normally, negative clauses in Hebrew narrative function as background, scene-setting devices and are relegated to the lowest rank of significance. In certain contexts, however, the fact that an event did not materialize is so critical to the plot that the negative clause receives prominence.[34] Such is the case with 3:10e, which functions as a second rank clause, directly supporting the preceding narrative verb (*wayyinnāḥem*).[35]

Canonical and Practical Significance

The Relationship between Divine Mercy and Human Repentance

Jonah's oracle, despite its brevity, sparks a remarkable movement of contrition and repentance that can only be attributed to God's mercy. The immediacy and thoroughness of the citizens' response stresses the power of God's word to inspire reform even on such a large scale as the great metropolis of Nineveh.

Furthermore, the fact that this narrative applies similar terminology to God's relenting from disaster as it does to human repentance from moral wrong suggests a significant connection between the two. God is responsive to human repentance because of his mercy.

At the same time, the narrative carefully avoids compromising divine freedom

---

34. Robert Longacre, *Joseph: A Story of Divine Providence* (Winona Lake, IN: Eisenbrauns, 2003), 82.

35. Ibid.

in any way. Though God's change of course from judgment to mercy was motivated by Nineveh's repentance, it was in no way *necessitated* by that repentance (3:9). God is presented as free both with regard to human repentance and with regard to the prophetic word. Neither human repentance nor the prophetic word forces God into a course of action. Thus, Jonah 3 provides a clear illustration of the principle expressed in Jer 18:7 – 10:

> If at any time I announce that a nation or kingdom is to be uprooted, torn down and destroyed, and if that nation I warned repents of its evil, then I will relent and not inflict on it the disaster I had planned. And if at another time I announce that a nation or kingdom is to be built up and planted, and if it does evil in my sight and does not obey me, then I will reconsider the good I had threatened to do for it. (NIV)

One should not, however, interpret God's freedom with regard to the divine word as implying any inefficacy with regard to that word or caprice on God's part. Whether Nineveh repents and is spared, or does not and is destroyed, the divine word is effective and vindicated. This is evident in two ways in the narrative. First, the narrative refuses to give any credit for Nineveh's repentance to secondary causes. While the curious reader may wish to know what providential circumstances inclined the proud and wicked Assyrians to respond so readily, the narrative keeps the reader's attention firmly fixed on the divine word as the only cause. Nineveh's remarkable repentance is therefore attributable to nothing but the power of God's word.

Second, the ambiguity of the oracle itself, expressed in the term "overturn" (*nehpāket*), indicates that the prophetic word is capable of generating multiple possibilities. The oracle's ambiguity serves two important theological purposes. On the one hand, it serves to express both God's justice and his mercy. Associations of the verb "overturn" with judgment revealed that God would not sit idly by and allow Nineveh to continue in her wickedness with impunity. At the same time, however, the verb's associations with reform and transformation indicate God's willingness to give Nineveh opportunity to repent and his willingness to respond favorably to that repentance.

On the other hand, the ambiguity of the verb "overturn" communicates a different message to Jonah than it does to Nineveh. In chapter 4, Jonah apparently picks up only on the destructive sense of the verb "overturn" and is therefore disappointed, even angry, that Nineveh's destruction did not follow. He suspected this might happen when he first received the divine commission. When YHWH gave him this message in the second commission (3:2d), however, Jonah understood the oracle to speak only of judgment and hoped that his errand was merely one of ensuring that the Assyrians knew the reason for Nineveh's certain demise. The oracle's ambiguity, therefore, exposes Jonah's heart to himself and to the reader, which brings the real issue out into the open where God can address it.

The citizens of Nineveh, however, recognize in the oracle the possibility of repentance and of forestalling the announced doom. Nineveh and her king understand both meanings and thus act accordingly. The oracle's ambiguity thus also reveals the hearts of the citizens and king of Nineveh, who are surprisingly receptive to the terse and unqualified proclamation. The contrast between the receptive, compliant people of Nineveh and the resentful, surly prophet is obvious and telling. Furthermore, the stage is set for God's dramatic demonstration of his own change of course when he shows clemency to Nineveh.

God's Ability and Willingness to Change his Mind

This last point of God's willingness and ability to change course raises another important theological issue. One can certainly feel the tension with regard to the clear teaching of this text that God can and does on occasion relent and change his plan with passages that declare the opposite (e.g., 1 Sam 15:29; Jer 4:28; 15:6; 20:16). Twenty-seven times the OT declares that God changes his mind about a chosen course of action. But on nine occasions it declares that he does not change his mind.[36] Believers tend to stress one of these affirmations to the neglect of the other. The biblical text, however, confronts the reader with both realities and demands that both be taken into account when relating to God.

Special circumstances always apply in contexts where the Bible affirms that God does not repent.[37] Most of these cases are related to covenantal obligations into which God voluntarily entered. In such cases, God has chosen to limit his options, and his commitment is irrevocable. Yet, one must be careful not to turn one of these affirmations into a general principle that governs the other, or to dismiss one as merely accommodative language that metaphorically attributes human qualities to God while insisting that the other is literally true.[38]

It is better to understand both affirmations as applying to different circumstances, depending on the nature of the divine communication involved.[39] Prophecy, generally speaking, is conditional. Unilateral covenants (i.e., covenants in which God unconditionally guarantees promises solely on the basis of his character), however, such as the Davidic and Abrahamic covenants, are irrevocable. With regard to the latter,

---

36. John T. Willis, "The 'Repentance' of God in the Books of Samuel, Jeremiah, and Jonah," *HBT* 16 (1994): 156.

37. Ibid, 159.

38. Ibid, 168.

39. Robert B. Chisholm Jr., "Does God 'Change His Mind'?" *BSac* 152 (1995): 387 – 99. Chisholm helpfully distinguishes between four kinds of divine forward-looking communication, each of which creates different circumstances in which God either leaves open or closes the possibility of a change in plans. These are (1) formal decrees, (2) informal decrees, (3) explicitly conditional statements of intention, and (4) implicitly conditional statements of intention. The first two of these express immutable pronouncements bearing directly on God's character or on the success of his redemptive purposes. The latter two create possibilities from which humans may choose. To that choice God then responds in a manner consistent with his character and larger purpose.

God indeed does not change course because he has voluntarily bound himself in order to guarantee a crucial outcome. With regard to the former, however, he can and does change his plan in response to human petitions and behavior. The key is to hold both truths as equally valid and equally important to understanding God's character. Both aspects of God's dealings with humans underscore his faithfulness and mercy. To dissolve one of these realities into the other is to make the same mistake Jonah made and to end up badly misunderstanding, and perhaps misrepresenting, God.

Clemency for Israel and for Her Enemies

The issue in Jonah, however, is not simply God's ability to change course from exacting punishment to showing clemency, but also on whose behalf God may graciously turn from judgment to mercy. One of the ways the book explores the scope of divine mercy is by means of echoing texts that feature YHWH's mercy for Israel in contexts where he is extending that same mercy to Israel's enemies. For example, the final verse of Jonah 3 describes God's relenting concerning Nineveh's punishment in terms that echo, nearly verbatim, the mercy he extended to Israel after her sin with the golden calf (Exod 32:14). The two texts are compared below.

	Table 6.1: Comparison of Exodus 32:14 with Jonah 3:10	
	Exodus 32:14	**Jonah 3:10**
Hebrew	*wayyinnāḥem yhwh ʿal hārāʿâ ʾăšer dibber laʿăśôt lĕʿammô*	*wayyinnāḥem hāʾĕlōhîm ʿal hārāʿâ ʾăšer-dibber laʿăśôt lāhem*
English	YHWH relented concerning the disaster that he had threatened to perform against his people.	God relented concerning the disaster that he had threatened to perform against them.

As the comparison shows, the two texts differ in only two respects. The first is that where Exod 32:14 has the divine name, "YHWH," Jonah 3:10 has the designation "God." This difference is due simply to the fact that the objects of mercy in Exodus are Israelites and therefore familiar with God's covenant name whereas in Jonah 3:10 they are Gentiles and thus familiar only with the general designation for deity. The second difference is the final phrase. Exodus 32:14 concludes with the phrase "against his people" with reference to Israel. Jonah 3:10 concludes with the phrase "against them" with reference to the inhabitants of Nineveh.

The close similarity between the two texts underscores the truth that YHWH's mercy is not exclusively for Israel's benefit. God's special relationship with Israel is not an end in and of itself, but a means to an end — the blessing of the nations (cf. Gen 12:1 – 3). It is not difficult to understand why Jonah had issues with the indiscriminate nature of YHWH's mercy. His mercy toward Assyria appeared to Jonah to create a serious conflict of interest with his covenant obligations to Israel. The question Jonah could not get around was how God could remain faithful to Israel while pardoning Assyria and thus assure Israel of destruction.

Many believers since have wrestled with Jonah's issue. At times God's mercy appears to allow injustice, perhaps even encourage injustice. It is at those moments that believers struggle most with the implications of God's mercy. Mercy toward one's enemies is the first imperative of the gospel for the simple reason that that is what God did when he took the initiative in reconciling sinners to himself by sending his Son. "For if, *while we were God's enemies*, we were reconciled to him through the death of his Son, how much more, having been reconciled, shall we be saved through his life!" (Rom 5:10 NIV, italics added).

Animals, Repentance, and God's Utopian Vision

The book of Jonah is not alone in claiming that animals have a role in petitioning for divine clemency. The prophet Joel encouraged a similar cooperation of humans and animals in petitioning YHWH for mercy when he summoned Judah to national repentance. Joel first noted that animals suffered the consequences of Judah's sin when the covenant curses were applied and drought and famine deprived them of their food.

> How the cattle moan!
> > The herds mill about
> because they have no pasture;
> > even the flocks of sheep are suffering. (Joel 1:18 NIV)

Joel directed YHWH's attention to the fact that even the animals were joining in the petition for divine mercy. The prophet seemed to think that this added weight to Judah's petition.

> Even the wild animals pant *for you*;
> > the streams of water have dried up
> > and fire has devoured the pastures in the wilderness. (Joel 1:20 NIV, italics added)

Finally, when YHWH announced through Joel that he had accepted Judah's repentance and had relented from the disaster he had planned, he addressed the animals directly, assuring them of their imminent relief.

> Be not afraid, you wild animals,
> > for the pastures in the wilderness are becoming green.
> The trees are bearing their fruit;
> > the fig tree and the vine yield their riches. (Joel 2:22 NIV)

Joel and Jonah share many affinities (call to repentance, fasting, sackcloth, mourning rites, the phrase "God may change his mind," and quotations from Exod 34:6 – 7). Among these is their portrayal of animals as participants, in some sense, in petitioning God for mercy. In fact, both books indicate that the animals' participation is an indication of the thoroughness and seriousness of the repentance.

The apostle Paul envisioned something similar in Rom 8:19 – 22 when he described all creation as groaning under the weight of the fall.

> For the creation waits in eager expectation for the children of God to be revealed. For the creation was subjected to frustration, not by its own choice, but by the will of the one who subjected it, in hope that the creation itself will be liberated from its bondage to decay and brought into the freedom and glory of the children of God.
>
> We know that the whole creation has been groaning as in the pains of childbirth right up to the present time. (NIV)

What is also clear from Paul's statement is that just as animals share in bearing the weight of the effects of the fall, so will they share in the glorious redemption of Christ and the resulting new creation. This is anticipated both in the flood narrative and in the book of Jonah. The emphasis on God's concern for all his creatures is unmistakable and finds confirmation in Jesus, who insisted that God is constantly mindful of even the sparrows (Matt 6:26; Luke 12:6 – 7).

The Abrahamic Covenant, Israel, and the Nations

YHWH promised Abraham that all families of the earth would experience divine blessing through the agency of Abraham's offspring (Gen 12:1 – 3). Jonah's mission to Nineveh serves as one example of this promise's fulfillment. God, through an Israelite prophet, turns an Assyrian city away from its impending destruction. The irony, of course, is that this particular Israelite prophet is resistant to the calling to "be a blessing" to a foreign nation. Jonah's resistance, however, does not prevent God from advancing the Abrahamic ideal in his ministry. In fact, God takes advantage of an opportunity through Jonah's interaction with the people of Nineveh to demonstrate for Jonah true repentance and the broad scope of divine mercy.

The repentance of Nineveh was remarkable for its orthodoxy and its depth. As the king's pronouncement indicated, the people of Nineveh went so far as to abandon their wicked and violent ways simply because Jonah delivered a terse oracle regarding their imminent destruction. In fact, Nineveh's contrition became a paradigm of genuine repentance elsewhere in Scripture. Jesus, for example asserted that the people of Nineveh would rise up in the judgment and condemn the Pharisees for their failure to repent in response to Jesus' teaching (Matt 12:41; Luke 11:30 – 32). The people of Nineveh repented at the minimal revelation offered by Jonah, but the Pharisees wouldn't repent in response to the fullness of revelation offered them by Christ.

It is this last notion that captured Paul's imagination. He started by explaining the odd dynamic at work in Israel's rejection of her Messiah in tandem with widespread Gentile conversion to Christ. Paul then suggested that God was actually provoking Israel to jealousy by means of Gentile repentance in order to motivate Israel's repentance as well:

> Again I ask: Did they stumble so as to fall beyond recovery? Not at all! Rather, because of their transgression, salvation has come to the Gentiles to make Israel envious. But if their transgression means riches for the world, and their loss means riches for the Gentiles, how much greater riches will their full inclusion bring
>
> I am talking to you Gentiles. Inasmuch as I am the apostle to the Gentiles, I take pride my in ministry in the hope that I may somehow arouse my own people to envy and save some of them. (Rom 11:11 – 14 NIV).

Jonah's reaction to Nineveh's repentance in 4:1 seems to foreshadow the jealousy Paul mentioned in Romans 11. Just as YHWH used the compliance of animals throughout the book of Jonah to expose the irony and severity of human rebellion, so he used the exemplary repentance of the Gentiles (the mariners and the citizens of Nineveh) to shame Jonah, and later the Jews as a whole, into embracing his scandalous mercy.

Jonah 4:1 – 4

C. Resentment of God's Mercy (Peak episode)

Main Idea of the Passage

In a fit of anger, Jonah objects to God's clemency, finally revealing that his problem with YHWH's commission from the beginning was his fear that divine justice would suffer at the hands of divine mercy. Since his worst fears have been realized, Jonah asks to die.

Literary Context

Jonah 4:1 – 4 parallels 2:1c – 11b (1:17c – 2:10b). It brings the second main section of Jonah to its climax. As in the preceding peak episode, the tension building between Jonah and YHWH culminates in prayer. But this time, Jonah's prayer takes the form of a complaint. Ironically, the complaint is provoked by the same mercy that inspired Jonah's earlier praise. The two prayers, therefore, serve as counterpoints, marking the twin peaks of the book's parallel structure.

This unit is also significant because it contains the first real dialogue between Jonah and YHWH. In previous episodes, either YHWH addressed Jonah and received no verbal response (1:1 – 2; 3:1 – 2), or Jonah addressed YHWH and received no verbal response (2:1c – 2:11b).

The book's second peak episode also reveals an alternating pattern. In the two pre-peak episodes (1:4a – 17b and 3:3c – 10) Jonah interacts with Gentiles: first with the mariners and then with the citizens of Nineveh. In the two peak episodes (2:1c – 10b and 4:1 – 4) Jonah interacts with YHWH. This basic rhythm is illustrated in Table 7:1.

Table 7.1: Alternating Pattern in Jonah's Pre-peak and Peak Episodes			
Jonah 1:4b – 2:1b [1:17b] PRE-PEAK 1	Jonah 2:1c – 11b [1:17c – 2:10b] PEAK 1	Jonah 3:3c – 10 PRE-PEAK 2	Jonah 4:1 – 4 PEAK 2
Jonah and Gentiles (The mariners)	Jonah and YHWH (Prayer)	Jonah and Gentiles (People of Nineveh)	Jonah and YHWH (Prayer/dialogue)

This pattern reveals a significant literary dynamic. Every encounter with Gentiles brings Jonah to a crisis point. These crises are followed by interactions with God in which Jonah experiences an emotional catharsis and a renewed invitation to embrace, rather than resist, God's mercy.

This alternating rhythm is coupled with intensification. Engagement with others (strangers/foreigners) alternates with communion with YHWH (thanksgiving for Jonah's salvation), resulting in an intensified engagement with others (enemies/foreigners), culminating in intensified communion with YHWH (argument over Nineveh's salvation).

II. From Compliant Acceptance to Angry Resentment: The Offense of God's Mercy (3:1 – 4:11, Macro Unit 2)
   A. A Second Chance at Compliance with God's Mercy (3:1 – 3b, Stage setting)
   B. Responsiveness to and the Responsiveness of God's Mercy (3:3b – 10, Pre-peak episode)
   C. Resentment of God's Mercy (4:1 – 4, Peak episode)
      1. Jonah's anger over YHWH's mercy (4:1)
      2. Jonah's complaint against YHWH's mercy (4:2 – 3)
      3. YHWH's challenge to Jonah's anger (4:4)
   D. An Object Lesson on the Justice of Divine Mercy (4:5 – 11, Post-peak episode)

Translation and Outline

(See the next page.)

Structure and Literary Form

Jonah 3:10 concluded with a negated clause ("And he did not do it," *wĕlōʾ ʿāśâ*), which restated and reinforced the outcome of Nineveh's repentance and YHWH's clemency. The author thus brought closure to the pre-peak episode. The initial narrative verb form in 4:1 ("this displeased," *wayyēraʿ*), therefore, resumes the plot line. Whereas the preceding sequence of narrative verbs had YHWH as their subject

Jonah 4:1–4

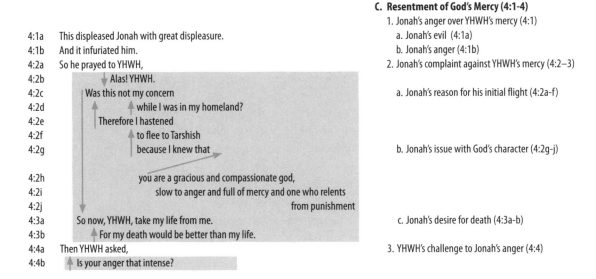

4:1a	This displeased Jonah with great displeasure.
4:1b	And it infuriated him.
4:2a	So he prayed to YHWH,
4:2b	Alas! YHWH.
4:2c	Was this not my concern
4:2d	while I was in my homeland?
4:2e	Therefore I hastened
4:2f	to flee to Tarshish
4:2g	because I knew that
4:2h	you are a gracious and compassionate god,
4:2i	slow to anger and full of mercy and one who relents
4:2j	from punishment
4:3a	So now, YHWH, take my life from me.
4:3b	For my death would be better than my life.
4:4a	Then YHWH asked,
4:4b	Is your anger that intense?

C. Resentment of God's Mercy (4:1-4)
1. Jonah's anger over YHWH's mercy (4:1)
   a. Jonah's evil (4:1a)
   b. Jonah's anger (4:1b)
2. Jonah's complaint against YHWH's mercy (4:2–3)

   a. Jonah's reason for his initial flight (4:2a-f)

   b. Jonah's issue with God's character (4:2g-j)

   c. Jonah's desire for death (4:3a-b)
3. YHWH's challenge to Jonah's anger (4:4)

(3:10), the two that launch the peak episode share an impersonal subject: "*This* displeased Jonah … and *it* infuriated him." When impersonal verbs express subjective experiences or emotions, they typically mark the person feeling the emotion with the preposition "to" ('*el*, or simply *lĕ*). Jonah is thus identified as the one experiencing grave displeasure and anger. After his brief oracle in 3:4, Jonah receded from view and played no further role in chapter 3. The shift of attention back to Jonah in 4:1, therefore, confirms the beginning of a new unit.

The unit breaks into three sections. A brief narrative describes Jonah's emotional reaction to Nineveh's deliverance (4:1). Jonah's prayer to YHWH follows, expressing his formal complaint regarding what he perceives to be a deception and an injustice (4:2 – 3). The unit concludes with YHWH's response to Jonah's complaint in the form of a question (4:4).

Emphasis falls here on the content of Jonah's complaint, which likewise consists of three sections. First, Jonah explains his initial flight: he feared the possibility that YHWH would spare Nineveh after YHWH's first commission. Jonah knew that prophetic condemnation usually implies an invitation to repent, a chance Jonah was unwilling to take. These concerns were allayed after the second commission when Jonah received the content of the message. His misperception that the oracle spoke unequivocally of judgment created certain expectations that were not met.

Second, Jonah complains that YHWH's character was precisely the reason he feared such a scenario. The source of the scandal was YHWH's readiness to relent even if the penitent was guilty of harming YHWH's people. Jonah perceives a flaw in the divine character when it comes to executing justice on Israel's enemies.

Finally, Jonah concludes his prayer with an explicit petition for death. He issues YHWH an ultimatum — either Nineveh must die or Jonah must die. Jonah cannot see how YHWH could simultaneously maintain his covenant faithfulness to Israel and grant clemency to Nineveh. Perhaps Jonah hopes to change YHWH's mind regarding Nineveh's fate.

In terms of genre, Jonah's prayer takes the form of a prophetic complaint similar to those uttered by Elijah (1 Kgs 19:4) and Jeremiah (Jer 11:18 – 23; 12:1 – 6; 15:10 – 21; 20:7 – 18). In particular, Jonah 4:2 – 3 is a prophetic complaint concerning the fulfillment of an oracle. Such complaints typically consist of three elements. The first is an invocation of YHWH that includes an accusation of injustice. The second is an oracle confessing some aspect of divine activity or of divine character that is relevant to the accusation of injustice. The third is a reproach that requests either an explanation or the correction of injustice.[1]

The author used this genre as a means of expressing Jonah's initial objection to the divine call of 1:1 – 2. Thus, the complaint form is subordinate to the commission narrative. Furthermore, Jonah's objection to the divine call is displaced. Rather than immediately following the commission as expected, Jonah's objection is strategically delayed until the second peak episode. The author thus makes the objection to the commission at the high point of the book's conflict and the trigger for YHWH's object lesson at the conclusion of the book.

Explanation of the Text

1. Jonah's Anger over YHWH's Mercy (4:1)

a. Jonah's Evil (4:1a)

The peak episode begins with a resumption of the motif of "evil" (*rāʿâ*). This time the word is applied to Jonah's emotional reaction to Nineveh's deliverance. While the noun has appeared frequently in the book, 4:1 is the first occurrence of the verb (*wayyēraʿ*). The author pairs the verb with the noun, stressing the intensity of Jonah's feelings: (lit.) "It was displeasing to Jonah, greatly displeasing" (*wayyēraʿ … rāʿâ*).

The concluding verse of Jonah 3 states that God relented concerning the "disaster" (lit., "evil," *rāʿâ*) he had threatened to perform on Nineveh. Just a few words later, the reader encounters the same root again, both as a verb and as a noun form, at the onset of the peak episode. The close proximity of these occurrences clarifies the close relationship between God's relenting concerning the "evil" he had planned for Nineveh and the great "evil" that now afflicts Jonah. God's clemency is the source of the unbearable offense.

By means of the repetition of the word "evil" throughout the book, the author has been working toward the connection of several closely related events. Nineveh's evil prompted YHWH to

---

1. Michael H. Floyd, "Prophetic Complaints about the Fulfillment of Oracles in Habakkuk 1:2 – 17 and Jeremiah 15:10 – 18," *JBL* 110 (1991): 398.

threaten "evil" upon the city. As a result, the citizens of Nineveh repented of their evil, and YHWH responded by graciously relenting from the "evil" he had planned to bring on Nineveh. That YHWH would relent from the "evil" that Nineveh so richly deserves is "a great evil" to Jonah. Interestingly, everyone is relinquishing "evil" except for Jonah.

With reference to Jonah the word *rāʿâ* has dual significance. On the one hand, Jonah is clearly displeased (*wayyēraʿ*). On the other hand, the displeasure is merely a symptom of a deep-seated evil (*rāʿâ*) within Jonah. Having dealt with Nineveh's evil, the narrative now turns to Jonah's "evil."

b. Jonah's Anger (4:1b)

The next verb also creates a link with the preceding episode. The text states that YHWH's clemency "infuriated him" (*wayyiḥar lô*). This verb derives from a root that literally means "to burn." It occurs in its noun form in 3:9d with reference to God's anger toward Nineveh (*ḥārôn*). Ironically, just as YHWH quenched his wrath, Jonah has kindled his. The reader is again reminded of how out-of-step Jonah is. The event that calmed God's wrath is the same event that has provoked Jonah's wrath.

2. Jonah's Complaint against YHWH's Mercy (4:2 – 3)

a. Jonah's Reason for His Initial Flight (4:2a-f)

Jonah's anger prompts him to address YHWH. The recurrence of the verb "to pray" (*wayyitpallēl*) connects this prayer to the one Jonah uttered from the fish's belly (2:2). These are the verb's only two occurrences in the book, and they invite comparison of Jonah's prayers. Ironically, the same mercy that inspired Jonah's praise when he was saved also provokes his complaint when Nineveh was saved.

The second notable feature is the resumption of the divine name "YHWH." Throughout the preceding episode, the name YHWH was carefully avoided as emphasis fell on God's interaction with Gentiles. The focus of attention now returns to Jonah, and the covenant name reappears. The author's strategic use of divine designations repeatedly raises the issue of the interrelationship of YHWH, the Gentiles, and Jonah.

Jonah opens his prayer with a strong interjection ("Alas, YHWH!" *ʾannâ yhwh*), which was last heard on the mariners' lips as they pleaded with YHWH to be absolved of responsibility for Jonah's death (using the same expression, transl. "We beg of you, YHWH," 1:14b). This interjection typically expresses the urgency and gravity of a request.[2] It was understandable in the context of the mariners' prayer as they petitioned YHWH in the midst of a violent storm. It seems out of place, however, at the opening of Jonah's complaint over Nineveh's deliverance and hints at a significant irony. What proved to be a crisis to the mariners was not treated as a crisis by Jonah, who slept during the storm. For Jonah, Nineveh's salvation is the true disaster (*rāʿâ*).

One would expect the initial interjection "Alas, YHWH!" to be followed by an urgent request, but the reader first hears Jonah's long-awaited explanation for his initial flight. The request is postponed until 4:3a. An understanding of Jonah's reason for initially fleeing the divine call becomes critical at this point.

Jonah begins his explanation with a rhetorical question: "Was this not my concern while I was in my homeland?" The question implies a shared knowledge between Jonah and YHWH to which the reader is only now introduced. Apparently,

---

2. Van der Merwe, Naudé, and Kroeze, *A Biblical Hebrew Reference Grammar*, 335.

a conversation transpired between YHWH and Jonah in the context of the prophet's initial calling that only now comes to the reader's attention. Jonah 4:2d, therefore, features another example of information gapping.[3] The author has aroused readers' curiosity by withholding this information until now, ensuring that readers will pay close attention to this dialogue. The author is about to reveal the key theological issue of the book and doesn't want readers to miss it.

Jonah proceeds to make the connection between his anticipation of Nineveh's deliverance and his decision to flee. He states, "Therefore I hastened to flee to Tarshish." The verb "I hastened" (*qiddamtî*), in the Piel stem, has the basic meaning of "getting in front of" something, "meeting" or "coming before" something. Its use in conjunction with the infinitive "to flee" (*librōaḥ*) is awkward and difficult to translate. In Late Biblical Hebrew, however, the verb can have the meaning "to hasten," which fits this context admirably.[4]

The author's choice of the unusual construction is likely rhetorical. The verb *qdm* derives from the same root as the Hebrew word for "east" (*qedem*) and thus strikes an ironic chord. YHWH had commanded Jonah to travel east toward Nineveh. Jonah, however, fled in the opposite direction, west. In fact, the entire clause here is framed by the poles of Jonah's journey. It starts with the verb re-lated to the direction "east" and ends with "Tarshish," the westernmost point on Israel's conceptual map. Jonah's own words condemn him. His use of a verb related to the cardinal direction "east" recalls his stubbornness, which resurfaces in this heated exchange with YHWH.

b. Jonah's Issue with God's Character (4:2g-j)

Jonah's complaint finally exposes the root issue underlying his conflict with YHWH. At its heart, this conflict was about Jonah's perception of an imbalance in the divine character. Divine justice was eclipsed by an indiscriminate mercy. From Jonah's point of view, the clemency God showed Nineveh jeopardized YHWH's covenant with Israel, which created a conflict of interest between his promises to Israel and the breadth of his mercy.

Interestingly, Jonah expresses his frustration with YHWH's character in terms of the divine attributes first articulated in Exod 34:6 – 7.[5] This confession appears numerous times throughout the Old Testament in a number of variations.[6] Jonah is selective with regard to his recitation of YHWH's attributes, focusing exclusively on his attributes of mercy. He quotes[7] the first line of Exod 34:6 nearly verbatim, except that he addresses it to YHWH in the second person rather than in the third person of Exod 34:6.

Jonah's recitation consists of two pairs of

---

3. Landes, "Textual 'Information Gaps,'" 275.

4. Clines, *Concise Dictionary*, 388.

5. Michael Fishbane, *Biblical Interpretation in Ancient Israel* (Oxford: Clarendon, 1988), 335 – 47. I side with Fishbane and the majority of interpreters in understanding Exod 34:6 – 7 to be the original form of this confession and therefore the basis for subsequent repetitions and variations.

6. 2 Chr 30:9; Neh 9:31; Pss 111:4; 112:4; and Sir 2:11 quote the first line of the confession, though the order of the attributes varies. Neh 9:17; Pss 86:15; 103:8; 145:8 quote the entire confession with slight variations. 2 Kgs 13:23 and Nah 1:3 do not appear to be direct quotations but rather strong echoes or allusions. Joel 2:13 and Jonah 4:2 are the two quotations that depart most noticeably from the traditional formula by both an addition and a deletion of a line. See Thomas B. Dozeman, "Inner-biblical Interpretations of Yahweh's Gracious and Compassionate Character," *JBL* (1989): 207, n. 2.

7. I understand Jonah to be quoting Exod 34:6 – 7 with modifications that accrued to the tradition through its repeated use over time. Sasson argues against characterizing Jonah 4:2 as a quotation, claiming that the Hebrew conjunction "that" (*ki*) does not introduce quotations (Sasson, *Jonah*, 279). He offers no support for this claim, and most standard grammars provide examples in which *ki* introduces quoted speech. See, e.g., Arnold and Choi, *Guide to Biblical Hebrew Syntax*, 154 – 55.

attributes, followed by the addition of a line concerning YHWH's readiness to relent from punishment, apparently drawn from Moses' appeal in Exod 32:12 – 14. The first pair of attributes is "gracious and compassionate" (*ḥanûn wĕraḥûm*). The first of these terms carries the idea of favor especially toward those who are disadvantaged. The second, related to the noun "womb," refers to maternal concern and compassion.

The second pair of attributes is "slow to anger and full of mercy" (*'erek 'appayim wĕrab-ḥesed*). "Slow to anger" translates a Hebrew idiom that literally means "long nostrils," with reference to the visible flaring of nostrils that accompanies anger. The point of the idiom is that YHWH's wrath is not easily excited. It takes a lot to move him to anger. The second attribute refers to the frequency with which YHWH gives more than is deserved or required. This same term occurred in Jonah's earlier prayer (2:8), and the comments on that verse explore the term in detail.

The final attribute stands alone and serves as the climax of the description of YHWH's character, namely, YHWH's readiness to relent concerning punishment. The wording of this attribute may be inspired by Moses' intercession in Exod 32:12. Moses asked YHWH: "Turn from your fierce anger; relent and do not bring disaster on your people."[8] The phrase also recalls the final lines of the king of Nineveh's proclamation, where he expressed the hope that "God may … relent and recover from his intense anger" (3:9b-d). Thus, it appears that Jonah's version of the traditional creed finds its inspiration in the context of Exod 32 – 34, where Moses prevails on YHWH to grant Israel mercy.

Of particular importance for the book of Jonah are two changes to the traditional formula. These changes match Joel's recitation of Exod 34:6 – 7 in Joel 2:13. The three texts are compared below.

Table 7.2: Joel's and Jonah's Modified Quotations of Exodus 34:6 – 7		
Exodus 34:6 – 7	**Joel 2:13**	**Jonah 4:2**
YHWH, YHWH a deity (who is) compassionate and gracious,		
He is compassionate and gracious,	You are a gracious and compassionate god,	You are a gracious and compassionate god,
slow to anger and full of mercy and faithfulness	slow to anger and full of mercy	slow to anger and full of mercy,
who administers mercy to thousands of generations,		
who forgives offense, crime, and immorality,		
but will certainly not acquit (the guilty),		
who applies the punishment due the fathers to the children and the grandchildren, to the third generation and to the fourth generation.		
	and who relents from punishment.	and who relents from punishment.

---

8. Dozeman, "Inner-biblical Interpretations," 219.

It appears that Joel and Jonah reflect the same version of this confession that each has adapted to his context. Of particular interest is the fact that both Joel and Jonah omitted the attribute of justice featured in the last two sections of Exod 34:7. They say nothing regarding YHWH's refusal to acquit the guilty or his extending punishment to succeeding generations of the disobedient.

Joel omitted these parts of the confession because he quotes Exod 34:6 – 7 as the basis for a season of fasting, prayer, and repentance in Judah. Emphasis in this setting naturally fell on YHWH's attributes of mercy rather than his attributes of justice. Judah was not appealing to YHWH for justice but for mercy. Similarly, Jonah omitted YHWH's attributes of justice because of the act of divine clemency he has just witnessed, an act of clemency that, from Jonah's perspective, conflicted with divine justice.

Another departure from the confessional formula is the addition of the line "and who relents from punishment." Both Joel and Jonah added this element to the quotation. Joel did so as an expression of hope intended to motivate Judah's repentance. Jonah added it as the culmination of his accusation that YHWH's indiscriminate mercy undermined justice. Comparison of Jonah's and Joel's adaptation of this quotation highlights the prophets' rhetorical and, sometimes, ironic appeal to Israelite tradition.[9]

Jonah was distressed to discover that the divine attributes listed in Exod 34:6 – 7, which elsewhere express YHWH's disposition toward Israel, also express YHWH's disposition toward Assyria. Jonah suspected that YHWH might extend the same mercy to Assyria he had extended to his own people. Thus, Jonah fled. After witnessing Nineveh's repentance and YHWH's rescinding of the city's destruction, Jonah realizes that his initial impression was correct. As a result, Jonah reverts to his staunch opposition to YHWH's decision to spare Nineveh.

c. Jonah's Desire for Death (4:3)

Jonah's complaint has been building toward an appeal that he finally introduces with the conjunction + the temporal adverb "so now" (wĕʿattâ). In this context, this expression has logical rather than temporal force, indicating that the petition is predicated on the preceding observations, "Please, take my life" (qaḥ-nāʾ ʾet-napšî). The imperative "take" (qaḥ) establishes the mainline of the direct discourse.[10] The mainline was postponed by an embedded narrative designed to explain the problem addressed in the complaint and to establish the basis for the appeal (4:2).[11] Jonah prefers death to life in a world where Israel's enemies are absolved by Israel's own God. Jonah is issuing YHWH an ultimatum, in an attempt to force YHWH to choose between Jonah and Nineveh: "Either destroy them, or destroy me!"

Jonah uses his life as a bargaining chip, believing that YHWH will give in rather than kill his prophet, or risk jeopardizing his covenant with Israel. Once again, the context of Moses' intercession for Israel in Exod 32 – 34 provides the background and inspiration for Jonah's ultimatum. Just as Moses laid his life on the line when begging YHWH to pardon Israel (Exod 32:32), so Jonah lays his life on the line when begging YHWH to destroy Nineveh. This

---

9. Ibid., 215 – 16.

10. According to Tucker (*Jonah*, 89), this clause is off the mainline because the imperative is preceded by wĕʿattâ. This, however, would leave Jonah's speech without a mainline since no clause-initial imperatives appear. While it is true that the

X + imperative construction typically departs from the mainline to mark a new topic, in the case of Jonah 4:3 this construction is the most prominent feature of the discourse to which all other clauses are subordinate.

11. Rocine, *Learning Biblical Hebrew*, 425.

connection suggests that Jonah's real goal is not death, but a reversal of YHWH's decision to spare Nineveh. All of the preceding references to Exod 32 – 34 have been preparing the reader for Jonah's ironic identification with Moses and for his dramatic appeal for a rescinding of YHWH's clemency.

3. YHWH's Challenge to Jonah's Anger (4:4)

The verb "and he said" (*wayyō'mer*) briefly returns to the narrative's mainline to introduce YHWH's response to Jonah. The response takes the form of a question, "Is your anger that intense?" (*hahêṭēb ḥārâ lāk*). Translations differ considerably regarding the precise meaning of this verse. The verb form (Hiphil infinitive absolute of *yāṭab*) is capable of a variety of nuances, and the syntax is difficult. The translation offered here understands the verb to convey the idea of doing something "well, thoroughly, or utterly."[12] The emphasis falls on the intensity of Jonah's anger because the prophet has requested death. YHWH responds by questioning such intense anger. He draws attention to Jonah's overreaction as the indicator of the prophet's underlying problem. The question is repeated in the book's final episode (4:9), where it sets the stage for YHWH's closing remarks.

The word YHWH uses for anger (*ḥārâ*) literally means "heat." It recalls the author's description of Jonah's emotional state in 4:1 ("it infuriated him" [*wayyiḥar lô*]) as well as the royal decree's description of the intensity of the divine wrath YHWH rightly directed toward Nineveh (3:9, *ḥārôn*). The reader's attention is redirected back to the beginning of the episode and, consequently, to Jonah's disposition of heart. His anger has exposed the real issue, and YHWH clarifies this with his question.

YHWH's words are remarkably measured. He demonstrates in his dealings with both Nineveh and Jonah the attributes Jonah just listed. YHWH asks Jonah a probing question. One might have expected YHWH to respond more forcefully. He had killed prophets for similar acts of disobedience (cf., e.g., 1 Kgs 13:20 – 25). Dealing with Jonah in accordance with his deserts, however, would only reinforce Jonah's skewed perspective of divine justice. YHWH's purpose all along has been to correct the prophet's misperception of the relationship between justice and mercy. Wolff eloquently captures the spirit of the question by stating, "Yahweh's initial reaction to Jonah's rebellious resignation is a positively tender kindness, which sets about bringing the sulky Jonah to a proper self-examination."[13]

Canonical and Practical Significance

Moses, Joel, Jonah and the Nations

The Explanation section discussed in some detail the important relationship between Jonah 4:1 – 4; Exod 32 – 34; and Joel 2:12 – 17. One additional aspect of their interrelationship remains to be explored. I have already suggested that the additional element in the traditional creed that Jonah and Joel share, YHWH's readiness to relent from punishment, comes from Moses' cry to God in Exod 32:12. The question that remains is how Jonah came to apply this aspect of YHWH's character to his

12. Clines, *Concise Dictionary*, 152.   13. Wolff, *Obadiah and Jonah*, 169.

dealings with the nations. Even Joel's expression of this attribute is in the context of YHWH's sparing Israel.

The author of Jonah understands the prophet's experience as an illustration of the principle articulated in Jer 18:7 – 10, which is itself an extension of Moses' appeal to YHWH's readiness to relent from punishment.

> If at any time I announce that a nation or kingdom is to be uprooted, torn down and destroyed, and if that nation I warned repents of its evil, then I will relent and not inflict on it the disaster I had planned. And if at another time I announce that a nation or kingdom is to be built up and planted, and if it does evil in my sight and does not obey me, then I will reconsider the good I had threatened to do for it. (NIV)

The key terms in this text, "relent" and "disaster," echo Moses' appeal in Exod 32:12. Jeremiah, however, generalized YHWH's readiness to relent from punishment as an aspect of his relationship with all nations and not just with Israel. This divine action flows out of his character and not simply out of his covenant. Jonah's experience with Nineveh represents the historical precedent for Jeremiah's insight, and the author connects the two.[14]

Thus, Exod 32 – 34; Joel 2:12 – 17; and Jonah 4:1 – 4, when read together, establish a critical connection between Israel's fate and the fate of the nations. In Exod 32:12 Moses dissuaded YHWH from destroying Israel for their idolatry by drawing attention to what this would mean for YHWH's reputation among the nations: "Why should the Egyptians say, 'It was with evil intent that he brought them out, to kill them in the mountains and to wipe them off the face of the earth'?" (NIV). Moses hinted at the achievement of a larger goal that would be sabotaged by Israel's annihilation — the revelation of YHWH's redemptive purposes for all creation.

What Moses hinted at in Exod 32:12, Joel stated more clearly. He called the priests and ministers of YHWH to weep and suggested that they plead with YHWH for mercy with these words: "Spare your people, Lord. Do not make your inheritance an object of scorn, a byword among the nations. Why should they say among the peoples, 'Where is their God?'" (Joel 2:17 NIV). Like Moses, Joel made the connection between Israel's fate and the fate of the nations. It is clear in Joel 2:17, however, that Israel's destruction would have potentially undermined God's will for the nations. Israel's destruction would have caused the nations to question the reliability, power, and mercy of Israel's God.

What was tangential in Joel 2:1 – 17 becomes central in Jonah 4:1 – 4. In this text, a Gentile nation rather than Israel is the recipient of divine mercy. God is moving rapidly toward his larger goal. The author of Jonah, however, anticipates a theological dilemma that YHWH's mercy toward the nations will create for Israel. What would

---

14. Fishbane, *Biblical Interpretation*, 346.

this mercy mean for Israel's status as YHWH's covenant people when the very nation YHWH spared remained hostile to Israel/Judah? Thus the prophet Jonah sees an inverted relationship between Nineveh's fate and Israel's fate. Whereas Moses and Joel saw Israel's destruction as detrimental to the nations' acceptance of YHWH, Jonah sees Nineveh's deliverance as detrimental to Israel's survival as YHWH's covenant people.

YHWH, by contrast, views Nineveh's deliverance as an opportunity to discipline his own people in preparation for their role in revealing YHWH to the nations. Jonah's perception of the situation is limited by his inability to understand the larger goal suggested by Moses and Joel. He can only perceive the more immediate result of Nineveh's deliverance: Assyria's resurgence, domination of God's people, and the eventual destruction of Israel. Isaiah 49:1 – 6 presents both Jonah's point of view and YHWH's point of view in dialogue.

> Listen to me, you islands;
> > hear this, you distant nations:
> Before I was born the LORD called me;
> > from my mother's womb he has spoken my name.
> He made my mouth like a sharpened sword,
> > in the shadow of his hand he hid me;
> he made me into a polished arrow
> > and concealed me in his quiver.
> He said to me, "You are my servant,
> > Israel, in whom I will display my splendor."
> But I said, "I have labored in vain;
> > I have spent my strength for nothing at all.
> Yet what is due me is in the LORD's hand,
> > and my reward is with my God."
> And now the LORD says —
> > he who formed me in the womb to be his servant
> to bring Jacob back to him
> > and gather Israel to himself,
> for I am honored in the eyes of the LORD
> > and my God has been my strength —
> he says:
> "It is too small a thing for you to be my servant
> > to restore the tribes of Jacob
> > and bring back those of Israel I have kept.
> I will also make you a light for the Gentiles,
> > that my salvation may reach to the ends of the earth. (NIV)

Isaiah 49:4 expresses the same sentiment Jonah felt but from the perspective of the exile. Israel, like Jonah, felt Israel's work was in vain because it ended in her exile.

YHWH, however, saw beyond the apparent impasse to a future in which a sancti-fied Israel would serve as the medium of divine revelation to the nations. The gospel of Luke and Acts chronicle the outworking of this vision through a restored Israel, whose people serve as Jesus' witnesses "in Jerusalem, and in all Judea and Samaria, and to the ends of the earth" (Acts 1:8 NIV).[15]

Moses, Jonah, Nahum, and the Nations

Jonah and Joel are not the only minor prophets who allude to Exod 34:6 – 7. Nahum appealed to this traditional confession as well. Significantly, Nahum high-lights that part of the confession that Jonah and Joel omit — YHWH's attribute of justice. Since Nahum's prophecy deals with Nineveh's destruction long after Jonah's eighth-century setting, it serves as a counterpoint to the book of Jonah. This is par-ticularly evident in Jonah's and Nahum's complementary quotations of this tradi-tional Israelite creed. These quotations are compared with Exod 34:6 – 7 below.

Table 7.3: Jonah's and Nahum's Quotation of Exodus 34:6 – 7		
Exodus 34:6 – 7	**Jonah 4:2**	**Nahum 1:3**
YHWH, YHWH, a deity (who is) compassionate and gracious	You are a gracious and compassionate god,	YHWH is
slow to anger and full of mercy and faithfulness	slow to anger and full of mercy,	slow to anger
who administers mercy to thousands of generations		
who forgives offense, crime, and immorality		
but will certainly not acquit (the guilty)		but YHWH will certainly not acquit (the guilty)
who applies the punishment due the fathers to the children and the grandchildren, to the third generation and to the fourth generation.		
	and who relents from punishment	

This comparison illustrates that Nahum's different context and content — Nineveh's destruction at the hands of Babylon — highlights the very divine attribute that Jonah implicitly questions. It also illustrates, however, that both texts retain the creed's emphasis on YHWH's patient nature ("slow to anger"). These two observa-tions combine to make a significant point regarding the relationship of the book of

---

15. David Seccombe, "The New People of God," in *Witness to the Gospel: The Theology of Acts* (ed. I. Howard Marshall and David Peterson; Grand Rapids: Eerdmans, 1998), 349 – 72.

Jonah to that of Nahum. Jonah misconstrued YHWH's mercy toward Nineveh as a denial of his justice and a betrayal of his covenant to Israel. Nahum clarified, however, that, in reality, YHWH's act of clemency was simply his patient grace, reserving judgment until Nineveh had ample opportunity to proceed from momentary repentance to a permanent change of character. It also postponed destruction so that Nineveh might serve as YHWH's instrument for disciplining Israel and Judah.

In this sense, Israel and Assyria shared a parallel experience of YHWH's patient grace. Moses persuaded YHWH to postpone punishment of Israel's idolatry so that Israel could serve as a display of divine grace to the nations. Similarly, Hezekiah persuaded YHWH to postpone Jerusalem's destruction so that the city's deliverance could be a testimony to the nations of YHWH's superiority over idols and of his sovereignty over all superpowers (Isa 36 – 39; cf. esp. 36:18; 37:9 – 12, 20). In a parallel manner, Nineveh was spared in the book of Jonah so that she could serve YHWH's purposes as his disciplinary rod (Isa 10:5).

These postponements of judgment, however, were not indefinite. Eventually, YHWH's justice had to be satisfied with regard to both Jerusalem and Nineveh, both of whom fell to Babylon. The difference was that Nineveh fell never to rise again (Nah 1:9, 14), whereas Jerusalem was restored as a testimony to YHWH's faithfulness, mercy, and power.

Two important theological points emerge from this comparison. First, Jonah's concerns regarding divine justice were not completely dismissed. YHWH ensured that justice was served. YHWH, however, allowed abundant time for repentance. His wrath patiently waited as his grace ran its course. God's people, however, often grow impatient for God's justice, not realizing that instant justice serves neither YHWH's nor humanity's interests (2 Pet 3:9).

Second, Jerusalem and Nineveh illustrate the inverse relationship that existed between Israel and the nations. On the one hand, God spared Israel for the sake of the nations because universal blessing and salvation came through this people. On the other hand, God spared the nations for the sake of Israel because their hostility to Israel refined her faith in God and provided a context in which Israel could learn and demonstrate mercy for enemies.

Jonah 4:5 – 11

D. An Object Lesson on Divine Mercy and Divine Justice (Post-peak episode)

Main Idea of the Passage

YHWH performs an object lesson in which he delivers Jonah from the desert heat only to revoke that deliverance later. Jonah's anger over God's reversal exposes Jonah's double standard and vindicates the justice of God's decision to spare Nineveh.

Literary Context

Jonah 4:5 – 11 constitutes the book's post-peak episode. Post-peak episodes provide a degree of resolution to the conflict that climaxed in the preceding peak episode.[1] Jonah 4:5 – 11 does this by narrating YHWH's response to the ultimatum Jonah expressed at the conclusion of his prayer: "So now, YHWH, take my life from me, for my death would be better than my life!" (4:3). YHWH responds to Jonah's anger with an object lesson designed to trap Jonah in his own theological inconsistency. YHWH follows the object lesson by explaining its significance.

This post-peak episode is unique in the book of Jonah in that it is the only unit lacking a parallel. It stands outside the parallel structure that organizes the rest of the book; this suggests its role as a commentary on the narrative. The lack of a parallel, however, does not mean that it lacks strong connections with previous episodes. A number of events in 4:5 – 11 bear marked similarity to previous events in the narrative. For example, Jonah's departure from the city in 4:5 abruptly concludes the dialogue between YHWH and Jonah in 4:1 – 4, leaving YHWH's question ("Is your anger that intense?") unanswered. This silent departure is reminiscent of Jonah's

---

1. Robert E. Longacre, *The Grammar of Discourse* (New York: Plenum, 1983, 1996), 38.

initial flight when he left YHWH's presence without explanation (1:3). Such a similarity may signal Jonah's regression to his original rebellion.

Furthermore, Jonah's request for death and YHWH's question, both of which first occur in 4:1 – 4 (the peak episode), are repeated almost verbatim in 4:5 – 11. These repetitions spark the resumption of the dialogue interrupted by Jonah's abrupt departure in 4:5. The continuation and completion of this dialogue mark 4:5 – 11 as the book's post-peak episode.

II. From Compliant Acceptance to Angry Resentment: The Offense of God's Mercy (3:1 – 4:11, Macro Unit 2)
   A. A Second Chance at Compliance with God's Mercy (3:1 – 3b, Stage setting)
   B. Responsiveness to and the Responsiveness of God's Mercy (3:3c – 10, Pre-peak episode)
   C. Resentment of God's Mercy (4:1 – 4, Peak episode)
→ **D. An Object Lesson on Divine Mercy and Divine Justice (4:5 – 11, Post-peak episode)**
      1. Jonah's vigil for YHWH's response (4:5)
      2. YHWH's object lesson on divine mercy (4:6 – 8)
      3. God's final challenge to Jonah's anger (4:9 – 11)

Translation and Outline

(See the next page.)

Structure and Literary Form

The book's final episode consists of three sections. The first one reports Jonah's retreat to a desert region east of Nineveh.[2] Jonah's second silent flight from YHWH's word returns the reader to the story's main plot. A series of narrative verb forms (*wayyiqtol*) follows, relating Jonah's activities in his desert retreat. The first section concludes with a break in the report of Jonah's activity as the author pauses to indicate Jonah's purpose in retreating to the desert (4:5e).

The focus shifts to YHWH's activity in 4:6a. This second section relates an object lesson God offers Jonah by means of a plant, a worm, and wind. God initiates all of the actions, and Jonah simply responds. In fact, the section can be subdivided on

---

2. It is important to keep in mind that the author of Jonah is less interested in the actual geography, topography, and climactic conditions of Nineveh's environs than he is the symbolism of the desert. The book of Jonah was addressed to a Judean audience, which likely had little knowledge of Nineveh's actual climate and used their own frame of reference for interpreting the author's use of setting. For a Judean, the east was associated with the desert.

Jonah 4:5–11

| | | **D. An Object Lesson on Divine Mercy and Divine Justice (4:5—11)** |

4:5a Jonah departed from the city,

4:5b and sat east of the city.

4:5c He built himself a hut there,

4:5d and sat under it in the shade

4:5e until he could see what would happen in the city.

4:6a Then YHWH God appointed a plant,

4:6b and it grew over Jonah

4:6c to serve as a shade over his head

4:6d to deliver him from his misery.

4:6e Jonah rejoiced over the plant with great joy.

4:7a Then God appointed a worm.

4:7b When dawn came the next day,

4:7c it attacked the plant,

4:7d and the plant withered.

4:8a As the sun climbed higher,

4:8b God appointed a cutting, easterly wind,

4:8c and the sun attacked Jonah's head.

4:8d He grew faint,

4:8e and asked himself to die.

4:8f He said,

4:8g My death is better than my life.

4:9a God asked Jonah,

4:9b Is your anger over the plant that intense?

4:9c He answered,

4:9d My anger is so intense I could die!

4:10a YHWH said,

4:10b As for you, you pitied the plant,

4:10c over which you exerted no effort,

4:10d nor did you grow it,

4:10e which overnight appeared

4:10f and overnight perished.

4:11a But as for me, must I not pity Nineveh, the great metropolis,

4:11b in which live more than 120,000 persons

4:11c who do not know their right from their left,

4:11d as well as many animals?

D. An Object Lesson on Divine Mercy and Divine Justice (4:5—11)

  1. Jonah's vigil for YHWH's response (4:5)
    a. Jonah's movement away from YHWH (4:5b)
    b. Jonah's return to the wilderness (4:5c-e)

  2. YHWH's object lesson on divine mercy (4:6-4:8)
    a. God's appointment of a plant (4:6a-b)
    b. God's purpose for the plant (4:6c-d)

    c. Jonah's joy over the plant (4:6e)
    d. God's appointment of a worm (4:7a)

    e. God's purpose for the worm (4:7b-d)

    f. God's appointment of a wind (4:8a-b)
    g. God's purpose for the wind (4:8c-d)

    h. Jonah's despondence over the plant's demise (4:8e-g)
  3. God's final challenge to Jonah's anger (4:9-11)
    a. God's call to self-reflection (4:9a-b)
    b. Jonah's self-vindicating response (4:9c-d)

    c. Jonah's self-pity vs. YHWH's mercy (4:10-11)
      i. The plant as a symbol of divine mercy (4:10a-d)

      ii. The plant as a symbol of divine justice (4:10e-f)

      iii. Nineveh as an object of divine mercy (4:11)

the basis of Jonah's two responses to God's activity. God's appointment of a plant symbolizes his merciful activity, to which Jonah responds with great joy (4:6). God's appointment of the worm and the wind symbolizes his judgment (4:7), to which Jonah responds with despondence (4:8).

Jonah's brief soliloquy in 4:8g serves as a transitional clause that brings closure to the object lesson (4:5a). Jonah's statement in 4:8g ("my death is better than my life") repeats his petition in 4:3b, and it opens the door for YHWH to return to his initial question (4:4b). Thus begins the third section, consisting of a dialogue between YHWH and Jonah, in which YHWH again challenges Jonah's objections to divine mercy.

In terms of genre, Jonah 4:5 – 11 bears several affinities with YHWH's interview with Elijah when he fled from Jezebel (1 Kgs 19:3 – 18). A comparison of the common elements of the stories appears in the table below.

| Table 8.1: Comparison of 1 Kgs 19:3 – 18 to Jonah 4:5 – 11 ||
1 Kgs 19:3 – 18	Jonah 4:5 – 11
1. Elijah flees to the desert (19:3)	1. Jonah flees to the desert (4:5a-b, 8a-b)
2. Elijah sits under a broom tree (19:4)	2. Jonah sits under a plant (4:5c-d, 6a-d)
3. Elijah in despondence requests death (19:4)	3. Jonah in despondence requests death (4:8e-g)
4. YHWH poses the same question twice (19:9, 13)	4. God poses the same question twice (4:4b, 9b)
5. YHWH communicates through nature (19:11 – 13)	5. God communicates through nature (4:6 – 8)

The strong similarities suggest that the author is deliberately alluding to the Elijah narrative, but not for the purpose of simple comparison. Rather, the similarities serve to underscore two significant contrasts. First, whereas Elijah was despondent over his failure to bring Israel to repentance, Jonah is despondent over his success at bringing Nineveh to repentance. Second, whereas the Elijah narrative is succeeded by a story portending retribution for Elijah's enemies and vindication for the prophet, Jonah 4:5 – 11 ends with uncertainty. The reader is left wondering whether Jonah ever embraces YHWH's objectionable mercy. Furthermore, the book's first readers were keenly aware that Nineveh's unabated rise to power eventually did lead to Israel's exile (722 BC).

The author thus satirizes Jonah's behavior by means of an ironic comparison with Elijah. Since the best characterization of 1 Kgs 19:3 – 18 remains Fohrer's suggestion of a "story of divine encounter,"[3] Jonah 4:5 – 11 falls within this same genre but with elements of satire.

---

3. G. Fohrer, *Elias* (2nd ed.; Zurich: Zwingli, 1968), 38 – 42, cited in Long, *1 Kings*, 202.

Explanation of the Text

1. *Jonah's Vigil for YHWH's Response (4:5)*

Jonah 4:5a resumes the main storyline with a narrative verb (*wayyiqtol*) informing the reader that Jonah left the city. The verb form "Jonah departed" (*wayyēṣēʾ yônâ*) leaves the impression that this departure follows immediately upon YHWH's question, "Is your anger that intense?"[4] Jonah once again silently fled the divine presence, leaving YHWH's question unanswered (4:4). Such a response is consistent with Jonah's disposition and his previous behavior.

The impression that Jonah again fled confrontation with YHWH is subtly confirmed by the next clause: "[He] sat east of the city." The direction of Jonah's travel is opposite that of his initial flight. This time it is "east" (*miqqedem*). The author emphasizes the direction of Jonah's movement for two reasons. First, the word "east" creates a sound play with Jonah's statement in 4:2e that he had "hastened" (*qiddamtî*) to flee YHWH's calling. In fact, both words derive from the same three letter root, *q-d-m*. The connection serves to associate Jonah's initial flight with his action in 4:5, which suggests that this eastward movement is a resumption of Jonah's previous rebellion.

A second reason for the author's emphasis on Jonah's eastward movement is that it links to an important motif in Genesis. The author often evokes images and themes from Genesis because of its panhuman perspective. In Genesis, eastward movement often symbolizes humanity's departure from God's will.[5] For example, Adam and Eve's expulsion from Eden leaves the banished couple "east" of their former paradisiacal home. Cain's departure from YHWH's presence, an allusion made earlier in connection with Jonah's initial flight, ends in his settling "east of Eden" (*qidmat-ʿēden* [Gen 4:16]). The builders of Babel are in the process of migrating east when they decide to stop and build a city as a monument to their fame (Gen 11:2). Finally, when Lot separated from Abram and settled near Sodom and Gomorrah, the text notes that he "traveled east" (Gen 13:11). These references to eastward migration in Genesis mark stages in humanity's drift away from God.[6] Similarly, Jonah's movement east of the city seems to signal the prophet's return to his previous rebellion.

Jonah erects a hut shelter (*sukkâ*), reminiscent of the "booths" (*sukkôt*) that the Israelites used during their desert journey to Canaan (Lev 23:34 – 43). The hut, therefore, evokes images of the desert, recalling Israel's wilderness sojourn. It is the first indication of the inhospitable nature of Jonah's surroundings. Just as Jonah's first flight from YHWH led him to the inhospitable, turbulent sea, his second flight leads him to the inhospitable, arid desert. Both environments symbolize chaos and death in biblical thought and correspond to Jonah's spiritual state.[7]

---

4. Some commentators argue that this verb actually refers to Jonah's departure from the city immediately following the fulfillment of his commission. The action of 4:5, according to this perspective, occurred prior to the preceding dialogue between Jonah and YHWH and the *wayyiqtol* form should be rendered as a pluperfect (so Wolff, *Obadiah and Jonah*, 169; Stuart, *Hosea – Jonah*, 504; and Heimerdinger, *Topic, Focus, and Foreground*, 88). As Sasson points out, however, this is not a natural reading of the text's grammar (Sasson, *Jonah*, 288). Ma-

gonet suggests that Jonah's departure is a response to YHWH's query and that it corresponds to his initial flight to the sea in 1:3 (Magonet, *Form and Meaning*, 58 – 60). I have adopted Magonet's reading in this commentary for reasons that will become clear below.

5. Hamilton, *Genesis, Chapters 1 – 17*, 235.

6. Gordon J. Wenham, *Genesis 1 – 15* (WBC; Waco, TX: Word, 1987), 238 – 39.

7. Perry, *The Honeymoon Is Over*, 70 – 73.

Jonah assumes his station under the hut for two purposes. The first is to enjoy its shade (*ṣēl*), a term often associated with YHWH's protection (Pss 17:8 [7]; 36:8; 57:2 [1]; 91:1; 121:5; Isa 49:2; 51:16; Hos 14:8 [7]). Ironically, in this context the term refers to shade of Jonah's own making. The second purpose for Jonah's perch under the hut is to wait and see what will happen in the city (*ʿad ʾăšer yirʾeh mah-yihyeh bāʿîr*). It seems odd that Jonah would wait to see what Nineveh's fate would be when the narrative makes clear that the city's fate has already been determined, announced by the author (and presumably by God) and acknowledged by Jonah.

An explanation for this peculiarity in the narrative may be found in the recognition that Jonah's prayer in 4:1 – 4 was, in reality, a thinly veiled request that YHWH rescind his mercy to Nineveh. Jonah had already witnessed YHWH's willingness to alter course when he relented of the judgment he had planned for the city. Jonah's request for death, like Moses' request to be blotted out of YHWH's book, was intended to move YHWH to change course.

In light of this understanding of 4:1 – 4, Jonah sat under his hut waiting to see if any change might occur in the outcome that he so vehemently protested. Jonah likely envisions two possibilities. One is that Nineveh's repentance will quickly evaporate as the citizens instinctively revert to wickedness and violence.[8] This might result in YHWH's rescinding his mercy if his clemency had been motivated strictly by Nineveh's repentance.

The other possibility is that YHWH might do for one of his own what he had done for Nineveh — change his mind. Jonah understands that YHWH is compassionate, but surely divine justice will win the day. It is for such a change that Jonah waits in the desert — the same setting where YHWH changed his mind for Moses.

2. YHWH's Object Lesson on Divine Mercy (4:6 – 4:8)

The focus of attention returns to YHWH in 4:6a, where he is introduced for the first time in the book as "YHWH God" (*yhwh ʾĕlōhîm*). The author is typically deliberate about his use of divine designations, and it is reasonable to assume that he has a reason for introducing this combined designation at this point in the narrative.[9] In fact, throughout the remainder of Jonah 4 the author's preferred designation for God is Elohim, with the divine name, YHWH, appearing only in the introduction to YHWH's final question to Jonah (4:10a). This preference for Elohim throughout a scene focused on YHWH's relationship with Jonah is out of character for this author, who normally reserves this name for contexts focused on God's relationship with non-Israelites.[10]

The reason for the author's departure from his typical practice is difficult to determine without considering the distribution of divine names throughout the book. If in fact the author has some rationale for shifts in divine designations, it must be discerned by analyzing each designation in context to determine if there is a pattern. The table below illustrates the distribution of divine designations throughout the book in terms of three discernible narrative voices: the author's voice, the non-Israelite voice, and Jonah's voice.[11]

---

8. This was the position of the medieval Jewish commentator, David Kimhi, and it remains a viable interpretation. See Perry, *The Honeymoon Is Over*, 164 – 65, for a recent defense.

9. Goldstein, "On the Use of the Name of God," 75 – 76.

10. Ibid.

11. Ibid, 76 – 78. These categories of voice are based on Goldstein's fine analysis. She includes a fourth, God's voice, but since God never refers to himself by a divine designation, I have not included her fourth category in my analysis. The data she includes under the designation of "God's voice" is actually the author's voice introducing divine speech. Therefore, I include this data under the designation "the author's voice."

Table 8.2: Divine Designations in the Book of Jonah				
	Elohim	**god[12]**	**YHWH**	**YHWH Elohim**	**El**
Author	3:3, 5, 10 [2x]; *4:7, 8, 9*	1:5; 2:2	1:1, 3 [2x], 4, 10, 14, 16 [2x]; 2:1, 2, 3, 8, 10, 11; 3:1, 3; 4:4, 10	4:6	
Non-Israelites (mariners/people of Nineveh)	1:6; 3:8, 9	1:6	1:14 [2x]		
Jonah		1:9; 2:7	1:9; 2:6, 7; 4:2, 3		4:2

The table illustrates that for a book of only four chapters, the author uses a surprising number of designations for God. It also illustrates that the author's default designation for God is the divine name YHWH. Whenever the author departs from this designation, the author is stressing a particular aspect of God's character, or of God's relationship to humanity and creation. Jonah, with only one exception, refers to God as YHWH, and on two occasions follows this with a qualifying designation (1:9, "god of heaven," and 2:7, "my god"). The exception is when Jonah refers to God as "El" when he quotes Israel's traditional confession from Exod 34:6 (Jonah 4:2).

Non-Israelites in the book refer to God as Elohim. The one exception is when the mariners invoke YHWH twice (1:14), which they are only able to do on the basis of Jonah's use of the divine name in his confession (1:9). Other non-Israelite references to deity are either designating other gods or referring to Jonah's personal deity, whom they do not yet know.

The evidence in general supports the rule that when God's relationship to non-Israelites is in view, the designation Elohim occurs. When God's relationship to Jonah is in view, or when the au-

thor is relating the story to a presumably Jewish audience, the designation YHWH occurs. The difficulty occurs in 4:6 – 9. These verses are italicized in the table because these occurrences of Elohim and YHWH/Elohim break the pattern of chapters 1 – 3. In a context focused on God's relationship to Jonah, the author suddenly shifts to Elohim.

The reason for this change in divine names in 4:6 – 9, however, may be related to another principle at work in Jonah. We have already noted the author's tendency to draw heavily from Genesis in order to communicate the scope of YHWH's mercy. The first time the designation YHWH Elohim occurs in the Old Testament is Gen 2:4, at the beginning of the account of Adam's creation: "This is the account of the heavens and the earth when they were newly made, on the very occasion YHWH Elohim made earth and heavens." This designation for God dominates the Genesis narrative to the end of chapter 3. It appears to serve as a transitional name that identifies Israel's covenant God, YHWH, with the God of creation who, throughout Gen 1, is called Elohim ("God").[13]

Such a transitional name for God serves the purposes of Jonah's author admirably as the author presses the point of YHWH's universal sovereignty

---

12. Recall here the footnote on "god of heaven" in 1:9, that the designation *'ĕlōhîm* may either serve as a reference to deity in general, or as a non-Israelite designation for the one true God, the God of Israel, for which I have used the lowercase

"god." For the most part, only when "God" stands alone in the text do I use uppercase G.

13. Jean L'Hour, "Yahweh Elohim," *RB* 81 (1974): 524 – 56.

and mercy. In Jonah, however, the transition moves in the opposite direction. Genesis uses YHWH Elohim as a transition from the exclusive use of Elohim (God) in Gen 1 to the dominant use of YHWH in Genesis 4 – 50. The movement is from the universal perspective to the particular perspective. In contrast, Jonah uses YHWH Elohim as a transition from the dominant use of YHWH to the dominant use of Elohim.[14] The movement is from the particular perspective to the universal perspective. In other words, the author is once again taking us back to creation, back to its emphasis on the global dimensions of YHWH's mercy.

If the author is inverting Genesis' use of the compound divine name, then the shift in divine designation in 4:6 – 11 is not an aberration from the author's usual principle. The emphasis in 4:6 – 11 is on God's object lesson designed to teach Jonah the universal scope of divine mercy. The transition from "YHWH" to "Elohim," marked by the compound "YHWH Elohim" (4:6), is a sound rhetorical move given the author's point.

God takes an indirect approach when he confronts Jonah's issue with the perceived injustice of divine mercy. Like the storm at sea, God uses nature in an elaborate object lesson designed to change Jonah's perspective regarding the relationship of justice and mercy. He begins by appointing a plant (*wayĕman yhwh-'ĕlōhîm qîqāyôn*). The author uses the same verb with reference to the plant that he used with reference to the fish in 2:1a (1:17a). Both served as God's instruments for delivering Jonah. The fish delivered Jonah from the consequences of his rebellious flight. The plant was designed to deliver Jonah from the misery of his conflict with God (4:6d). Thus, both the fish and the plant are symbols of the grace that God extends to Jonah.

Attempts to identify the species of the plant have been largely unsuccessful because this designation (*qîqāyôn*) occurs only here in the Hebrew Bible. The most popular suggestions are vine, gourd, or castor oil plant.[15] The author, however, is less interested in botanical precision than he is in the plant's function and symbolism. The plant joins with other features of the narrative to establish connections with 1 Kgs 19, where Elijah sat under a broom tree awaiting a response from YHWH. The difference in Jonah 4 is that the plant is a special creation of YHWH Elohim, raised up specifically for this object lesson. In this respect, the plant recalls Gen 2:8 – 9, where we find the account of Eden's creation and YHWH Elohim's provision of all kinds of trees and shrubbery for human enjoyment and sustenance.

The plant serves two purposes. First, it provides "shade" (*ṣēl*) for Jonah. Mention of the word "shade" reminds the reader of Jonah's hut, which he constructed for this same purpose. One may wonder why God provides Jonah with additional shade when his hut is already meeting this need. The plant serves as God's indication of the inadequacy and futility of Jonah's attempt to provide his own shade. Jonah's hut does not stand a chance against the elements of his harsh surroundings. God's plant was the counterpoint to Jonah's hut, representing God's gracious and abundant provision.[16]

The plant's second purpose is "to deliver him

---

14. Hesse and Kikawada, "Jonah and Genesis 1 – 11," 6 – 9. Eric Hesse and Isaac Kikawada were the first to notice an inversion of the story line of Gen 1 – 11 in the book of Jonah. While I cannot accept their thesis in its entirety or in many of its details, I do see merit to their arguments for the inversion of Gen 1 – 3 in Jonah 4:6 – 11.

15. For a full discussion of various proposals and their strengths and weaknesses, see Wolff, *Obadiah and Jonah*, 78 – 80, 169 – 70, and Sasson, *Jonah*, 290 – 92.

16. John H. Walton, "The Object Lesson of Jonah 4:5 – 7 and the Purpose of the Book of Jonah," *BBR* 2 (1992): 47 – 57.

from his misery" (*lĕhaṣṣîl lô mērāʿātô*). The infinitive "to deliver" (*lĕhaṣṣîl*) creates a sound play with the word "shade" (*ṣēl*); the reader is reminded of Jonah's hut erected for the purpose of providing Jonah "shade" (*ṣēl*, 4:5). The author again hints at the inadequacy of Jonah's own constructs, be they physical or ideological.

The author's word for the threat from which Jonah needs to be delivered is the familiar term for evil/disaster/misery (*rāʿâ*). In this instance, the word carries a double entendre. It refers both to Jonah's physical misery in the heat of the sun as well as to his internal bitterness — the literal evil entrenched in Jonah's heart. The repetition of the word "evil" (*rāʿâ*) exposes once again the fact of Jonah's moral equivalence to Nineveh, the city that has been characterized as "evil" from the outset of the book. Jonah is no better than Nineveh if the same hatred and disregard for human welfare resides in his own heart.

The author describes Jonah's response to God's provision of the plant in terms that parallel his response to God's mercy on Nineveh. The text says, "Jonah rejoiced over the plant with great joy" (*wayyiśmaḥ … śimḥâ gĕdôlâ*). The reader immediately recognizes one of the author's favorite rhetorical devices: the combination of a verb with an etymologically related noun. The rhetorical device recalls the description of Jonah's opposite emotional state at the beginning of Jonah 4, "This displeased [Jonah] with great displeasure" (*wayyēraʿ … rāʿâ gĕdôlâ*). By this means the author emphasizes that divine mercy provoked two radically different reactions in Jonah. When extended to Jonah's enemies, divine mercy was displeasing, but when Jonah himself was the beneficiary of such mercy, he was overjoyed.

The next stage in God's object lesson is the appointment of a worm. The familiar verb already used of the fish and the plant appears again, "God appointed" (*wayĕman*). The repetition of this verb alerts the reader to the fact that the worm contributes to Jonah's deliverance though its role is decidedly different than that of the plant. Whereas the plant symbolized God's mercy, the worm symbolizes God's judgment.

In fact, the word "worm" (*tôlaʿat*) frequently serves as an image of divine judgment or profound human despair and humiliation (Deut 28:36 – 39; Job 25:4 – 6; Ps 22:7 [6]; Isa 14:11; 41:14; 66:24). The creature designated by this term conjures thoughts of death and the grave. Thus, the worm is an appropriate teaching tool for God's object lesson here since Jonah sits at the intersection of divine judgment, his own despair, and his request to die (4:3, 8d-g).

The day immediately following the appearance of the plant, the worm "attacks" (*wattak*) the plant, and it withers away. The use of the militarily charged term "attack" for the worm's action against the plant plays on Jonah's worst fears regarding God's decision to spare Nineveh. Such clemency virtually guaranteed an enemy attack on God's own people. The point of the worm's attack on the plant is to demonstrate the effect of God's judgment prevailing over his mercy. Jonah is about to experience the very scenario that he wished on Nineveh — the withdrawal of mercy and the execution of strict justice.[17]

The withering of the plant left Jonah exposed to the sun's intense heat. With the temporal clause "as the sun climbed higher," the author emphasizes that the day is advancing to noon and Jonah is getting hotter. At the very moment Jonah most needed the plant, God takes it away, which places Jonah in the very situation he wished on Nineveh.

---

17. Walton, "The Object Lesson," 56 – 57.

The heat of the sun is soon accompanied by a "cutting, easterly wind" (*rûaḥ qādîm ḥārîšît*). For the second time, God employs the wind as a means of getting Jonah's attention (cf. 1:4). This time the wind is described as "cutting" and "easterly." Both adjectives are important and require clarification. The term "cutting" (*ḥārîšît*) occurs only here in the Hebrew Bible. Its precise meaning continues to elude interpreters. The simplest interpretation understands the word as an adjective derived from a root meaning "to plow" or "to cut."[18] The wind, therefore, is sharp, biting, or cutting, intended to wear down Jonah's stubbornness.

The second adjective,[19] "easterly" (*qādîm*), resumes the pun with the verb "I hastened" (*qāddamtî*, 4:2e) and the "eastward" (*qedem*, 4:5b) direction of Jonah's departure from the city. The wind, therefore, serves as a further warning to Jonah of his estrangement from God because of his rejection of divine mercy.

God's purpose for sending the wind becomes clear in 4:8c-d. God intends to expose Jonah to an experience of unmitigated justice. The author uses the same verb for the sun's assault on Jonah as that used for the worm's assault on the plant, "[The sun] attacked [*wattak*] Jonah's head." Just as in the storm at sea (1:4b – 2:1b [1:17b]), creation joins God in a conspiracy against Jonah, subjecting him to the fate he wishes on Nineveh. Once again the militaristic language plays on Jonah's fears that Assyria will destroy Israel. The verb thus brings the issue of divine justice and its execution by means of Gentile agents into sharp focus.

Jonah languishes under God's display of pure justice and repeats his wish to die. This time, however, his request is not designed to strengthen his petition (4:3). Jonah genuinely desires death as an escape from the unmitigated justice of God. Jonah's second request also differs from the first in that it is not directed to YHWH, but to himself. The text says literally, "He asked himself to die" (*wayyiš'al 'et-napšô lāmût*). The direct object of the verb in this clause is the Hebrew word *nepeš*. It basically means "throat," but depending on context, it can also mean "life," "individual," or "soul." When the word is combined with a pronoun, it frequently takes on a reflexive sense and can be rendered "self."[20] Such is the case here; Jonah is directing his petition to himself.

The author's word choice implies that Jonah has moved from talking to God to talking to himself. Jonah's refusal to embrace the full implications of divine mercy has resulted in the prophet's turning inward. Dialogue becomes soliloquy because Jonah chooses isolation over reconciliation.

Jonah's soliloquy repeated his request to YHWH recorded in 4:3b, "My death is better than my life" (*ṭôb môtî mēḥayyāy*). This repetition here proves ironic. Previously, Jonah viewed death as preferable to witnessing God's mercy for Nineveh. This time, however, Jonah views death as preferable to the withdrawal of divine mercy from himself. The contrast brings into sharp relief the inconsistency of Jonah's application of mercy and justice. If he wishes God to deal in strict justice with Nineveh, then he must be prepared to experience that strict justice himself. If, however, he wishes God to treat him mercifully, then he must be prepared to embrace the extension of God's mercy to others.

---

18. *HALOT* (Study Edition), 1:353, 357. Cf. also Tucker, *Jonah*, 98 – 99.

19. In the Hebrew text, the adjective "easterly" actually precedes the adjective "cutting." The Hebrew word order, however,

coincides poorly with colloquial English; thus the translation has flipped the order for the sake of English style.

20. Clines, *Concise Dictionary*, 280.

3. God's Final Challenge to Jonah's Anger (4:9 – 11)

God does not give up on Jonah even when the prophet turns inward. God engages Jonah again by repeating the question that he had asked previously (4:4). This time, however, God focuses the question on Jonah's anger over the plant's demise rather than on his anger over Nineveh's deliverance. God asked, "Is your anger *over the plant* that intense?" By asking the question this way, God distances the discussion from the issue of Nineveh's deliverance.

Jonah responds to God's question emphatically: "My anger is so intense I could die!" (*hêṭēb ḥārâ-lî ʿad-māwet*). Jonah's response closely matches YH-WH's question with the exception of the interrogative particle and the prepositional phrase "over the plant." Jonah replaces this last prepositional phrase with a different one, "until death" (lit., *ʿad-māwet*). This phrase is often an idiomatic way of expressing the superlative or lending emphasis to a statement.[21] It probably has that meaning here. Because of the frequency with which the word "death" and related terms appear in this text, however, it is best to retain some connection with its literal meaning. The translation, "My anger is so intense I could die" represents a good compromise.

The word that both God and Jonah have used for the prophet's anger (lit., "heat"; *ḥārâ*), recalls Jonah's emotional state at the beginning of chapter 4 and plays off of the oppressive heat of Jonah's surroundings. The author again uses the climate in Jonah's environment to externalize the prophet's disposition, which thus facilitates the self-reflection called for by God's question.

God finally succeeds in getting a response out of Jonah. Jonah's answer sets the stage for God's clos-ing speech by providing the basis for a comparison that God will use to make his point. God's initial question to Jonah (4:4) implied that Jonah's anger over Nineveh's deliverance is both inappropriate and excessive. God's second question, however, implies the opposite. Jonah's anger over the sudden and unexplained removal of the plant is appropriate and understandable. God had extended mercy to Jonah via the plant and then revoked it, exposing Jonah to potentially lethal elements (recall the verb "attacked," *wattak*). Jonah experienced unmitigated justice, and he did not like it. The capricious change in God's actions was contrary to his attributes listed in 4:2 and properly provoked Jonah's anger. Jonah is now in a position to sympathize with YHWH's hesitancy to execute judgment and his refusal to rescind the mercy he has shown Nineveh.

Though Jonah answers God's question with a self-vindicating spirit, his response is truer than he realizes. He is, in fact, right to be angry about receiving mercy only to have it snatched away. The issue is not that Jonah, or Nineveh, has a right to God's mercy. Rather, the issue is that God's character is such that upon granting mercy, he follows through and remains true to his offer.

YHWH proceeds to make his final argument by means of a comparison. The author introduces these closing remarks with the words, "YHWH said." Significantly, the divine name reappears for the book's finale. Since 4:6a, the author has used the designation Elohim exclusively. What accounts for his return to the designation YHWH at this point?

The shift creates an ironic inversion of the use of the divine name in the rest of the book. Up to this point, Elohim (God) has been used with reference

---

21. Thomas, "Unusual Ways of Expressing the Superlative," 219 – 21; Gershon Brin, "The Superlative in the Hebrew Bible: Additional Cases," *VT* 42 (1992): 116 – 17.

to God's relationship with non-Israelites, emphasizing the universal scope of divine mercy and love. YHWH, by contrast, has been used with reference to Israel's covenant Lord, mostly with respect to God's dealings with Jonah but also with respect to the mariners who have come to know YHWH through Jonah's testimony.

In Jonah 4:6 – 9, Elohim deals with Jonah precisely because Jonah needs a lesson in the universality of divine mercy. When Nineveh returns to the narrative spotlight in 4:10 – 11, however, the author uncharacteristically reverts to YHWH. The reason for this return to God's covenant name is to remind Jonah again of YHWH's purpose for his special covenant with Israel. God desires to enter into covenant with Assyria, and all other nations as well, through Israel's mediation (cf. Isa 19:23 – 24). In fact, Jonah's mission has been a foreshadowing of this eventual redemptive goal. Interestingly, Jonah 4 concludes in a manner similar to Jonah 1. At the end of Jonah 1 the Gentile mariners invoke the name YHWH in gratitude for his mercy toward them, and at the end of Jonah 4 the name YHWH occurs with reference to God's mercy toward Nineveh. The author seems intent on emphasizing the nations' acknowledgment of YHWH by means of Israel's mediation.

YHWH set up his argument as a contrast between himself and Jonah as indicated by the emphatic pronouns at 4:10b ("As for you" [*'attâ*]) and 4:11a ("But as for me" [*wa'ănî*]). The contrast focused on two important differences between Jonah's disposition and YHWH's disposition. First, Jonah continues to turn inward while YHWH turns outward. YHWH notes that Jonah pitied (*ḥastā*) the plant.[22] The point is not that Jonah pitied the plant, but that the plant's demise has moved him

to self-pity. Jonah is upset over the withdrawal of God's mercy in the form of the plant. His distress is understandable. YHWH, however, was outwardly focused.

The second contrast has to do with the relatively minor implications of Jonah's self-concern compared to the far-reaching implications of YHWH's concern for Nineveh. Jonah's situation jeopardized only one person — himself. The consequences of his death in the desert would be relatively insignificant. Yet, Jonah recognized that even the individual is a legitimate object of YHWH's mercy and that the removal of that mercy is tragic.

YHWH, by contrast, pitied Nineveh. The city's destruction would have jeopardized thousands of people, not to mention a multitude of animals. YHWH could no more abide the thought of rescinding his mercy for that city than Jonah could abide the thought of losing YHWH's mercy. The stakes, however, are much higher for the object of YHWH's pity.

YHWH's first point is that Jonah's experience of the plant was completely gratuitous. Jonah had no claim over the plant or right to the plant. YHWH established this fact with the first of two relative clauses: "over which you exerted no effort, nor did you grow it." The plant was YHWH's gift to Jonah that shaded the prophet, but it also exposed the inadequacy of his attempts to shade himself.[23] The verb "you did not grow it" (*giddaltô*) underscores the plant's role as YHWH's instrument. The verb derives from the same root as the adjective "great" (*gādôl*), thus aligning the plant with Nineveh, the wind, the storm, and the fish — all of which YHWH has employed in his prophet's education.[24]

The author expressed the gratuitous nature of the plant in terms reminiscent of Gen 2:5 – 10,

---

22. *HALOT* (Study Edition), 1:298.
23. Walton, "Object Lesson," 51.

24. Jenson, *Obadiah, Jonah, Micah*, 92.

where YHWH Elohim created plants and cared for them even before humans existed. In fact, YHWH Elohim planted Eden and filled it with trees before placing Adam in it. This was a gift to Adam and was not the result of Adam's husbandry. The connection with Gen 2:5 – 10 emphasizes that YHWH's mercy is for all humankind.

YHWH's second point was that the plant withered just as quickly as it appeared because of divine caprice. YHWH expressed this in the second of the two relative clauses: "which overnight appeared and overnight perished." What Jonah wished on Nineveh, YHWH performs on Jonah — a withdrawal of his mercy. YHWH's point is that what upset Jonah about the demise of the plant is precisely what upset YHWH about Jonah's desire to see a reversal regarding Nineveh's fate. It would be a capricious act contradictory to YHWH's character, and it would subject a host of humans as well as animals to destruction.

YHWH proceeds to his main point. His argument assumes that Jonah's distress over the plant's demise is legitimate. The point of contrast has to do with the greater legitimacy of YHWH's distress over Nineveh's potential destruction. YHWH expresses this in the negative so as to assume Jonah's point of view for the purpose of exposing its absurdity: "But as for me, must I not pity Nineveh? [*lōʾ ʾāḥûs ʿal nînĕwēh*]." The second part of the comparison, therefore, takes the form of a rhetorical question.[25]

By stating Jonah's position in such bald terms, YHWH demonstrates to Jonah the inconsistency of his position. Jonah reserves the right to be distressed over his own experience of unmitigated divine justice, but he disallows YHWH's right to be distressed over the prospect of executing such justice on Nineveh. How can Jonah hold such a position after confessing that "deliverance belongs to YHWH" (2:10c [2:9c])?

Jonah's position appeared all the more ridiculous as YHWH elaborated on the potential impact of Nineveh's destruction. For the fourth time in the book, YHWH referred to Nineveh as a "great metropolis" (*ʿîr gĕdôlâ*). YHWH reinforces his argument with some impressive statistics. The city was home to "more than 120,000 human beings" (*harbēh mištêm-ʿeśrēh ribbô ʾādām*). The infinitive "to be more than" (*harbēh*) launches a series of puns on words derived from the root *r-b-b*, meaning "to be many, to multiply." It is followed by *ribbô* (10,000) and the final word of the book, "many" (*rabbâ*).

The stacking of words derived from this root emphasizes the significant loss of life involved in Jonah's wish for strict justice. YHWH's reluctance to punish was in part motivated by a desire to avoid such a tragic loss. Significantly, the author did not offer Nineveh's repentance as not a factor

---

25. Though it is true that YHWH's words in 4:11 are not explicitly marked as a question in the Hebrew text, the context suggests that YHWH is continuing his Socratic approach to Jonah's education that began with his initial question in 4:4. Hebrew frequently poses questions with no interrogative markers in situations where the question can be easily inferred from the context (Arnold and Choi, *Guide to Biblical Hebrew Syntax*, 187). This is especially true of negated clauses.

Interpreters of the book of Jonah are almost unanimously agreed on this reading of 4:11. Two notable exceptions are Alan Cooper and Philip Guillaume, both of whom argue that YHWH asserts at the end of Jonah that he will in fact destroy the city per Jonah's oracle. Their arguments, however, are unconvincing and fail to interpret the closing line in the light of the book's thrust as a whole. See Alan Cooper, "In Praise of Divine Caprice: The Significance of the Book of Jonah," in *Among the Prophets* (ed. Philip R. Davies and D. J. A. Clines; Sheffield: Sheffield Academic, 1993): 144 – 63; Philip Guillaume, "The End of Jonah Is the Beginning of Wisdom," *Bib* 87 (2006): 243 – 50. For a successful refutation of Cooper and Guillaume, see ben Zvi, *Signs of Jonah*, 14 n. 1, 17 n. 11.

in YHWH's decision not to rescind the threat of destruction. Nineveh's deliverance was an act of divine mercy motivated by YHWH's compassion.

The number 120,000 is not intended to be an accurate assessment of Nineveh's population. Rather, this was a standard expression for a multitude or an innumerably large quantity, related to ancient Near Eastern mathematics, which was based on units of 60 (a sexagesimal system).[26] This same number occurs elsewhere in the Old Testament to emphasize a great quantity.[27] The point is that the exercise of strict justice in Nineveh's case would have resulted in a significant loss of life.

This great multitude is further defined as those "who do not know their right from their left." YHWH employed a phrase that occurs frequently with reference to proper Torah observance in Israel. God often warned Israel not to turn to the right or to the left as they walk the path of obedience (Deut 5:32; 17:11, 20; 28:14; Josh 1:7; 23:6). These references indicate that this language is associated with Israel's access to special revelation, which distinguished for Israel between the right and the left. Nineveh, however, had no such access to YHWH's special revelation. He took this into account when administering his justice and mercy.

Finally, YHWH concluded with a surprising final reason for his clemency, "as well as many animals." This statement recalls the animals' participation in the penitential rites demanded by the king in Jonah 3. YHWH took notice of this. The inclusion of the "animals/beasts" (*bĕhēmâ*) combines with the mention of "human beings" (*ʾādām*) earlier in the verse to recall once again Genesis 2 and its emphasis on YHWH's intimate connection with both humans and beasts (2:19–20). YHWH's mercy was remarkably circumspect, especially compared to Jonah's narrow perspective. YHWH thought even of the animals who would suffer in such destruction. Jonah thought only of himself.

As the book closes, the reader is left to wonder: How did Jonah respond? Did he repent? Did he rebut? Or did he retreat further into himself? The author opted not to tell us. Rather, the reader is left with YHWH's question, "Must I not pity Nineveh?" (4:11a).

Canonical and Practical Significance

Paul's opening words in Rom 11:22 serve well as a heading for Jonah 4:5–11. The apostle says, "Consider therefore the kindness and sternness of God" (NIV). The book of Jonah's final section is an exploration of the relationship between these two aspects of God's character, which, from a human point of view, often appear in tension. When God allows humans to go unchecked for extended periods of time, the faithful join the chorus of psalmists who ask the question, "How long O, LORD?"

Jonah, however, has stopped asking this question. He is tired of asking "How long?" and has moved on to pressing God to act immediately. Jonah's concerns are legitimate and have been shared by many faithful saints throughout history. The danger exists, however, that such faithful questioning may turn into bitter resentment of

---

26. *CANE* 3 and 4, 1948–49.

27. Cf. Judg 8:10; 1 Kgs 8:63; 1 Chr 12:38 [37]; 2 Chr 7:5; 28:6; Jdt 2:5, 15; 2 Macc 8:20; 12:20.

the grace that was once a source of joy. Peter addressed this danger when he offered encouragement to beleaguered saints.

> The Lord is not slow in keeping his promise, as some understand slowness. Instead, he is patient with you, not wanting anyone to perish, but everyone to come to repentance. But the day of the Lord will come like a thief. (2 Pet 3:9 – 10a, NIV)

Peter's exhortation focused on a frustration that God's people often have with the patience of God's wrath. Believers, like Jonah, are often tempted to view God's reluctant wrath as indecisiveness or inconsistency. This perspective, however, is an indication that faith has turned inward and that believers have lost sight of the bigger picture of God's redemptive activity. Therefore, Peter redirects the concern for justice by reminding his audience of the universal scope of God's compassion. Believers are encouraged to balance their eagerness for the consummation of God's kingdom expressed in the prayer "Lord, come quickly!" with a long-suffering that desires, along with God, to see everyone come to repentance. Prayer, therefore, is often the painful collision of a believer's impatient hope with God's patient grace.

Interestingly, when Peter speaks of God's patience, he speaks of it as directed not to "them" but to "you." He says, "[God] is patient *with you.*" By stating it this way, Peter reminds believers that they were once the beneficiaries of God's patient grace and that it is now their calling to bear injustices in mercy when that same patient grace is extended to others. The memory of our own salvation enables us to embrace the scandal of God's patient mercy as we impatiently anticipate and pray for our Lord's return.

Peter also affirms, however, that judgment is coming. The day of the Lord is like a thief biding its time, patiently waiting for the right moment — a moment that only God the Father knows (Matt 24:36). God will not bear with sin and injustice indefinitely. In this respect, the book of Nahum is an important complement to the book of Jonah. The city that God spared in the book of Jonah, he destroyed in the book of Nahum. Contrary to Jonah's fears, YHWH's mercy does not eclipse his justice. It just postpones it, opening the door to the satisfaction of divine justice through reformation rather than ruin.

Until the day of Lord comes, believers should serve as agents of mercy, encouraging and rejoicing in repentance, however feeble it may be. This means that we must adopt Jesus' ethic of loving our enemies and interceding on behalf of our oppressors. As Christ stated in the beatitude in Matt 5:7, "Blessed are merciful, for they will be shown mercy." Similarly, Jesus' parable in 18:23 – 33 suggests a vital relationship between the receipt and the demonstration of mercy. A slave, who owed his master an enormous sum, was forgiven his debt. He then turned around and required immediate payment of a measly sum from a fellow slave. Upon hearing this, the master subjected the wicked slave to torture until his entire debt was paid. Believers are motivated to show mercy, both by the memory of mercy already received and by the anticipation of the fullness of God's mercy in the future. Jonah, however, jeopardizes his participation in the fullness of divine mercy by refusing to remember and share the mercy he has already received.

In fact, Jonah's behavior at the close of the book is reminiscent of the older brother in the parable of the prodigal son (Luke 15:11 – 31) This brother could not bring himself to share in his father's joy over his younger brother's repentance. Like the older brother, Jonah isolated himself in his bitterness and exchanged joy for despair over a perceived imbalance in the scales of God's justice. As James warns, "judgment without mercy will be shown to anyone who has not been merciful. Mercy triumphs over judgment" (Jas 2:13 NIV).

Scripture Index

Subject Index

Abrahamic covenant, 88

accents, 98

anger
    Jonah's, 151 – 52, 156, 171
    slow to, 159

animals
    inclusion of, 139, 145 – 46, 174

Ashshur Dan III, 33, 135

Assyria, 33, 36, 40, 53 – 55, 88, 155

author, of Jonah, 34

banishment, from YHWH's presence,
    62 – 63

belly, 102, 104, 106

Ben Sirach, 28

Bible, the Christian, 29

Book of the Twelve, the, 26 – 27

bowels, 75

calling, 82, 86, 107

canonical context, 25 – 30

cargo, flinging, 74, 75, 84

casting lots, 76, 77, 89

chiasm, 51, 69, 70, 99, 111

climate, 40

cola, 97 – 98

colon, 97 – 98, 106

commission, the
    clarification of, 126
    from God, 48 – 49
    narratives, 50 – 51
    nature of, 52
    submit to, 122 – 25
    YHWH's, 61, 63

compliance, with God's mercy, 122 – 26

confession, 93

context
    canonical, 25 – 30

    historical, 30 – 32
    literary, 36 – 42

covenant, 88, 110, 112, 133, 146, 172

creation
    serves as messenger, 73, 89

cutting, the term, 170

date, of composition, 34

death
    desire for, 155, 170
    journey from, 104
    request for, 58,162

desert, symbolism of the, 162, 165

discourse markers, 42 – 44

divine retribution, 35

dry ground, 123

eastward, symbolizes, 165, 170

Eleazar, mentions Jonah's, 116

election
    Israel's, 37, 41, 86 – 88
    meaning of, 86

Elijah, 58, 64, 116, 151, 164, 168

Elohim, designation of, 131, 166 – 68,
    171. *See also*, God, YHWH

evil
    Nineveh as, 61
    repented of their, 141
    the word, 55 – 56, 151 – 52, 169

exodus, the, 117 – 18

faith
    Jonah's confession of, 69
    in YHWH, 74

false prophets, 72

fasting, 77

fear
    of judgment, 90
    the mariners', 74

    of YHWH, 79, 84

fish, the
    in the belly of, 102, 104
    Jonah in, 85, 95
    responds by, 114
    and the ship, 104
    symbol of grace, 168 – 69

flight, Jonah's, 51, 56 – 60, 62, 63, 162,
    165

flinging, 74, 75, 84

genre, 36 – 37

Gentiles, 118, 128
    aversion to, 58
    extending it to the, 36
    repentance of, 147

geography, symbolic use of, 40

God. *See also*, Elohim, YHWH
    changes his mind, 143
    character of, 171, 174
    designation of, 131, 144, 166 – 68

gods
    cried out to, 74
    will(s) of the, 84

grace
    gift of, 63
    response to, 109
    symbol of, 95

historical context, 30 – 32

hut, the, 166, 168 – 69

information gapping, 56

interpretation
    the book's, 25 – 26
    starting point for, 30

intertextuality, 41

Israel
    election of, 41, 86, 87, 88
    mercy for, 61

Author Index